THE SPIRIT OF ARISTOPHANES

THE SPIRIT OF ARISTOPHANES
Essays in Honor of Jeffrey Henderson

EDITED BY DUSTIN W. DIXON
AND MARY C. ENGLISH

EDINBURGH
University Press

Edinburgh University Press is one of the leading university presses in the UK. We publish academic books and journals in our selected subject areas across the humanities and social sciences, combining cutting-edge scholarship with high editorial and production values to produce academic works of lasting importance. For more information visit our website: edinburghuniversitypress.com

© editorial matter and organisation Dustin W. Dixon and Mary C. English 2024, 2025
© the chapters their several authors 2024, 2025

Edinburgh University Press Ltd
13 Infirmary Street
Edinburgh EH1 1LT

First published in hardback by Edinburgh University Press 2024

Typeset in 11/13 Minion Pro
by Cheshire Typesetting Ltd, Cuddington, Cheshire

A CIP record for this book is available from the British Library

ISBN 978 1 3995 1197 1 (hardback)
ISBN 978 1 3995 1198 8 (paperback)
ISBN 978 1 3995 1199 5 (webready PDF)
ISBN 978 1 3995 1200 8 (epub)

The right of Dustin W. Dixon and Mary C. English to be identified as the editors of this work has been asserted in accordance with the Copyright, Designs and Patents Act 1988, and the Copyright and Related Rights Regulations 2003 (SI No. 2498).

Contents

Editors' Acknowledgments	vii
List of Contributors	viii
A Note on the Text	xi
Preface Mary C. English and Dustin W. Dixon	xii

1	Female Genitalia Onstage in Aristophanes Amy Richlin	1
2	'Let Loose the Melodies of Holy Hymns': Voice, Agency and Gender in Aristophanes' *Birds* Daniel Libatique	19
3	Performing Ritual Sacrifice in Aristophanes' *Peace* and *Birds* Mary C. English	38
4	Political Ambition and Poetry in Aristophanes' *Birds* and Plato's Aristophanes I-Kai Jeng	49
5	Sophocles and Happy Endings Anne Mahoney	64
6	Heroism in the Middle in Sophocles' *Philoctetes* Emily Austin	76
7	διδαγμάτων ἥδιστον: Storytelling and the Origin of Religion in the Sisyphus Fragment (43 Fr. 19 *TrGF*) Andrew Ford	90
8	The Whetstone of Love: Helen's Blemished Beauty Dustin W. Dixon	103

9 Virginity and the Post-mortem State of the Body: Reading
   Mary and Hippolytus in Dialogue   119
   Chris Synodinos

10 Literal Truth, Mythic Truth and Narrative in Longus's
   Daphnis and Chloe   131
   William Owens

11 The Body's Borders: Violation and the Visual in the *Carmina
   Priapea*   144
   Tyler T. Travillian

12 What Are the Goals of Lucretius's *De Rerum Natura*?   160
   James J. O'Hara

13 Not So Funny After All: On Deconstructing (and
   Reconstructing) the Text of Petronius   178
   John Bodel

Index   204

Editors' Acknowledgments

We offer enthusiastic appreciation to the volume's contributors, who have been generous and exemplary colleagues from even before we approached them with the idea for this volume. We thank Pat Johnson for her encouragement and her efforts that facilitated bringing the contributors together. James Uden, Chair of the Department of Classical Studies at Boston University, graciously allowed us to announce the volume at the 2022 Aurelio Conference in honor of Jeff Henderson. Rachel Bridgewater and Isobel Birks of Edinburgh University Press have shepherded the project expertly through every stage of publication, from peer review to press. We are grateful to the anonymous readers of the proposal and of the volume for their suggestions, which have improved the collection immensely. Our research assistant Jada Caldwell's meticulous attention to detail has improved every page. The cover image was created and designed by Jonathan Becker, and we thank him for his enthusiastic efforts to make this image for us. His masks and art can be found on his website, www.theater-masks.com.

Above all, we thank you, Jeff, for your erudition, generosity, passion and wit, all of which you have shared with us and with countless others. Cheers.

Contributors

Emily Austin is Associate Professor of Classics and the College at the University of Chicago. Her first book, *Grief and the Hero: The Futility of Longing in the Iliad* (2021), explores the nexus of grief, anger and action in the *Iliad*. Her current book project focuses on ancient conceptions of solitude.

John Bodel is W. Duncan MacMillan II Professor of Classics and Professor of History at Brown University. His research focuses on ancient Roman social and cultural history, epigraphy and Latin literature, especially the Roman novels of Petronus and Apuleius. Since 1995, he has directed the U.S. Epigraphy Project, the purpose of which is to gather and share information about ancient Greek and Latin inscriptions in American collections.

Dustin W. Dixon is Assistant Professor of Classics at Grinnell College. He is co-author of *Performing Gods in Classical Antiquity and the Age of Shakespeare* (2021), and he has published articles on ancient tragedy and comedy, fragmentary drama and classical receptions.

Mary C. English is Professor of Classics and General Humanities at Montclair State University, where she teaches Latin and Greek at all levels as well as courses in mythology, ancient drama and theater history. Currently, she is co-editor of the *Thornton Wilder Journal*, a new peer-reviewed journal which she helped to launch in 2020. With Lee M. Fratantuono, she edited a collection of essays entitled *Pushing the Boundaries of Historia* (2018); and with Georgia L. Irby, she authored *A Little Latin Reader* (2011; 2nd edn, 2017) and *A New Latin Primer* (2015). She also has written on the staging of ancient comedy and the reception of Greek drama by contemporary American playwrights.

Andrew Ford is Charles Ewing Professor of Greek Language and Literature and Professor of Classics Emeritus in the Department of Classics at Princeton University. His interests center on the intersections between Greek literature, literary history and literary criticism from Homer through Aristotle.

I-Kai Jeng is Associate Professor of Philosophy at National Taiwan University. His research focuses on Plato's conceptualization of philosophical discourse in relation to other discursive modes and genres of ancient Greece. He is currently researching the philosophical significance of dramatic aspects of Plato's late dialogues.

Daniel Libatique is the Vincent J. Rosivach Assistant Professor of Classical Studies at Fairfield University. He earned his PhD from Boston University in 2018, with a dissertation on which Jeffrey Henderson was a reader. His research interests include gender, narratology, Greek drama and Augustan poetry, and his publications on those issues have appeared in venues such as *Helios*, *New England Classical Journal*, *Classical Quarterly* and *Classical World*. He is co-editor with Fiona McHardy of *Diversity and the Study of Antiquity in Higher Education: Perspectives from North America and Europe* (2023).

Anne Mahoney is Senior Lecturer in Classical Studies at Tufts University. She works on meter and poetics, and on later neo-Latin.

James J. O'Hara is the George L. Paddison Professor of Latin at the University of North Carolina, Chapel Hill. He is the author of *Death and the Optimistic Prophecy in Vergil's Aeneid* (1990); *True Names: Vergil and the Alexandrian Tradition of Etymological Wordplay* (1996; expanded edn, 2017); *Inconsistency in Roman Epic: Studies in Catullus, Lucretius, Vergil, Ovid and Lucan* (2007); and classroom commentaries on *Aeneid* 4 (2011) and 8 (2018). His current project is a monograph entitled *Teaching, Pretending to Teach, and the Authority of the Speaker in Roman Didactic and Satire*.

William Owens is Professor Emeritus of Classics at Ohio University. His research focuses on the representation of slavery in Greek and Roman texts, most recently, the Greek novels in *The Representation of Slavery in the Greek Novel* (2020). As a graduate student at Yale University, he read Aristophanes with Jeffrey Henderson.

Amy Richlin is Distinguished Research Professor of Classics at UCLA. She has published on Roman sexuality, Roman women's history and the theory of sexuality since 1981, and she turned to work on Roman comedy around 2000. Her book *Slave Theater in the Roman Republic: Plautus and Popular Comedy* (2017) won the Goodwin Award of Merit from the Society for Classical Studies in 2018. Jeffrey Henderson first introduced her to Aristophanes at Yale in 1974.

Chris Synodinos has received his doctorate in Classics from Boston University and is currently Visiting Assistant Professor in the Department of Language, Literature, and Culture at Clark University, in Worcester, Massachusetts.

Tyler T. Travillian is Director of Louisiana Scholars' College at the Northwestern State University of Louisiana. His primary areas of interest are Latin poetry and historiography of the late Roman Republic and early Empire, especially how gender and sexuality are represented in poetry and how historians assert claims about truth and reality in their texts. He teaches classical literature and history.

A Note on the Text

Unless noted otherwise, all translations of Greek and Latin texts are original, and, in honor of Jeff, the Greek and Latin texts follow the most recent edition in the Loeb Classical Library.

In the notes and the bibliographies, we follow the *Oxford Classical Dictionary* for abbreviations of ancient authors and titles of ancient works; we follow *L'Année philologique* for abbreviations of scholarly journals.

Preface
Mary C. English and Dustin W. Dixon

αἱ Χάριτες, τέμενός τι λαβεῖν ὅπερ οὐχὶ πεσεῖται
  ζητοῦσαι, ψυχὴν εὗρον Ἀριστοφάνους.
The Graces, seeking to occupy a shrine that would not falter,
  found the spirit of Aristophanes.
                    Aristophanes T-130 [= Plato, Epigram 14]

Let us ponder, for a moment, a few of the questions generated by this charming, enigmatic epigram. What are those characteristics of Aristophanes' spirit or soul (ψυχή) that attracted the Graces to it? What makes his spirit so resilient that it does not falter? What happened to this spirit after Aristophanes' body, not afforded the same resiliency as his soul, perished? Did his soul, like those described in the Platonic myth of Er, find a new body, or new shrine? In different ways, such questions about the Aristophanic spirit animate the essays in this volume. Although resolving these questions is beyond our scope – for how can one speak conclusively about spirit? – we do hope to contribute new perspectives on Aristophanic comedy, its vibrancy and its legacy. Our journey begins naturally with Aristophanes' comedies as well as with a few of the comic and the tragic poets who shared his stage, and then we proceed to later authors who, some more overtly than others, embody the enigmatic spirit of Aristophanes.

Each chapter is written by a student of Jeffrey Henderson, to whom this volume is dedicated. His scholarly energies have sparked many questions about the defining qualities of Aristophanic comedy – its innovative verve, intellectual heft, radical impulse, unabashed deviance – questions that turn out, as Jeff's own work shows, to transcend the world of the fifth- and fourth-century stage.

Amy Richlin opens the collection with an essay that pays tribute to Jeff's groundbreaking work on obscenity. Richlin surveys the deictic moments in Aristophanes' comedy where female bodies, and in particular their genitalia, are on display and the source of (crude) jokes and of comic action.

She then considers how female genitalia are described and displayed in the mimes of Herodas and in the *Rudens* of Plautus. Daniel Libatique also grounds his work on gender and on subversion of genre in Aristophanes. In this first of three chapters on Aristophanes' *Birds*, Libatique traces how Aristophanes reconfigures Sophocles' tragic presentation of the myth of Tereus into comic material. Libatique is interested in the dynamics of speech and of silence and how the two poets handle the voices of Tereus and Procne (and Philomela). Mary English approaches *Birds* from a different perspective and argues that Aristophanes capitalizes on the political optimism of 414 BCE to subvert religious norms by having Peisetaerus use the prayers and the implements of sacrifice to advance his comic agenda, a practice that Aristophanes also employs earlier in *Peace*. Even though Aristophanes mocks religious conventions in these plays and teases the audience with possible acts of *asebeia*, he is careful not to endorse behavior that is too subversive to the polis. In the final chapter on *Birds*, I-Kai Jeng explores the intersection of utopia, political fantasy, eros and the power of poetry in this play, and then using the *Birds* as a heuristic, Jeng teases out how Aristophanes' myth told in Plato's *Symposium* contains a similar message about fantasy.

After these chapters treating, primarily, Aristophanes' comedies, the next set of essays shifts focus to his contemporaries and will make, in various ways, new connections within and beyond fifth-century drama. Anne Mahoney challenges our understanding of perceived generic markers and their development in literary criticism of tragedy as she explores tragedies with happy endings. Though such questions of genre often stimulate discussion of Euripidean tragedy, Mahoney's research on the extant and the fragmentary plays of Sophocles shows that Sophocles, too, contributed to a bold expansion of traditional tragedy. Emily Austin then offers a chapter on Sophocles' response to epic notions of heroism in his *Philoctetes*; she draws on the grammatical concept of the middle voice in ancient Greek to show that Philoctetes' heroism is not active (as in Homer) or entirely passive. With the next chapter, Andrew Ford considers the Sisyphus fragment (43 Fr. 19 *TrGF*) attributed to Critias. Situating this fragment in the context of fifth-century sophistic discourse, Ford argues that the fragment's characterization of the origin of religion is not ironic, as other scholars have maintained, but instead expresses a pleasure in fabulation. An interest in storytelling also motivates Dustin Dixon's chapter as he looks at how comic and tragic playwrights as well as Ovid and Lucian subvert their audiences' expectations of Helen's paradigmatic beauty by depicting an imperfect, even ugly Helen. He explores how this alternative tradition of Helen's appearance still manifests the dangerous allure of Helen in her physical form. Chris Synodinos continues the engagement with questions of corporeality and of reception by discussing the post-mortem transformation of

Mary's body in the *Transitus Mariae* and by contrasting it with the deformity of Hippolytus's corpse after his rejection of Aphrodite. Thus, Synodinos's essay reminds us of the long, wide-ranging tradition that uses the body as locus for not only ontological but also theological debates.

The final cluster of essays turns our attention to how later Greek and Latin literature renewed some of the dynamics of classical Athenian literature and of Aristophanic comedy in particular. William Owens considers how Longus thinks about genre, narrative and truth within the text of *Daphnis and Chloe* itself. By engaging ancient ideas about myth, history and fiction, Longus, Owens argues, plays with the concepts of literal and mythic truths and thus distinguishes the novel genre from other modes of storytelling, such as that of New Comedy. Tyler Travillian, turning to the male form and masculinity, invites reconsideration of the standard reading of the *Carmina Priapea*. He traces how, in these poems for the aggressively masculine Priapus, the gaze – and its ambivalent nature in Rome – can both uphold and subvert notions of Roman masculinity. James O'Hara discusses Lucretius's goals in writing *De Rerum Natura*, situating Lucretius's epic in the context of other so-called didactic epics and arguing that Lucretius's *De Rerum Natura* shows more concern with the style and the pleasurable effects of his poetry than with its scientific and philosophical content. Finally, John Bodel leads us through challenges of interpreting the fragments of Petronius's *Satyrica* and argues that the work's narrative techniques serve the satiric portrait of the figure at the center of the Quartilla episode: Quartilla herself.

Readers familiar with Jeff's scholarship will recognize our inspiration in some of his most influential work. Many of us trace our own investigations back to his pioneering study of obscenity in *The Maculate Muse: Obscene Language in Attic Comedy*, first published in 1975 by Yale University Press, with a revised edition published in 1991 by Oxford University Press. And to his work on the dynamics of ideology of ancient comedy, especially Aristophanic comedy, in 'The *Dēmos* and the Comic Competition', published as part of the volume *Nothing to Do with Dionysos? Athenian Drama in Its Social Context* in 1990. And to his challenging of accepted scholarly paradigms in 'The *Satyrica* and the Greek Novel: Revisions and Some Open Questions' in 2010. Yet these are only a few examples of how his work, whose breadth is difficult to capture succinctly, has inspired us. Indeed, few scholars have explored the intersections of classical literature, political ideology, civic culture, identity, obscenity and translation in as vibrant and productive ways as Jeff. He is best known for his thrilling scholarship on the comedies of Aristophanes, which has shaped debates about the social and historical context of drama, ancient gender, sexuality and obscenity. Jeff's research has brought to new light those qualities of Aristophanes that made him a celebrated poet at times and a dangerous one in less open-minded times.

Jeff, like the comic poet who has attracted much of his attention, treats the highbrow and the bawdy with the same critical eye.

What strikes us as particularly significant of Jeff's scholarship is not that he simply reveals Aristophanes' 'relevance' – an overused term in popular literary criticism – to us today but that he challenges and, importantly, permits his readers to engage with insights into the human condition offered by Aristophanes, a sharp and provocative observer of it. As General Editor of the Loeb Classical Library and as translator himself, Jeff has made classical texts more accessible to a wider audience of experts and enthusiasts. At the helm of the Loeb Classical Library, he has expanded the Library's offerings to include a number of ancient works that would otherwise be unavailable to a general audience, and he has launched the digitized Loeb Classical Library online, which allows a vast corpus of ancient Greek and Latin literature to be carried in a pocket. Through his own translations, Jeff has revealed the enduring vivacity of classical literature for a world that often strives to cast these texts as mere relics of the past. We think of his own translations of Aristophanes for the Loeb Classical Library, which won a Charles J. Goodwin Award of Merit from the Society for Classical Studies in 2001 (then the American Philological Association), as well as *Three Plays by Aristophanes: Staging Women* (first published in 1996) and his recent *Three More Plays by Aristophanes: Staging Politics* (2022). These latter two volumes reveal how Aristophanes' insights into sex, gender and politics remain vital reading not only for the histories of politics and of gender but also for turns in our own sexual and political cultures. As Richlin notes in the conclusion to her chapter, Jeff published the first edition of *The Maculate Muse* in the liberatory atmosphere of the sexual revolution and the second edition at a time when he perceived the nation was reverting to sexual conservatism. We need not linger on why Henderson has recently published, in *Staging Politics*, three plays capturing Aristophanes' biting critiques of Athenian political popular culture.

To be sure, Aristophanic comedy is not a panacea for our age. Reading Aristophanes, or any ancient author, requires one to wade into a maculate past that tolerated, even embraced, misogyny, xenophobia, classicism, homophobia. Though Aristophanes was not as radical as we might have hoped or in the ways we might have wanted, he was a radical, nevertheless. He challenged his audiences to question their world, their culture, their politics, their literature, their habits, their long-held beliefs and their ideas newly in vogue. This, too, has been a vital part of Jeff's career, both investigating and renewing the Aristophanic impulse to engage his audience in vigorous intellectual debate. Jeff spent his career uncovering how fifth-century drama was part of the civic fabric of the city of Athens, how the same comedians who reveled in lowbrow humor also tried to engage, even shape, thinking on some of the most important and controversial issues facing the body politic.

We hope that readers will find within our essays the desire to investigate and to honor this impulse.

Works Cited

Henderson, Jeffrey. 1991. *The Maculate Muse: Obscene Language in Attic Comedy*. Oxford: Oxford University Press.

———. 1992. 'The *Dēmos* and the Comic Competition'. In *Nothing to Do with Dionysos? Athenian Drama in Its Social Context*, edited by John J. Winkler and Froma I. Zeitlin, 271–313. Princeton: Princeton University Press.

———. 1998–2008. *Aristophanes*, 4 vols. Cambridge, MA: Harvard University Press.

———. 2010a. 'The *Satyrica* and the Greek Novel: Revisions and Some Open Questions'. *International Journal of the Classical Tradition* 17: 483–96.

———. 2010b. *Three Plays by Aristophanes: Staging Women*, 2nd edn. Abingdon and New York: Routledge.

———. 2022. *Three More Plays by Aristophanes: Staging Politics*. Abingdon and New York: Routledge.

CHAPTER 1

Female Genitalia Onstage in Aristophanes
Amy Richlin

In the autumn of 1972, fresh from his four-year PhD at Harvard, Jeffrey Henderson began teaching at Yale, which is where I met him when I arrived in the autumn of 1973 to start my own PhD.[1] He would have been about twenty-six; I was twenty-one. He was working on converting his Harvard dissertation into his first book, *The Maculate Muse* (1975), and was usually to be found in the bleak underground cloaca linking Sterling Library with the Cross-Campus Library, smoking, deep in some early commentary and ready to tout its virtues. His powers of concentration were remarkable, but he always used to say, 'One trip to the dry cleaner and your whole research day is shot', a truth I have often passed on to my own students. We both came from northern New Jersey, and in him I happily recognized the street humor I grew up with. I took a course with him in 1974 in which we read *Acharnians*, *Lysistrata*, and part of *Frogs*, and when I came to write my own dissertation it was a chance remark of his in the spring of 1976 that set me on my course: 'Why don't you do *Maculate Muse* in Latin?' That was the beginning of all the work I have done since; my own lexical dissertation, completed in 1978, then turned into *The Garden of Priapus* (1983; I was slower). Henderson moved from Yale to Michigan, then to USC in 1982 and, as chair there, made it possible for me to move there myself in 1989; in 1991, before he moved from USC to Boston University, he brought out the revised edition of *Maculate Muse* with Oxford, encouraging me to do the same with *Garden of Priapus* (1992). He was the one who got me to study Freud's *Jokes and Their Relation to the Unconscious* and Gershon Legman's

1 My thanks to the editors for their forbearance in difficult times, to Angeliki Tzanetou for kind help with access, and to my colleague Brent Vine for his generous eye. A shout-out to three students in my last-ever Comedy class, spring 2020 – Andrew Stratton, Jazmine Villalino and Yeliz Yoruk – for showing how to take your broken heart and make it into art; and to Ralph Flores and the Troubadour Theater Company for bringing *Lysistrata* to life in plague time and teaching me so much. To Jeff, thanks from the bottom of my heart.

Rationale of the Dirty Joke; he was the one who taught me to think seriously about what makes jokes funny.

When it came to his work, he was fearless, ready to deal with Aristophanes word for word. It is hard now to realize how revolutionary this work was; obscene content was then outside the boundaries of scholarly labor. In the first edition of *Maculate Muse*, he refers with asperity to 'the small number of responsible critics who have dealt with obscenity'.[2] Indeed, when you think about how omnipresent the sexual and scatological are in people's daily lives, it is exasperating that scholarly decorum has made it so rare a topic of research in the humanities, leaving it all to the anthropologists, who are not usually interested in literature. The Anglophone circulation of Bakhtin's work gave humanists a way in, starting in the early 1980s (so he appears in my chapter on theory). But it was Henderson's strictly philological and lexical survey that first made it clear how integral the obscene was to Old Comedy and, by delineating its form in detail, simultaneously documented the workings of the Athenian sex/gender system, so that, for me, *The Maculate Muse* stands as the origin of writing the history of ancient sexuality. Kenneth Dover had taken steps in that direction, and served Henderson as a good friend and sponsor, but by the time Dover published *Greek Homosexuality* in 1978 he had a knighthood; in 1975, Henderson was three years into his first Assistant Professorship.[3]

Moreover, his even-handedness led him to discuss *all* Aristophanes' words, no matter how currently taboo. In discussing here the ways in which female genitalia were displayed on the ancient stage, I am following the model set in *The Maculate Muse*, and, as will be seen, some of my own discoveries already appeared *in nuce* in Henderson's footnotes (as I belatedly found). There is more to be said. To this day, what one of my students could only comfortably discuss as 'lady parts' are widely felt to be unfit for the classroom and are certainly hard to find in classical journals.

Staging Female Genitalia in Aristophanes

Henderson begins *Maculate Muse* with chapters on the literary and performance context for obscenity in Aristophanes and on theoretical approaches that elucidate the work done by the plays' obscene language. He settles on Freud as the best approach, and it is a fact that, when it comes

---

2 Henderson (1975, 36 n. 2).
3 On Dover's status in 1978, see Halliwell (2016, vii). For the horrified reactions to Henderson's proposed dissertation topic, see the opening of the preface to the revised edition (1991, vii), including the advice that he write it in Latin. Here he also comments on his own youth ('a novice scholar'), and incidentally on the speed with which he produced his pioneering research on a difficult author ('if I had given myself more than one year to write a dissertation').

to understanding texts that express fear and loathing of female genitalia, the best of the few explanations offered are psychoanalytic, in the work of Karen Horney and Julia Kristeva. The real thunderbolt in the theory chapter is the well-supported argument that Aristophanes' audience found female genitalia attractive,[4] posing a strong contrast, as I came to find, with the attitudes expressed in Roman invective. Cunnilingus, as Henderson shows, is spoken of onstage as yummy,[5] another big contrast with Roman sensibilities.[6] Alongside food, he sketches out a wide range of metaphors used to denote female genitalia, pointing out the common theme of hiddenness and secrecy;[7] paradoxically, however, it seems that conventional costumes in Old Comedy allowed for a bodysuit that had some representation of female genitalia visible on the outside of the costume, presumably on the actor's lower belly as well as between his legs.

Henderson suggests that the lack of euphemisms for female genitalia stems from the plays' pervasive objectification of the female body for the benefit of male members of the audience.[8] The use of actual women to play the role of mute nudes onstage – showgirls – is disputed, but certainly many scenes involve the specularization of a female body, whether in drag or in the flesh, and by characters onstage as well as by the audience, who are often cued by the characters' words and movement.[9] (The erotic effect on the Athenian audience of male actors costumed as naked women is something else again; this was a significant element in early Roman comedy, but the question, usually dismissed for Old Comedy, is beyond my scope here. Note that, if and when such roles were played by men, their bodysuits would have erased and replaced the actor's own gen-

---

4 Henderson (1975, 52).
5 Henderson (1975, 52).
6 For revulsion against female genitalia in Latin, see Richlin (1983/1992, 113–16) and (2014). On Roman disgust for oral sex in general, see Richlin (1983/1992, 26–9 and 108–9).
7 Henderson (1975, 45).
8 Henderson (1975, 55); cf. Compton-Engle (2015, 44).
9 On the mute nude female characters in Aristophanes, see Zweig (1992) (some roles played by men wearing female bodysuits, others played by sex workers); Marshall (2000) (with comparative evidence from southern Italy); Revermann (2006, 157–9), in a nuanced discussion of 'comic ugliness'; Lambert (2018), with a broader consideration of both theory and characters than I can give here. Compton-Engle, in an authoritative study of comic costume, lists this among unanswerable questions at the outset (2015, 4), but offers arguments on the 'grotesque comic *somation*' for female characters as well as male, with illustrations (figs 6, 7, 19). See Mastromarco (2023) on nudity (unresolved). Hughes (2012, 212–13) dismisses both possibilities, arguing that onstage bodies are left to the imagination: not a tenable position, considering the material record. For visual and tactile cues, and 'ogling conventions', see Compton-Engle (2015, 44 and 50). For the powerful effect mute characters in Roman comedy can have through body language, see Klein (2015).

italia, an even more drastic move than the superimposition of the comic phallus.[10]) Henderson leans toward these bodysuits in a note: 'probably included simulated sexual organs and pubic hair', giving three instances where the text cues something visible (*Wasps* 1373ff.; *Peace* 891ff.; *Lys.* 87ff.).[11] But even a brief survey of Henderson's own catalogue of metaphors for female genitalia produces five probable additions to these instances, and a thorough review of the corpus would, I think, reward study.[12] In addition, two major scenes – the division of Reconciliation in *Lysistrata*, and the sale of the 'piggies' in *Acharnians* – involve extended displays of female bodies in which the genitalia play a central part. Especially fascinating is the suggestion of 'simulated sexual organs', of which there is indeed some trace in the text.

Of the eight short examples, four are cued by onstage ogling of a mute female character, sometimes coupled with feeling, poking, squeezing; all involve some kind of deixis. Most familiar is the ogling of the Theban, Ismenia, as the women gather at the start of *Lysistrata* (87–9):

ΜΥΡΡΙΝΗ νὴ Δί' ὡς Βοιωτία
καλόν γ' ἔχουσα τὸ πεδίον.
ΚΑΛΟΝΙΚΗ καὶ νὴ Δία
κομψότατα τὴν βληχώ γε παρατετιλμένη.

Myrrhine She certainly looks like Boeotia,
with all her lush bottomland.
Calonice Indeed,
and with her bush most elegantly pruned.[13]

All translations meant to be read as poetry, or literature, or performance text, get caught between idioms original and current; academic exegesis is able to unpack jokes more closely. So here, 'with all her lush bottomland' (sounds like a reference to the newcomer's backside) translates the text's simple 'She's got a nice plain (πεδίον)' – just like Boeotia's famous farmland; 'bush' translates the text's more specific βληχώ, 'pennyroyal', which to save the joke might be transposed to an English word with similar connotations, like 'clover'. In *Maculate Muse*, Henderson explains: 'pennyroyal is used jokingly by Lysistrata to refer to the Boeotian girl's neatly depilated *campus muliebris*, with a clever reference to the smooth, fertile plains of that region'; he adds a

---

10 For drag in Greek drama, see Rabinowitz (1998); in early Roman comedy, Richlin (2017, 281–303) and (2024). On male nudity on the comic stage, see Compton-Engle (2020).
11 See Henderson (1975, xi n. 8) and (1991, xv n. 8).
12 Henderson (1975, 130–48).
13 Translation from Henderson (2000) with lines breaks added.

note on pennyroyal's 'small, hairy leaves'.[14] These lines follow those in which the Spartan Lampito is ogled by Lysistrata, Calonice and Myrrhine, and Lampito explicitly complains (84) that they are fingering her ('Hey, you're feeling me up like a beast for sacrifice!').[15] The verb there, ὑποψαλάσσετε, bears the LSJ translation 'touch softly', but the basic verb ψάλλω means 'pluck', like a harp, suggesting Lampito is pinched. For the ogling of Ismenia to work onstage, her lower belly would have to be visible, probably as her clothes were pulled up in front by the others rather than through nudity or see-through lingerie (not yet motivated), and the comment on the [clover] is perhaps also a tactile cue, cuing a plucking movement on 'pruned' (since 'pluck' is the literal meaning of the verb παρατίλλω).[16]

The ogling at the end of *Wasps* is expedited by the fact that the object of the onstage gaze is an *aulētris*, a 'flute-girl': a sex worker who played at parties, lightly clad. Caught sneaking off with her by his killjoy son, as he brandishes a torch (1331), the old man Philocleon hands her the torch (1361–2) and then insists that she *is* a torch he has picked up in the marketplace, the same kind of dehumanizing joke seen in other examples here. Like other straight men, the son, Bdelycleon, is skeptical (*Wasps* 1373–7):

BD. δᾷς ἥδε;
PH.   δᾷς δῆτ'. οὐχ ὁρᾷς ἐσχισμένην;
BD. τί δαὶ τὸ μέλαν τοῦτ' ἐστὶν αὐτῆς τοὐν μέσῳ;
PH. ἡ πίττα δήπου καομένης ἐξέρχεται.
BD. ὁ δ' ὄπισθεν οὐχὶ πρωκτός ἐστιν οὑτοσί;
PH. ὄζος μὲν οὖν τῆς δᾳδὸς οὗτος ἐξέχει.

BD. This is a torch?
PH.   Yes, a torch. Don't you see its cleavage?
BD. And what's this dark patch in the middle?
PH. That's easy: pitch coming out when it's hot.
BD. And behind here, isn't this an arsehole?
PH. No, that's a knothole sticking out of the torch.[17]

---

14 Henderson (1975, 135, #129); see also Henderson (1975, 136, #136) for more on the Boeotian plain.
15 Translation from Henderson (2000). Compton-Engle (2015, 50) points out that Lampito is the only non-mute ogled character, so that she has a voice with which to complain about her treatment: speaking, so definitely played by a male actor.
16 So also Compton-Engle (2015, 51): 'the hem of the Boeotian's tunic must have been lifted enough to reveal the pubic hair painted on her *somation*, a practice attested on vase paintings'. The presence at all of pubic hair on mute ogled characters is disputed, depending on whether or not you believe total hairlessness was the goal of appearance-conscious women in Aristophanes; for brief discussion, see Smith (2013).
17 Translation from Henderson (1998b).

Earlier in the scene, Philocleon addresses the girl as χοιρίον, translated by Henderson as 'my little pussy', as he urges her to hang onto his phallus and promises he will 'buy your freedom and keep you as a concubine' (1353). This enslaved girl is constituted by her genitalia, just as the objectification turns her into a torch that is 'split by a crack' (ἐσχισμένην; again, here, 'cleavage' suggests the wrong body part, but Henderson's discussion points lower down, to 'the notion of the cunt as a split or crack').[18] In a separate discussion of this passage, Henderson further suggests that the 'pitch' refers (favorably) to women's genital secretions (that is, hot and wet),[19] but the 'dark patch in the middle' surely evokes the whole central focus of the genital area, picking up on 'split by a crack', just as the πρωκτός ('anus') is visible from the back (the girl is rotated in place, or Bdelycleon walks around her to get a good look).[20] Here, especially, we might infer a drawing in plan, as it were, of bodily orifices on the bodysuit.

In *Peace*, Trygaeus enters, accompanied by Theoria and another mute nude, at 819, and Theoria then has quite a while to strike poses, though, according to a later cue to strip, she is still somewhat clothed. The House Slave must, then, flip up her skirt when he checks out her πρωκτός (876, in a comic formation that would have to be transposed as 'only comes around once every four years, like the Olympics'). He then 'traces her outlines' (879) and claims he is looking for a σκηνή for his penis (πέει) for the 'Isthmian games' (880). 'Isthmian' here suggests, as elsewhere, the place between the legs.[21] The σκηνή here ostensibly means a tent, a place to stay (thus πρωκτός as orifice/tent flap), but the σκηνή as stage is entirely appropriate for Theoria's identity, as we will see. At 886 Trygaeus orders Theoria to put her 'outfit' (σκευήν) on the ground[22] so he can show her to

---

18 Henderson (1975, 147, #196). It should also be noted that ἐσχισμένην is a conjectural emendation by August Meineke, for codd. ἐστιγμένην, 'tattooed'. A tattooed mark would befit a slave and might also point to the flute-girl's pubic hair, and possibly ἐστιγμένην might have something to do with Philocleon's claim that the torch comes from the agora where it was dedicated to the gods (1372, so 'stamped'?), but all current editors adopt Meineke's emendation without comment, I assume because at 1361 Philocleon refers to the torch as δετάς, 'bundle of sticks'. But images of such torches show the sticks tightly bound together. Based on other ogling scenes, the word must describe her genital area, but neither ἐσχισμένην nor ἐστιγμένην seems convincing to me.
19 Henderson (1975, 145, #183).
20 Compton-Engle (2015, 73) is noncommittal. The sense of πρωκτός as 'anus, asshole' is secure – cf. Henderson (1975, 26) – so that, when this body part is ogled, the ogler is somehow looking at the orifice, not just at the buttocks; perhaps lines like this cue the ogled to bend over. See further below on Theoria in *Peace*.
21 Henderson (1975, 137, #143) takes the House Slave to be using 'Isthmian games' to refer to Theoria's 'cunt', but surely this is a continuation of his gaze at the πρωκτός.
22 It would be convenient for the House Slave checking out Theoria's body at 876 if Theoria had been naked on her entrance, in which case σκευήν here would refer

the Council; he urges them to 'lift her legs in the air' (889), then points to Theoria's 'cooker', as the House Slave chimes in (891–3):

ΤΡΥΓΑΙΟΣ τουτὶ δ' ὁρᾶτε τοὐπτάνιον.
ΟΙΚΕΤΗΣ οἴμ' ὡς καλόν.
διὰ ταῦτα καὶ κεκάπνικεν ἄρ· ἐνταῦθα γὰρ
πρὸ τοῦ πολέμου τὰ λάσανα τῇ βουλῇ ποτ' ἦν.

Trygaeus Just look at this cooker of hers!
House Slave My, she's a fine thing!
Now I see why she's scorched:
before the war, she used to be the Council's trivet![23]

This is explicated in *Maculate Muse*, 'She is blackened down below [pubic hair] because the council used to put their pots [phalli] there for cooking before the war.'[24] More exactly, Trygaeus points out her 'roasting oven' (ὀπτάνιον), and the slave's comment on how nice it/she is leads to the explanation 'That's why it/she is all smoky: before the war it/she was the λάσανα for the Council'. The plural noun λάσανα, translated '*trivet or stand for a pot*' in LSJ, denotes a kind of support stand, usually for a chamberpot; here, in the context of cooking, then, it suggests a stand for a roasting pan, a vivid evocation of Theoria's legs as support for a hot, smoky oven, with the suggestion of ample use.[25] When Trygaeus displays Theoria to the Council, he urges them to look (ὁρᾶτε τὴν Θεωρίαν, 887; σκέψασθ', 888); he repeats the command to look in 891, adding the insistent τουτί. Theoria in the play is the mute companion of the mute Peace, and because θεωρία has the extended meaning 'sight, public spectacle', and in the play she represents festival displays as a benefit of peace, her name has been given translations like 'Showtime', 'Festival', or (so Henderson) 'Holiday'; its basic meaning, though, is just 'viewing', or 'spectatorship', so when she is embodied and made object of the gaze of characters and audience, she is a walking example of the Droste effect. And, like every good *mise en abyme*, like the flute-girl in *Wasps*, Theoria has a dark patch visible at her center, inviting entry. Trygaeus goes on to invite the Council members to use Theoria in a violent gang rape, thinly disguised as festival events (894–905).

to props; but for the wording at *Peace* 886, cf. *Lys.* 637, where the Old Women urge each other to 'put that stuff on the ground' as they strip. For the Chorus's cues in *Lysistrata*, see Compton-Engle (2020, 413).
23 Translation from Henderson (1998b) with line breaks added.
24 Henderson (1975, 142–3, #163).
25 For Aristophanic associations between female genitalia, heat and ovens in the context of Greek theories about the female body, see duBois (1988, 121–3).

A fourth deictic moment comes up in *Birds*, or so it appears in Henderson's catalogue, where he argues that χρυσόν at *Birds* 670 is a pun on κυσός, 'the female member ... a word whose root notion seems simply to be an opening or hole'.[26] Tereus, the Hoopoe, has just summoned his wife Procne the nightingale, who enters (666) dressed as a bird/flute-girl.[27] Peisetaerus exclaims over her beauty, Euelpides expresses a wish to spread her thighs apart (669), and Peisetaerus follows up with 'What marvelous *gold* she has, just like a young girl!' (ὅσον δ' ἔχει τὸν χρυσόν, ὥσπερ παρθένος, 670).[28] The translation in the Loeb has morphed into 'She's got quite a choker, like a debutante',[29] but this sequence of jokes zooms in from the general to the coital, so a genital reference would not be surprising (maybe 'choker' is meant to be one? – a very difficult pun to replicate in English).

In all these deictic instances, the shtick involves acting out a *blason*, the poetic device where an eroticized body is praised part by part, often top to toe (in *Lysistrata* the same effect is achieved by sequential scoping of three newcomers onstage). Exclamations track the gaze: 'What a ...!' It is noteworthy that the *blason* in Roman elegy conspicuously omits female genitalia, 'as if', I once wrote, 'there were a blank space in the middle of the woman'.[30] The very technique of this shtick supports Henderson's argument about the attractiveness of female genitalia in Old Comedy; there is a desire to view.

Four other instances from Henderson's catalogue involve cues for stage action that would require female characters flashing their genitals in order to put wordplay across to the audience. As staging makes clear in live performance, the back-and-forth challenges of the semichoruses of old men and old women in *Lysistrata* involve much wild bodily display. At 683 the Old Women shout at the Old Men, 'I'll let my sow loose' (λύσω τὴν ἐμαυτῆς

---

26 Henderson (1975, 131, #109). For a possible related usage, see Stroup (2004, 61-2) for χρυσίον as a pet name at *Lys.* 930; she ties it to the association between prostitutes and metals, but perhaps it means 'Blondie'.

27 Henderson (1975, 147, #190) argues, based on usage outside comedy given in #189, that ἀηδών at *Birds* 207-8 and 664 'seems to be an obscene pun on the bird-name of the hoopoe's wife (represented onstage by a flute-girl)', in other words, that this word, 'singer', an epithet of the nightingale, is also a metaphor for female genitalia; he stresses Peisetaerus's excited line, 'Call her out here, by heaven, so we can see the *bird*!' (emphasis original; θεασώμεσθα τὴν ἀηδόνα). If so, this would be another instance in which the mute female character is summed up by her genitalia, again with an emphasis on viewing, although she is not yet in view: anticipatory, like many deictic receptions in Plautus (Richlin 2017, 295-303).

28 Translation from Henderson (1975, 131), emphasis original.

29 Henderson (2000, 113).

30 For the *blason* in Roman elegy, see Richlin (1983/1992, 44-7; 2014, 78, with n. 33). One of the press readers for *Garden of Priapus*, around 1980, remarked of this observation, 'Well, there *is* a blank space!' Evidently not on the Attic stage.

ὖν ἐγώ), or, as Henderson explains, 'the older women threaten the men with the power of their cunts',[31] ὗς being the mature form of the 'piggy' denoted by χοῖρος.[32] Again in the opening scene, when Calonice swears loyalty to Lysistrata (113–14), Henderson suggests that the phrase τοὔγκυκλον | τουτὶ καταθεῖσαν might bear the double sense 'pawn my shawl/lay down my cunt', adding that 'We must suspect also that the deictic demonstrative pronoun indicates byplay on stage.'[33] Certainly the leap from ἔγκυκλον, 'wrap', to 'cunt' would need a visual cue.[34] Even more difficult to put across would be the clever play on ἐς χέρας/ἐσχάρας, 'into the arms'/'the labia' (*Thesm.* 912), perverting a line from Euripides' *Helen*:[35] only a timely bump and grind, or skirt flip, would clarify the joke in the vowel shifts (sensitive though audiences may have been to diction). Finally, a joke at the start of *Assemblywomen* might well be underscored by a skirt flip; as Henderson translates, 'Wouldn't it be a fine thing if the Assembly happened to be full and one of us, pulling up her clothes to get over those already seated, should flash her ... Phormisius!' (*Eccl.* 95–7).[36] This kind of joke, it seems to me, does come close to a ladylike euphemism, no matter how proverbially hairy Phormisius was; again, my students in class have used 'See you next Tuesday' instead of the taboo C-U-N-T. The word here translated 'flash' is δείξειε, the eponymous deictic verb, in use, for example, at *Birds* 666 when Tereus calls out Procne to show herself.

This array of small episodes – flashes – contextualizes the two showstoppers that focus on female genitalia: the dividing-up of Reconciliation in *Lysistrata* and the piggies scene in *Acharnians*. Reconciliation has attracted much recent attention. Lysistrata calls her onstage at 1114, with a simple 'Where is ...?' Reconciliation then stands there, posing, to motivate the ithyphallic (1136) Athenian and Spartan delegations to come to terms. A Spartan exclaims, ὁ πρωκτὸς ἄφατον ὡς καλός! ('The asshole – how unspeakably lovely!', 1148); the Athenian, in turn, exclaims, κύσθον γ' οὐδέπω καλλίονα ('I've never seen a lovelier cunt!' 1158).[37] The exclamations and the verb of seeing (carried over from 1157) are familiar from the shorter ogling episodes. Then the men begin to divide up Reconciliation as if she embodied Greece itself: the Spartan asks for τὤγκυκλον (1162; cf. above on the use of this word earlier in the play), which he specifies to

---

31 Henderson (1975, 132, #114).
32 See Compton-Engle (2015, 54 n. 134); Farmer (2020, 432–5) on the choruses.
33 Henderson (1975, 139, #147).
34 Cf. the Spartans' request at *Lys.* 1162, for a feature on the body of Reconciliation; the line is discussed by Henderson (1975, 139, #147) and by Compton-Engle (2015, 57), where she cautiously identifies it as a 'rounded part' of Reconciliation's body.
35 Henderson (1975, 143, #164).
36 Henderson (1975, 148, #197).
37 Translation from Henderson (2000 and 2010).

mean 'Pylos', translated by Henderson as 'Back Door'.³⁸ The Athenians then ask what *they* can fuck (τίνα κινήσομεν, 1166), and Lysistrata tells them to choose another χωρίον (1167, 'place') – possibly, with a stage pause before the word, a pun on χοιρίον, 'little pussy'.³⁹ The Athenians comply (1168–70), pointing (τουτονί) and requesting '[place name that sounds like 'sea urchin', a visual metaphor for the female genitalia] and the Melian Gulf (κόλπον)': '"Melian" refers to apple-like buttocks and "Gulf" (κόλπος) to the anus'. Indeed, since this 'gulf' is somehow ὄπισθεν ('behind' – cf. ὄπισθεν above at *Wasps* 1376), I do not see how this can be anything but anal despite the Spartans' prior claims.⁴⁰

Sarah Stroup sets Reconciliation up as a culminating example in her analysis of the play, pointing out the tiny agency she gets when Lysistrata urges her to lead the Athenians and Spartans by their phalli if they will not cooperate (1119); on the other hand, she is 'pornified', '*not even a person*'.⁴¹ In fact ogled characters are often dehumanized: Procne, as a bird; the flute-girl in *Wasps*, as a torch; Theoria, an embodied abstraction; and the piggies. Compton-Engle rightly remarks that Reconciliation's body parts are played as 'territory available for penetration';⁴² indeed, the Athenian reacts (1173) by saying he wants to plow naked, while the Spartan then wants to spread manure (1174).⁴³ The question of who played Reconciliation, a male actor in a bodysuit or a naked woman, stands at the center of the debate about mute nudes; Compton-Engle suggests that this scene is 'intended precisely to violate convention'.⁴⁴ Modern productions like to experiment; some-times, as in the 2021 Getty Villa production, a glamorous dancer is replaced by a male actor in the same getup;⁴⁵ Michael Lambert opens his extensive theoretical analysis of the scene with a South African production in which Reconciliation was played by a 'naked female blow-up doll', which exploded.⁴⁶ It is clear, in any case, that the female genitalia aroused enthusiasm in the original.

38 τοὔγκυκλον is translated here by Henderson (2000 and 2010) as 'this abutment', and see n. 34 for Compton-Engle's interpretation; but since the sense is 'wraparound', surely here it refers, like 'Pylos', to the πρωκτός.
39 For the suggestion of a similar pun at *Wasps* 849–50, see duBois (1988, 156), in a discus-sion of woman's body as writing tablet.
40 On the sea urchin, see Henderson (1975, 142, #161). On the Melian Gulf, Henderson (1975, 149, #203), despite other contexts in which κόλπος = 'cunt' (1975, 140, #151).
41 Stroup (2004, 62–8).
42 Compton-Engle (2015, 56–7).
43 For the metaphor of female body as field/furrow, widespread in Greek literature, see duBois (1988, 39–85); Henderson (1975, 8 and 166) differentiates between 'grand' and obscene uses of this imagery, but duBois shows the point of the continuity.
44 Compton-Engle (2015, 159 n. 145).
45 See also Given (2011).
46 Lambert (2018, 35).

The piggies scene in *Acharnians* (719–819) takes the display of female genitalia to another level, animalizing two young girls as they are turned into χοῖροι, complete with trotters and snouts. The Megarian arrives via the orchestra as the first customer in Dicaeopolis's private market, accompanied by his two young daughters; they are all starving, and the Megarian intends to sell the two girls, first disguising them as χοῖροι, then lugging them along in a sack. They are, then, very small. The whole scene depends on the double entendre whereby the girls are simultaneously piglets and female genitalia; Dover's analysis tracks the joke by this semantic fluctuation,[47] but the word χοῖρος in various forms appears twenty-four times in eighty lines (739–819), suggesting that the word itself is a laugh no matter when it is used.[48] The girls are specularized, in the same shtick used in *Wasps* of the girl/torch: τουτὶ τί ἦν τὸ πρᾶγμα ('What's this supposed to be?'), asks Dicaeopolis; χοῖρος ναὶ Δία ('A piggy, by Zeus!'), replies the Megarian (767); αὗτα 'στὶ χοῖρος; ('Isn't that a piggy?', 781), the Megarian insists.[49] Dicaeopolis, unfooled, plays the straight man. The scene is full of the cues that become familiar in Aristophanes' later plays: along with the deictic pronouns and the verb ἐπίδειξον, an invitation to feel them (766), and multiple uses of forms of καλός (765, 766, 788, 792). Analysis of the wordplay does not take in the visual impact of watching the two small figures spoken of as pussies and joked about as tasty when cooked on a skewer (796), or as turning into 'cunts' when they grow up (κύσθος, 782; 789); or the audible impact of hearing the piggies squeal on cue (776–80, 800–3).

Lauren Taaffe, in a brisk discussion, calls this scene 'arguably the most gruesome example of black humor in Aristophanes' repertoire' and identifies the girls as 'living synecdoches', 'stripped of language';[50] she speculates that these characters might have been played by boy actors.[51] That children were sold as sex slaves very young is well illustrated by the story of Neaera (ps.-Dem. 59.18; cf. Metagenes fr. 4 KA). The crudity of the scene has often led scholars to associate it with the lost performance form known as Megarian farce, but Henderson argues that Old Comedy was perfectly capable of generating a scene like this, and the piggies do fit right in with the shorter ogling scenes.[52] It is not that shtick like this does not circulate.

---

47 Dover (1972, 63–5).
48 Olson (2002, *ad* 738–9), discussing χοῖρος, argues against Henderson's specific definition of this word as 'the pink, hairless cunt of young girls', but it does seem that the age of the girls and the contrast with their grown-up state marks them as hairless pink piglets.
49 Translation from Henderson (1998a).
50 Taaffe (1993/2014, 28–9).
51 Taaffe (1993/2014, 157 n. 19).
52 For an extended argument that this scene depends on Megarian farce, see Konstantakos (2012, 120–49); the idea was vehemently rejected by Henderson (1975, 23–4 and 223–8).

When Dicaeopolis protests that the χοῖρος 'belongs to a human being' (ἔστιν ἀνθρώπου γε, 774), the Megarian replies, 'It belongs to me!' (ἐμά γα, 775), a joke that plays off the girls' obvious powerlessness and their father's rights as their *kyrios*. The same joke is used by Plautus in *Persa*, father to daughter as he tells her of his plan to let her be sold to a pimp: no problem, 'since you're mine' (*quae sis mea*, 340). A joke about a girl's *porcus* shows up briefly in Plautus's *Rudens*, which brings us to the diffusion of this shtick throughout the Mediterranean comic soup.

Staging Female Genitals Outside Athens

Time passed; war gave way to war; comedy in Athens changed. Meanwhile, in the new world after Alexander, a journeyman poet possibly from Cos staged (probably) some comedy sketches at the court of Ptolemy II in Alexandria in the 270s. Herodas's mimes are now known for their artificial language (imitating the iambos of three hundred years before), and the circumstances of their production are debated.[53] In later mime it is certain that naked women were part of the show; did Herodas have a lovely assistant? Or did he play all the roles himself, like Richard Pryor doing standup? Several of his mimes call for multiple players (in flogging scenes, for example), and his second *Mimiambus*, it seems to me, would work best with an actual naked woman, for she is the center of the sketch, a display within the play. Uniquely in ancient literature, a self-identified *kinaidos* is the main character; he is also a pimp, and he delivers a courtroom speech complaining about a violent customer who has broken into his house and assaulted one of his prostitutes.[54] The pimp summons her (*Mim.* 2.65–71):

> δεῦρο, Μυρτάλη, καὶ σύ·
> δεῖξον σεωυτὴν πᾶσι· μηδέν' αἰσχύνευ·
> νόμιζε τούτους οὓς ὁρῆις δικάζοντας
> πατέρας ἀδελφοὺς ἐμβλέπειν. ὁρῆτ' ἄνδρες,
> τὰ τίλματ' αὐτῆς καὶ κάτωθεν κἄνωθεν
> ὡς λεῖα ταῦτ' ἔτιλλεν ὠναγὴς οὗτος,
> ὅτ' εἷλκεν αὐτὴν κἀβιάζετ' …

> … Come forward, Myrtale, you, too:
> show yourself to everybody – don't be ashamed before anyone,
> just pretend these jurymen you see

---

53 See Hunter (1993).
54 Sapsford (2022, 80–3) has much to say about the intertextual features of this mime, but naturally is interested in the *kinaidos* rather than Myrtale. I here follow the text and interpretation of Rusten and Cunningham (2002).

are (your) fathers and brothers looking on. Men, you see?
The plucked places of her, both below and up on top –
how smooth that angel has plucked her,
while he was dragging her and raping her …

Like Procne, like Reconciliation, out she comes, on cue; like Procne, like Reconciliation, like Theoria, like Ismenia, like the flute-girl in *Wasps*, Myrtale takes center stage and says nothing, while bystanders point out features of her body.[55] Her depilation, normally the mark of beauty, is here scraped over by a second, violent 'depilation', presumably effected by stage makeup. The pimp tells her not to be ashamed, as if she had any honor left to lose (joke). Like Reconciliation, Myrtale is doubly displayed, both to the imaginary audience within the stage action and to Herodas's audience, who also double as the stage audience; moreover, as a slave displayed by a pimp, she here revisits the experience of a slave on the block or a brothel slave on show.[56] And the whole joke works just as well in real life, since the mime actress is also available for sex: a staple of subsequent social history. The pimp's encouraging words to Myrtale to imagine the jurymen as fathers and brothers is surely a joke about the respectable audience as potential customers, with a slight whiff of incest: a cruel joke, since, as slaves, neither Myrtale nor the mime actress has legal kin, and, if she could even remember a father and brothers, what horror would be hers and theirs at this sight?[57] The depilation, the deictic markers, the verbs of seeing, the exclamation 'how', the violence – all are familiar from the Aristophanic genital displays considered above, but Herodas, like all sketch comics, is working in more closely with the audience.

Aristophanes is far better known than Herodas, so that the staging of Myrtale has not been often treated from a feminist perspective.[58] The pimp's speech is commonly compared with Hypereides' speech on behalf of the prostitute Phryne, a case he was said to have won by presenting her in court and tearing her clothes to display her breasts; the kinship between the law and the comic stage in this case has been the subject of some

---

55 Body parts κάτωθεν κἄνωθεν probably refer to genitalia and armpits, for the depilation of which see *Eccl.* 60–70, and remarks by McClure (2015, 70–1).
56 See Richlin (2017, 114 and 281–303, esp. 301–2) for this convention in the plays of Plautus.
57 On the joke, Nairn (1904, 24 *ad* 68): 'Considering Myrtale's profession there is certainly an exquisite impudence in the words' – typical of the patronizing tenor of critical remarks, as will be seen. Legal kin for Greek slaves: perhaps for slave families held by a single owner, but not for a sex slave owned by a pimp or a mime actress probably owned by the lead mime.
58 A major exception here is, unsurprisingly, Page duBois (2007), who leads an essay on violence against slaves with this passage in Herodas.

discussion.⁵⁹ As for the body parts that were plucked, Walter Headlam, in his magisterial 1922 edition, translation and commentary, decided that what was plucked – or 'rent', as he put it – was Myrtale's clothing, while the rape turns into 'tousled' and *kinaidos* is translated 'low fellow';⁶⁰ at least the first part was called out immediately upon publication by A. E. Housman, who comments that the mistake about plucking 'argues some innocence of mind'.⁶¹ He translates the Greek into Latin, and explains that the joke is that Myrtale is plucked only as 'an ordinary feature of the feminine toilet', as Herodas's audiences would have known perfectly well: 'the height of [the pimp's] impudence'. Why? Because whores come ready plucked, so the complaint that Thales plucked her involves a proverbial impossibility like 'taking the breeks off a Highlander'. This analysis of the joke has influenced further discussion, as for example in the standard commentary in English: 'Myrtale …, the object of Th[ales]'s affection, appears in person and displays her "injuries"'.⁶² The inverted commas are picked up elsewhere; but if ὠναγὴς is to be taken as sarcasm, as Cunningham argues, I see no reason why the adjacent λεῖα ταῦτ' ἔτιλλεν should not be so as well (figuratively, = 'scraped raw'). The pimp has just complained about actual damage to his house (63–5), a standard komastic event that no one takes to be a lie here. Meanwhile the woman turns into a standing joke.

A lifetime later, at the other end of the Mediterranean, Roman comedy was going strong, forged in the crucible of the Second Punic War. Just as in Athens, people needed something to laugh at in hard times, and then again in the boom times that followed in the 190s; only two of Plautus's plays can be securely dated, but they all belong somewhere in this eventful period, when human trafficking exploded. *Rudens* suffers from a spatial as well as a temporal dislocation, being set in Cyrene, and on the beach. As the play opens, two enslaved prostitutes are washed up on shore after a storm at sea; in their opening song they complain about how their clothing has been reduced to wet rags, and this feature draws comments from others who meet them. Clearly, their bodies – almost certainly bodysuits worn by male actors – are glimpsable. As they take refuge at the altar before a beachside

---

59 So Ziogas (2017, 89), in a discussion of the Phryne case, with brief use of Agamben on the *corpus*. The editor of the collection on law and literature in which Ziogas's essay appears saw fit to use the lurid Gérôme painting of Hypereides stripping Phryne as the jacket illustration, as did Konstantinos Kapparis in *Prostitution in the Ancient Greek World* (2019), and as, surprisingly, did Allison Glazebrook in her recent *Sexual Labor in the Athenian Courts* (2021). Sex always sells. For the specularizing reception of Phryne, see Morales (2012), with a brief but telling glance at Herodas *Mim.* 2 (2012, 78 n. 21).
60 Headlam (1922/2001).
61 Housman (1922, 109).
62 Cunningham (1971, 95, *ad* 2.65–78), explicitly following Housman.

shrine to Venus, they excuse their bedraggled condition to the goddess, and a male slave who befriends them calls attention to their genitals (699–704):

PALAESTRA ... elautae ambae sumus opera Neptuni noctu,
ne indignum id habeas neve idcirco nobis vitio vortas,
si quippiam est minus quod bene esse lautum tu arbitrare.

TRACHALIO Venus, aequom has petere intellego: decet aps te id impetrari;
ignoscere his te convenit: metus has id ut faciant subigit.
te ex concha natam esse autumant, cave tu harum conchas spernas.

Palaestra We both had a bath, thanks to Neptune, last night,
so's you don't get insulted or fault us for this –
if you think anything's less than well washed somehow.

Trachalio Venus, I know these women ask what's fair: it's right they should get this from you;
it's proper for you to forgive them: fear forces them to do it.
They say you were born from a *concha*, so don't you scorn their *conchas*.

The final joke makes it clear what the point at issue is: the women are sitting on the altar of Venus with nothing between it and their skin.[63] The joke is unusually crude for Plautus, who rarely makes genital jokes, much less about female genitals, but one of the few others is in *Rudens*: *cum sucula et cum porculis* ('with your little sow and your piglets', 1170), a joke that depends on what Varro says is the use of 'pig' by 'our women, especially nannies' to mean 'maiden's genitals'. Varro compares this with 'Greek women's' use of *choerus*.[64] Here the women, who are plastered to the altar of Venus, posing, without a word, through line 882, are displayed like the women in Aristophanes and Herodas, and their *conchae* at the center; unlike those women, however, these will be rescued from their pimp and married off, recovering, or gaining, a respectable status never available to Myrtale. The word κόγχη for 'vagina' does come up in Aristophanes, also in the mimes of Sophron[65] – pointed out by Henderson

---

63 For the possibility of female genital display in Roman costuming, see Marshall (2006, 64–5).
64 Varro *R* 2.4.10; see Richlin (2017, 409).
65 Fr. 24 in Rusten and Cunningham (2002).

in a footnote.⁶⁶ Here in Plautus, there is an extra thrill in the indeterminacy of the actor's body.⁶⁷

These textual traces of female genitalia on display are valuable because such display is rare in the material record, richly endowed with phalli as it is. Plenty of naked women in art, yes, but, as even Housman noted, generally airbrushed.⁶⁸ I always wonder about the central figure in the *Women at the Thesmophoria* vase, foot firmly planted where you would expect to see something else: what does it stand for? As for disembodied female genitalia, the 'coffee beans' catalogued by Stefanie Hoss perhaps give some idea of what a representation on a bodysuit might have looked like.⁶⁹

Jeffrey Henderson's Unusual Vision

How young we were, and living in young times; Henderson begins the 1991 preface by speaking of 1971, when he started his dissertation, as a time of 'cultural liberation', the time of the sexual revolution – and ends it by commenting that 1991 is 'an opportune time for re-release, in view of what seems to be a national reversion to sexual conservatism'; the reissue, he remarks, 'gives me an agreeable feeling of rebelliousness reminiscent of my student days'.⁷⁰ Again ahead of his time, he reminds the reader that 'there was an "other" Athens … that was more traditional and inclusive';⁷¹ contrast the programmatic exclusion of pussy in Plato. But his own attitude was fundamental; he 'had always been amused and fascinated by erotic art and literature'.⁷² It took a great man to bring the lady parts out of the shadows and into the daylight, which is where they belonged in Old Comedy. Jeffrey Henderson's candid eye set many free to see what was there, should they wish to. A great legacy, and, fifty years later, more necessary than ever.

Works Cited

Compton-Engle, Gwendolyn. 2015. *Costume in the Comedies of Aristophanes*. New York: Cambridge University Press.
———. 2020. 'Male Stage-Nudity in Aristophanes'. *ICS* 45: 399–423.
Cunningham, I. C. 1971. *Herodas: Mimiambi*. Oxford: Clarendon Press.
Dover, K. J. 1972. *Aristophanic Comedy*. Berkeley: University of California Press.

---

66 Henderson (1975, 142 n. 183).
67 Richlin (2023).
68 Housman (1922, 110).
69 Hoss (2020).
70 Henderson (1991, x).
71 Henderson (1991, ix).
72 Henderson (1991, vii).

duBois, Page. 1988. *Sowing the Body: Psychoanalysis and Ancient Representations of Women*. Chicago: University of Chicago Press.

———. 2007. 'The Coarsest Demand: Utopia and the Fear of Slaves'. In *Fear of Slaves – Fear of Enslavement in the Ancient Mediterranean: Actes du XXIXe colloque international du groupe international de recherche sur l'esclavage dans l'antiquité*, edited by Anastasia Serghidou, 435–44. Besançon: Presses universitaires de Franche-Comté.

Farmer, Matthew. 2020. 'Choral Disrobing in Aristophanes'. *ICS* 45: 424–46.

Given, John. 2011. 'Staging the Reconciliation Scene of Aristophanes' *Lysistrata*'. *Didaskalia* 8.29: 189–97.

Halliwell, Stephen. 2016. 'Foreword: The Book and Its Author'. In *Greek Homosexuality*, 3rd edn, edited by K. J. Dover, vii–xiv. London: Bloomsbury Academic.

Headlam, Walter. 2001 [1922]. *Herodas: The Mimes and Fragments*. Edited by A. D. Knox. London: Bristol Classical Press.

Henderson, Jeffrey. 1975. *The Maculate Muse: Obscene Language in Attic Comedy*. New Haven: Yale University Press.

———. 1991. *The Maculate Muse: Obscene Language in Attic Comedy*. Rev. edn. New York: Oxford University Press.

———. 1998a. *Aristophanes: Acharnians, Knights*. Cambridge, MA: Harvard University Press.

———. 1998b. *Aristophanes: Clouds, Wasps, Peace*. Cambridge, MA: Harvard University Press.

———. 2000. *Aristophanes: Birds, Lysistrata, Women at the Thesmophoria*. Cambridge, MA: Harvard University Press.

———. 2002. *Aristophanes: Frogs, Assemblywomen, Wealth*. Cambridge, MA: Harvard University Press.

———. 2010. *Three Plays by Aristophanes: Staging Women*. 2nd edn. Abingdon and New York: Routledge.

Hoss, Stefanie. 2020. 'Barbie-Bodies and Coffee Beans: Female Genital Imagery in the Mediterranean and the North-West Provinces of the Roman Empire'. In *Un-Roman Sex: Gender, Sexuality, and Lovemaking in the Roman Provinces and Frontiers*, edited by Tatiana Ivleva and Rob Collins, 117–82. Abingdon and New York: Routledge.

Housman, A. E. 1922. 'Herodas II 65–71'. *Classical Review* 36: 109–10.

Hughes, Alan. 2012. *Performing Greek Comedy*. Cambridge: Cambridge University Press.

Hunter, R. L. 1993. 'The Presentation of Herodas' *Mimiamboi*'. *Antichthon* 27: 31–44.

Klein, Sophie. 2015. 'When Actions Speak Louder than Words: Mute Characters in Roman Comedy'. *CJ* 111: 53–66.

Konstantakos, Ioannis. 2012. '"*My Kids for Sale*": The Megarian's Scene in Aristophanes' *Acharnians* (729–835) and Megarian Comedy'. *Logeion* 2: 121–66.

Lambert, M. 2018. 'Mapping Women's Bodies and the Male "Gaze": Reconciliation in Aristophanes' *Lysistrata*'. *Akroterion* 63: 35–56.

McClure, Laura. 2015. 'Courtesans Reconsidered: Women in Aristophanes' *Lysistrata*'. *EuGeStA* 5: 58–84.

Marshall, C. W. 2000. 'Female Performers on Stage? (*PhV* 96 [*RVP* 2/33])'. *Text & Presentation* 21: 13–25.

———. 2006. *The Stagecraft and Performance of Roman Comedy*. Cambridge: Cambridge University Press.

Mastromarco, Giuseppe. 2023. 'Sexy Mutes on the Aristophanic Stage'. In *Page and Stage: Intersections of Text and Performance in Ancient Greek Drama*, edited by S. Douglas Olson, Oliver Taplin and Piero Totaro, 97–113. Trends in Classics – Supplementary Volumes 146. Berlin: Walter de Gruyter.

Méndez Dosuna, J. V. 2021. 'Milesian Wool'. *Mnemosyne* 74: 667–76.

Morales, Helen. 2012. 'Fantasising Phryne: The Psychology and Ethos of Ekphrasis'. *Cambridge Classical Journal* 57: 71–104.

Nairn, J. Arbuthnot. 1904. *The Mimes of Herodas*. Oxford: Clarendon Press.

Olson, S. Douglas. 2002. *Aristophanes: Acharnians*. Oxford: Oxford University Press.

Rabinowitz, Nancy Sorkin. 1998. 'Embodying Tragedy: The Sex of the Actor'. *Intertexts* 2: 3–25.

Revermann, Martin. 2006. *Comic Business: Theatricality, Dramatic Technique, and Performance Contexts of Aristophanic Comedy*. Oxford: Oxford University Press.

Richlin, Amy. 1983. *The Garden of Priapus: Sexuality and Aggression in Roman Humor*. New Haven: Yale University Press.

———. 1992. *The Garden of Priapus: Sexuality and Aggression in Roman Humor*. Rev. edn. New York: Oxford University Press.

———. 2014. 'Invective Against Women in Roman Satire'. In *Arguments with Silence: Writing the History of Roman Women*, 62–80. Ann Arbor: University of Michigan Press. Revised, with introductory essay, from *Arethusa* 17 (1984): 67–80.

———. 2017. *Slave Theater in the Roman Republic: Plautus and Popular Comedy*. Cambridge: Cambridge University Press.

———. 2024. 'Schrödinger's Pussy: Slave Actors and Fluid Desire in Early Roman Comedy'. In *The Methuen Drama Handbook of Gender and Theatre*, edited by Sean Metzger and Roberta Mock, 219–37. London: Bloomsbury Academic.

Rusten, Jeffrey, and I. C. Cunningham. 2002. *Theophrastus: Characters. Herodas: Mimes. Sophron and Other Mime Fragments*. Cambridge, MA: Harvard University Press.

Sapsford, Tom. 2022. *Performing the Kinaidos: Unmanly Men in Ancient Mediterranean Cultures*. Oxford: Oxford University Press.

Smith, Nicholas D. 2013. 'Two Obscene Jokes in Aristophanes' *Wasps* and *Peace*'. *Eirene: Studia Graeca et Latina* 49: 147–52.

Stroup, Sarah Culpepper. 2004. 'Designing Women: Aristophanes' *Lysistrata* and the "Hetairization" of the Greek Wife'. *Arethusa* 37: 37–73.

Taaffe, Lauren K. 2014 [1993]. *Aristophanes and Women*. Abingdon and New York: Routledge.

Ziogas, Ioannis. 2017. 'Law and Literature in the Ancient World: The Case of Phryne'. In *Law and Literature*, edited by Kieran Dolin, 79–93. Cambridge: Cambridge University Press.

Zweig, Bella. 1992. 'The Mute Nude Female Characters in Aristophanes' Plays'. In *Pornography and Representation in Greece and Rome*, edited by Amy Richlin, 73–89. Oxford: Oxford University Press.

CHAPTER 2

'Let Loose the Melodies of Holy Hymns': Voice, Agency and Gender in Aristophanes' Birds
Daniel Libatique

In Aristophanes' *Birds*, the shabby-looking hoopoe Tereus makes an intertextual reference to his tragic predecessor in the eponymous play by Sophocles: 'Sophocles mistreats me, Tereus, in this way in his tragedies' (τοιαῦτα μέντοι Σοφοκλέης λυμαίνεται | ἐν ταῖς τραγῳδίαισιν ἐμέ, τὸν Τηρέα, 100–1). An inflection point in the various versions of the Tereus, Procne and Philomela myth,[1] the *Tereus* treats the act of rape and glossectomy inflicted by the Thracian king Tereus upon Philomela, the sister of his Athenian wife Procne; the revenge that Procne and Philomela inflict upon Tereus through the murder of Itys, Procne's and Tereus's son, and the subsequent feeding of Itys to Tereus in a meal; and the transformation of all three into birds.[2] The wide body of scholarship on Sophocles' best-attested fragmentary play ranges from conjectures about and reconstructions of its plot,[3] to investigations of the play's familial or gender

---

1 See Libatique (2018b, 52–5); Scattolin (2013, 119); Sommerstein *et al.* (2006, 145–6); Monella (2005, 13 and 83–125).
2 Fr. 581 *TrGF* indicates that Tereus becomes both a hawk and a hoopoe. All versions of the myth indicate that the sisters transform into the nightingale and the swallow, but the play's fragments and hypothesis do not allow us conclusive insight into which bird each of the sisters is transformed into in this play in particular, a fact made more confusing by the general tendency of the Greco-Roman mythic tradition to switch the sisters' and birds' identities; see Libatique (2018b, 27–94). As far as Sophocles' play is concerned, the hypothesis, as reconstructed by Sommerstein *et al.* (2006, 160–1), contains a μέν-δέ construction that does not name which sister turns into which bird. However, external and roughly contemporaneous evidence such as Aeschylus's *Suppliants* 58–67 and *Agamemnon* 1136–49 suggests that Procne, the filicide, becomes the nightingale who sings mournfully for her son, while Philomela, whose tongue Tereus cuts out to prevent her from revealing his crime, becomes the swallow who twitters unintelligibly.
3 For example, see Milo (2020); Slater (2018); Libatique (2018a); Finglass (2016); Slattery (2016); Sommerstein *et al.* (2006, 141–95); Casanova (2003); Fitzpatrick (2001); Dobrov (2001, 105–32); Hourmouziades (1986); Kiso (1984, 51–86); Sutton (1984, 127–32); Calder (1974); Welcker (1839). (This is an augmented version of the list at Dova (2020, 75 n. 16).)

dynamics as gleaned from its fragments,[4] to examinations of its reception in later works such as Achilles Tatius's *Leucippe and Clitophon,* Ovid's *Metamorphoses* and, indeed, Aristophanes' *Birds*.[5] Scholarship in the last category, obviously invited by Aristophanes' direct reference to Sophocles, abounds with implications for reception, intertextuality and genre. The plot of Aristophanes' *Birds* centers around the Athenians Peisetaerus and Euelpides and their quest to found a civilization free of the social strictures and obligations of Athenian life. Tereus, transformed into a bird and revered amongst the community of birds, serves as their blueprint to fashion such a civilization with the same birds that Tereus has civilized out of their previous 'barbarian' state; he serves as the main characters' bridge from the human Athens into the avian Cloudcuckooland.

In this chapter, I contribute to this discussion of the interaction between Aristophanes' *Birds* and Sophocles' *Tereus* by exploring how Aristophanes' choices in attributing speech or silence to his characters allow him to flip the hierarchy of power in Sophocles' play upside down. While the fragments do not reveal whether or not Tereus was afforded a vocal role in Sophocles' play, Aristophanes establishes Tereus as a vocal primary character, endowed with many opportunities for direct speech, virtuosic singing and positive characterization. On the other hand, while Procne receives opportunities in Sophocles' play to express powerful emotions and lament her situation, Aristophanes casts her as a mostly mute object, whose body is intended for the visual consumption of the males both onstage and in the audience; she no longer speaks, let alone expresses any emotion or exercises any agency. These shifts from Sophocles' tragic precedents conform to normative gender expectations that will nevertheless be upended in the practices of Cloudcuckooland, a subversion of a subversion that highlights Aristophanes' penchant for emulative generic play.

Tereus as an Arbiter of Communication

Of the fragments of Sophocles' *Tereus*,[6] the only ones that may be attributed to Tereus as a speaker are 582[7] and 585.[8] However, even those possibilities

---

4 For example, Coo (2020, 48–51); Finglass (2020); Dova (2020); Coo (2013); Suter (2004).
5 For example, Dova (2020); Haley (2019); Privitera (2007, 41–54); Liapis (2006); Monella (2005); Curley (2003); Dobrov (2001, 105–32).
6 For the text of the hypothesis and fragments, I use Sommerstein *et al.* (2006, 141–95), but for fragment numbering, I use Radt (1977).
7 'Helios most revered light to the horse-loving Thracians' (Ἥλιε, φιλίπποις Θρῃξὶ πρέσβιστον σέλας).
8 'It is clear that these things are painful, Procne, but nevertheless those who are mortal must bear divine mandates readily' (ἀλγεινά, Πρόκνη, δῆλον· ἀλλ' ὅμως χρεὼν | τὰ θεῖα θνητοὺς ὄντας εὐπετῶς φέρειν).

are unclear; 582 could be spoken by any character, though ostensibly a Thracian one, while 585 could be spoken by the Chorus Leader or some confidante of Procne. It is difficult and dangerous to make an *argumentum ex silentio* and say that the lack of clear references to direct speech for Tereus in the fragments means that he did not speak at all in the play. Barring the discovery of new fragments, the lines of the play that are extant do not allow us much insight into Tereus's opportunities for speech.

His counterpart in Aristophanes' *Birds*, on the other hand, is afforded numerous opportunities not only for direct speech, as a major interlocutor with Euelpides and Peisetaerus for the first half of the play, but even virtuosic lyric *qua* birdsong when he summons Procne and the birds (209–62). As Nan Dunbar notes, 'As birds are nature's songsters, so Tereus is given here, to establish the note of high lyricism that permeates the play, an elegant, mellifluous invocation of his mate and a long, metrically elaborate lyric invocation of the birds which would need an actor with a good singing voice.'[9] The length of Tereus's lyric run, which is ostensibly supposed to summon the birds, both delays the Chorus's arrival and showcases the vocal dexterity of its singer, with its various meters intended to evoke different groups of birds.[10] Euelpides even comments metatheatrically on the beauty of the song and the singer's voice, right after Tereus's anapests and before his mélange of lyric meters: 'King Zeus, that avian voice! How it's turned the entire thicket into honey!' (ὦ Ζεῦ βασιλεῦ, τοῦ φθέγματος τοὐρνιθίου· | οἷον κατεμελίτωσε τὴν λόχμην ὅλην, 223–4).[11]

The power of Tereus's voice is clearly emphasized at 199–200 when Tereus claims that he taught the birds how to speak and thus civilized them out of their prior barbarian state: 'I lived with them for a long time and taught them speech, since they were barbarians before this' (ἐγὼ γὰρ αὐτοὺς βαρβάρους ὄντας πρὸ τοῦ | ἐδίδαξα τὴν φωνὴν ξυνὼν πολὺν χρόνον). The adjective βαρβάρους is particularly pointed when we consider how Tereus's race was cast, presumably pejoratively,[12] as βάρβαρος in

9 Dunbar (1998, 150–1).
10 Dunbar (1998, 155–8). See also Nooter (2019, 200–3), on the aural effects of the hoopoe's chirps: 'The hoopoe's history of shifts in identities, dramatic genres and lifeforms is thus signaled by his shifts between broken vocalizations and decipherable language' (202).
11 Sommerstein (1987, 41), takes τοῦ φθέγματος τοὐρνιθίου as referring to Procne's song. The translations of Henderson (2000, 47) and Roche (2005, 347) do not ascribe the φθέγμα to either Procne or Tereus explicitly. The fact that Tereus has sung from 209 to 222, but the nightingale is also singing at the same time, starting from 214, perhaps suggests that it is better to interpret τοῦ φθέγματος τοὐρνιθίου as referring to the combined song of both. We may look to the dual pronoun at 204, νῷν (τοῦ φθέγματος), a combination of the two voices, as textual support for this interpretation.
12 See Segal (1990, 110): 'From Euripides' contemporaries on to Livy, Horace, and Ovid, the Thracians are notorious for their warlike violence, lack of self-control, unreliability

Sophocles' play: 'The entire barbarian race is money-loving' (φιλάργυρον μὲν πᾶν τὸ βάρβαρον γένος, *Ter.* fr. 587). Here in *Birds*, on the other hand, the barbarian has become the civilizer. In fact, it is the act of teaching the birds Greek that enables the very plot of the play to advance:

> Tereus' activities of disseminating language are catalytic for this metacomedy, allowing Peisetairos' political career to mirror, among other things, the improvisational creativity of the playwright … [T]he comic Tereus' linguistic pedagogy opens for the Athenians a political future marked by wings that Aristophanes uses as signs of rhetorical prowess and comic freedom.[13]

Indeed, Tereus casts the birds' initial meeting with Peisetaerus as an opportunity to hear (and thus understand and interpret) his words: 'Now all attend the conference' (ἀλλ' ἴτ' εἰς λόγους ἅπαντα, 258),[14] but literally, 'Now all attend the λόγοι', or 'words', that the birds would not understand if it were not for Tereus's teaching. The act of teaching the birds Greek appears to have put Tereus in a position of power among them. For example, though they are initially angry when he reveals that he has summoned the birds to listen to two humans speak (310–35), he appeals to their relationship and their seeming subservience to him: 'It's right, and you should tend to my good graces' (καὶ δίκαιόν γ' ἐστὶ κἀμοὶ δεῖ νέμειν ὑμᾶς χάριν, 384).[15] The birds, for their part, agree that they have followed him faithfully in the past: 'Well, truly, we haven't yet opposed you in any matter' (ἀλλὰ μὴν οὐδ' ἄλλο σοί πω πρᾶγμ' ἐνηντιώμεθα, 385).

While Gregory Dobrov claims that Peisetaerus mirrors Aristophanes in the quote above, I argue that Aristophanes has a second analogue in Tereus, inasmuch as the playwright dramaturgically decides who is and is not allowed to speak in the course of the play and exercises control over the characters' voices. One thread that connects both the tragic Tereus and his comic analogue is each one's status as an arbiter of communication, in restrictive and permissive senses respectively. The tragic Tereus, through the glossectomy of Philomela, attempts to place an insurmountable physical block on her ability to communicate. His act of excision states clearly that he not only denies but forcefully precludes Philomela's right to exercise her own voice. The comic Tereus, on the other hand, arms the birds with the power of speech by teaching them Greek. He appears to have transferred to

---

in oaths, and drunkenness.' For an in-depth discussion of the Thracian–Athenian tensions in the *Birds*, see Hall (2020).
13 Dobrov (2001, 124).
14 Translation from Henderson (2000).
15 Translation of χάριν as 'good graces' from Henderson (2000).

the birds the power of communication that he stole from Philomela when he cut out her tongue, thereby cementing his liminal position between manhood and birdhood and enabling Peisetaerus to communicate with the birds in the first place and to persuade them to follow along with his plan. True enough, Aristophanes clearly effaces the glossectomy of Philomela from his conception of the Tereus–Procne relationship within *Birds*,[16] but the comic Tereus's citation of Sophocles' tragedy (100–1) will have caused the audience to think about its plot and characters, especially as they relate to their comic analogues or lack thereof. So, my statement above should be nuanced further: the *comic* Tereus appears to have transferred to the birds the power of communication that the *tragic* Tereus stole from Philomela when he cut out her tongue out.

Procne as a Sexy Songster (and Little Else)

The comparison of the comic Procne to her tragic predecessor reveals a deliberate shift in her characterization. Procne's lament for the status of women as marriageable objects at *Tereus* fr. 583, recently augmented by the discovery of *P.Oxy.* 5292,[17] reveals her to be outspoken and passionate, allowed to vocalize a remarkable rebuke of the social status quo. Procne's speech places her in a coterie of other outspoken tragic women, such as Deianira of *Trachiniae*[18] or Tecmessa of *Ajax*,[19] and other fragments such as 584[20] suggest that Procne's outspokenness was not limited to this single speech.

The character of Procne in *Birds*, on the other hand, does not speak directly at all and sings only when commanded to do so by Tereus or the Chorus. The relative lack of 'lines' for a female character in an Aristophanic play is perhaps not surprising, especially once we consider Carina de Klerk's recent quantitative analysis of male versus female speech in selected Attic tragedies and Aristophanic comedies. In particular, female characters speak a meagre total of 1.3 percent of the available words in the *Birds*.[21]

---

16 On which see Libatique (2018b, 137–9).
17 On which see Milo (2020), Finglass (2020), Libatique (2018a), Finglass (2016), and Slattery (2016).
18 On which see Finglass (2020); Libatique (2018b, 104–5); Finglass (2016, 76–80); Coo (2013, 360); Milo (2008, 39–40); Monella (2005, 89–91).
19 On which see Libatique (2018b, 105–7).
20 'I very much envy your life, especially if you haven't experienced a foreign land' (πολλά σε ζηλῶ βίου, | μάλιστα δ' εἰ γῆς μὴ πεπείρασαι ξένης).
21 de Klerk (2020, 147). On de Klerk's overall methodology in comparing Aristophanes to tragedy, however, see Martin (2021): '… the basis for comparison seems shaky at best. Picking three plays each from the three major tragedians – but the *earliest* plays of each, which includes *Suppliants*, *Medea* and *Antigone* – surely sets up skewed numbers. As

This lack of direct speech in the *Birds* does not necessitate that Procne be entirely silent, however. Andrew Barker argues that Procne's lack of direct speech contributes to her passive existence, as opposed to active participation, in the play's plot: 'in this play [*Birds*] she utters not a word. She offers no verbal account of herself which would help us to reconstruct her meaning, or to interpret her interactions with other characters in the drama ... she not only *says* nothing, but *does* nothing to propel the action on its way.'[22] But while Barker is correct in that Procne never engages in direct speech, it is perhaps unfair to divest her completely of agency as far as the plot's movement is concerned, since the play's characters make constant references to her singing, an aural medium which uses her voice in a manner different from simple direct speech and which helps to summon the birds and move the plot of the play forward. Tereus refers to her as σύννομε (209), literally 'harmonizer' or one who 'sings with [me]' (σύν + νόμος) in preparation for the song that will summon the birds.[23] He also spends most of the anapestic beginning to his lyric run focusing on Procne's beautiful music and its origins as a lament for their son ('my son and yours, much-bewailed Itys', τὸν ἐμὸν καὶ σὸν πολύδακρυν Ἴτυν, 212). Indeed, Procne's voice or song receives multiple references throughout this section of the play: she and Tereus share a single voice (νῷν τοῦ φθέγματος, 204); she sings the strains of holy song (λῦσον δὲ νόμους ἱερῶν ὕμνων, 210); she laments with her divine mouth (διὰ θείου στόματος θρηνεῖς, 211); she sings elegies that Apollo hears (Φοῖβος ἀκούων τοῖς σοῖς ἐλέγοις, 217); and before her actual entrance, the Chorus Leader calls her the harmonious nightingale (ἡδυμελῆ ξύμφωνον ἀηδόνα, 659). After she has appeared and Peisetaerus and Euelpides have pawed at her, the Chorus sings that she shares in their hymns (πάντων ξύννομε τῶν ἐμῶν | ὕμνων, 678-9), creates sweet noise (ἡδὺν φθόγγον ἐμοὶ φέρουσ', 681) and plays on the beautiful-sounding *aulos* the strains of spring (ὦ καλλιβόαν κρέκουσ' | αὐλὸν φθέγμασιν ἠρινοῖς, 682-3).[24] Her voice is mentioned in various ways by various entities, and her song, along with Tereus's (σύννομε, 209), causes the birds to gather, setting in motion the confrontation between the birds and the Athenians before Peisetaerus wins them over.

for Aristophanes, what if we had *Lemniai* or *Poiesis* to toss into the tally?' (emphasis original).
22 Barker (2004, 186), emphases original.
23 The appellation is picked up by the Chorus Leader at 659 when he calls Procne ἡδυμελῆ **ξύμφωνον** ἀηδόνα, 'the sweetly-singing **harmonious** nightingale', though φωνή and νόμος are only thematically and not linguistically related. ξύμφωνος appears in Tereus's address to Procne (221), but it modifies ὀλολυγή, the cry that arises from the gods during the choral dances initiated by Apollo at the nightingale's song. On νόμοι in the *Birds* more generally, see Konstan (1997, esp. 7).
24 See n. 25 on the relationship between Procne and the production's *aulētēs*.

However, as he did with Philomela and the birds, Tereus clearly acts as an arbiter of Procne's communication and exercises control over her voice by issuing imperative commands that form the impetus for her song: 'Stop sleeping and **let loose** the strains of holy song' (παῦσαι μὲν ὕπνου, | **λῦσον** δὲ νόμους ἱερῶν ὕμνων, 209–10). She appears to fulfil his commands by beginning to sing[25] at the asyndeton in the middle of 214: 'the asyndeton … is used deliberately to *prevent* the hearer from taking χωρεῖ as a generic present co-ordinate with θρηνεῖς [211], and to show that now, after the long invocation's steady flow, comes the fulfillment of the request, that is the Nightingale's song, which the audience will hear presently with their own ear'.[26] Tereus controls the output of Procne's voice, just as he did with the birds and just as his tragic counterpart did with Philomela.[27] Again, Aristophanes finds an analogue in Tereus. While Tereus dictates the commands, Aristophanes put the commands in his mouth and at the authorial and dramaturgical level decided to restrict Procne to birdsong, a marked change from the direct speech she expressed in Sophocles' *Tereus*.

The Chorus also assumes the role of an arbiter of communication and, as such, a controller of Procne's voice at the introduction to the parabasis when they address the nightingale (676–84):

ὦ φίλη, ὦ ξουθή,
ὦ φίλτατον ὀρνέων,
πάντων ξύννομε τῶν ἐμῶν
    ὕμνων, ξύντροφ' ἀηδοῖ,
ἦλθες ἦλθες ὤφθης,
ἡδὺν φθόγγον ἐμοὶ φέρουσ'.
    ἀλλ', ὦ καλλιβόαν κρέκουσ'

---

25 Her 'song' was most likely played by the *aulētēs*, the official flute-player of the production. Considerable scholarly debate about the relationship of the *aulētēs* to the character of Procne abounds, with Romer (1983) advancing the theory that the two were one and the same. Romer is followed by Barker (2004, 200–3): 'The character of the nightingale, then, is not played by an actor at all, but by the official aulete himself' (203); and, with considerable reservations and modifications, Taplin (1993, 107 and n. 6): 'If Prokne *did* act as an *auletris*, I would still take it that the official *auletes* supplied the actual music … with Prokne playing at play' (emphasis original).

26 Dunbar (1998, 153 *ad* 213–14). I have deliberately left off the end of Dunbar's full quotation ('after 222') because it is not entirely clear what she means; the point of Tereus's praise of Procne's song (214–22) is that it happens contemporaneously with the latter part of the anapestic run, not in anticipation of some future song that will be sung afterward.

27 Telò (2020, 222) notes that Procne's voice is also doubly muted by both the *aulos* and Tereus: '… Procne's singing voice is replaced by the backstage sound of the *aulos*. Although she provides the music, Tereus sings *instead of* her' (emphasis original).

αὐλὸν φθέγμασιν ἠρινοῖς,
ἄρχου τῶν ἀναπαίστων.

Oh, dear one, oh, trilling one, oh, dearest of birds, harmonizer with all of my songs, my sister nightingale, you came, you came, you've been seen, bringing me your sweet voice. But you who play the beautifully voiced *aulos* with the voice of spring, begin our anapests.

The Chorus picks up on Tereus's appellation for Procne, ξύννομε, 678 (cf. σύννομε, 209), and indeed on other aspects of his diction (ὕμνων, 210, 679; ξουθῆς, 214, with ξουθή, 676), thereby aligning themselves rhetorically with him. Another notable similarity is each one's use of imperative verbs. While Tereus begins his address with them (παῦσαι, 209; λῦσον, 210), the Chorus ends their initial address with one (ἄρχου, 684), which initiates the parabasis proper, appropriately for a verb meaning 'begin'. The positions of the imperatives and the anapestic meters create a sort of Procne-based ring structure, containing within it her only physical appearance onstage. The latter boundary of the ring structure may be extended more properly, however, into the first part of epirrhematic syzygy (737–52), in which the Chorus addresses the nightingale again. Lexical similarities abound between this section and Tereus's song, namely mentions of holy songs (ἱερῶν ὕμνων, 210; νόμους ἱερούς, 745), trilling jaws (γέννυς ξουθῆς, 214, 744), thick-leaved trees (φυλλοκόμου μίλακος, 215; μελίας ... φυλλοκόμου, 742) and ritual dances (χορούς, 219; χορεύματ', 746). Procne's actual act of singing is circumscribed in both instances by the direct commands of Tereus and the Chorus. She sings within the play, but Tereus and the Chorus decide when she is allowed to do so.

Within this ring structure is contained Procne's first and only appearance onstage, in which she is cast as a sexualized object for visual consumption. The scene may come at this point of the action as something of a surprise, given the long interlude between Procne's offstage 'singing' which began at 214 and her appearance here at 667. The scene occupies a narrative space between Peisetaerus's successful persuasion of the birds to adopt his plan and the execution of it, and so the question becomes why Procne is summoned to appear here and now, a demand that seems to interrupt the flow of the play. Gwendolyn Compton-Engle argues that this scene, placed at the point when the birds have become obedient and are no longer a threat to the Athenians, is a dramaturgical signpost of the transition from the Tereus section of the play to the parabasis. More specifically, Procne's beak, which Euelpides strips off (673–4), is a prop whose removal physicalizes the obviation of the threat of bodily harm and enmity from the birds.[28] Procne, as

---

28 See Compton-Engle (2007, esp. 124–6).

liminally situated between human and bird as Tereus, serves as a visual sign simultaneously of the anthropomorphic life that Peisetaerus and Euelpides want to reject and the avian life that they want to assume. Her appearance at this point of the play at which the transition is about to be made, then, prepares the audience for that transition.

The scene is so densely packed with visual and objectifying diction that it necessitates reproduction in full here (659–74):

ΧΟΡΟΣ	… τὴν δ' ἡδυμελῆ ξύμφωνον ἀηδόνα Μούσαις κατάλειφ' ἡμῖν δεῦρ' **ἐκβιβάσας**, ἵνα **παίσωμεν** μετ' ἐκείνης.
ΠΕΙΣΕΤΑΙΡΟΣ	ὦ τοῦτο μέντοι νὴ Δί' αὐτοῖσιν πιθοῦ. **ἐκβίβασον ἐκ** τοῦ βουτόμου τοὐρνίθιον·
ΕΥΕΛΠΙΔΗΣ	**ἐκβίβασον** αὐτοῦ, πρὸς θεῶν, αὐτήν, ἵνα καὶ νὼ **θεασώμεσθα** τὴν ἀηδόνα.
ΤΗΡΕΥΣ	ἀλλ' εἰ δοκεῖ σφῷν, ταῦτα χρὴ δρᾶν. ἡ Πρόκνη, ἔκβαινε καὶ **σαυτὴν ἐπιδείκνυ** τοῖς ξένοις.
ΠΕ.	ὦ Ζεῦ πολυτίμηθ', ὡς **καλὸν** τοὐρνίθιον· ὡς δ' **ἁπαλόν**, ὡς δὲ **λευκόν**.
ΕΥ.	ἆρά γ' οἶσθ' ὅτι ἐγὼ **διαμηρίζοιμ'** ἂν αὐτὴν ἡδέως;
ΠΕ.	ὅσον δ' ἔχει τὸν **χρυσόν**, ὥσπερ παρθένος.
ΕΥ.	ἐγὼ μὲν αὐτὴν κἂν **φιλῆσαί** μοι δοκῶ.
ΠΕ.	ἀλλ', ὦ κακόδαιμον, **ῥύγχος ὀβελίσκοιν** ἔχει.
ΕΥ.	ἀλλ' ὥσπερ ᾠὸν νὴ Δί' ἀπολέψαντα χρὴ ἀπὸ τῆς κεφαλῆς τὸ **λέμμα** κᾆθ' οὕτω **φιλεῖν**.
Chorus	But **bring out** here and leave with us the sweetly singing nightingale, harmonious with the Muses, so that we can **play** with her.
Peisetaerus	Oh, by Zeus, obey them! **Make** the bird **come out** from the sedge.
Euelpides	**Make** her **come** here, by the gods, so that we too may **see** the nightingale.
Tereus	If it seems right to them, we must do it. Procne, come out and **show yourself** to our guests.
PE.	Oh, much-honored Zeus, how **beautiful** this bird is; how **soft**, how **white**.
EU.	You know how sweetly I'd **split her legs**?
PE.	How much **gold** she has, like a maiden.
EU.	I think I'd like to **kiss** her too.
PE.	You wretch, she has a **beak with skewers**.

| EU. | By Zeus, you have to peel off the **shell** from her head, like an egg, and **kiss** her in that way. |

We are prepared for the presentation of Procne as an objectified plaything from the first mentions of the nightingale at 203 and 208, where Tereus's and Peisetaerus's choice of verbs (ἀνεγείρας, εἴσβαινε κἀνέγειρε respectively) act as sexual double entendres. The use of double entendres continues here into the Chorus Leader's statement of purpose at 660, 'bring her out to us and leave her here so that **we may play** with her' (κατάλειφ' ἡμῖν δεῦρ' ἐκβιβάσας ἵνα **παίσωμεν** μετ' ἐκείνης), where 'to play' (παίζειν) has clear erotic undertones. The nightingale's corporeal absence until this point in the play and the necessity of her coming from obscurity into plain view is underscored by the polyptoton and anaphora of ἐκβιβάζειν, 'to cause to come out (ἐκ-)', and its prefix ἐκ (ἐκβιβάσας, 660; ἐκβίβασον, ἐκ, 662; ἐκβίβασον, 663). The hypervisuality of Procne's body, even before she makes her first appearance, is evinced by the verbs of viewing (θεασώμεσθα, 664) and display (σαυτὴν ἐπιδείκνυ, 666). Then, once she appears, Peisetaerus and Euelpides place an inordinate, explicit amount of focus on her physical attributes: her softness and whiteness (ἁπαλόν, λευκόν, 668), her adornment in gold (χρυσόν, 670), her beak or whatever is covering her face (ῥύγχος ὀβελίσκοιν, 672; τὸ λέμμα, 674). The sexual component of the objectification is made quite explicit by Euelpides in his declarations of what he would like to do to her (διαμηρίζοιμι, literally 'to enter through the thighs', 669; and φιλῆσαί and φιλεῖν, 'to kiss', 671 and 674, respectively).

As mentioned above, the poet affords Tereus and the Chorus control over Procne's voice, but here, he grants the characters dominion over her body as well. Aristophanes causes the Chorus Leader, Peisetaerus and Euelpides to place exorbitant focus on her physical appearance to depict Procne as possessing less agency than the others. In this scene, she is a prop for pawing, in Peisetaerus's case (ὡς ... ἁπαλόν, 668),[29] or actual sexual contact, in Euelpides' case.[30] The tragic Procne and the comic Procne are

---

29 Sommerstein (1987, *ad* 668) objects to this interpretation: 'The scholia ... are hardly right to suppose that Peisetaerus is touching or stroking her as he speaks; a person may be called *hapalos* on a purely visual judgement (cf. *Thesm.* 192), and amatory handling by Peisetaerus at this stage would make Euelpides' subsequent vain attempts to kiss Procne into something of an anticlimax.' While the first point is certainly true in the case of *Thesm.* 192, it does not preclude the possibility of a tactile sense of ἁπαλός in *Birds*, as in, for example, Hom. *Il.* 17.49: ἀντικρὺ δ' ἁπαλοῖο δι' αὐχένος ἤλυθ' ἀκωκή, 'The spear point passed straight through his soft neck.' With regard to the second point, if Peisetaerus and Euelpides both physically caress Procne, her role in the play as an objectified plaything becomes undeniable and concrete; the play's protagonist would validate the advances of the bomolochic Euelpides if he joined in Euelpides' attempts at tactile contact.
30 On Euelpides' seeming success in kissing Procne after removing her facial covering, see Compton-Engle (2007, 118–20).

now as diametrically opposed as the tragic Tereus and the comic Tereus are. The tragic Procne, who used her voice to lament the plight of married girls and to express emotion, has lost that capacity for communication in her transition to the comic Procne; she does not say a word as Peisetaerus and Euelpides look and poke at her. All that remains for her is the ability to sing when commanded to do so and the endurance of the male gaze and touching in her capacity as a sexual object. She is the physical embodiment of the *erōs* that pervades the play in almost all respects[31] and the polar opposite of her outspoken, powerful tragic predecessor. Procne's reversal complements the reversal experienced by Tereus, from an enigmatic character in Sophocles to a virtuosic lyricist in Aristophanes, and establishes each character as operating along normative gender expectations for Aristophanes' audience: a vocal man, a silent woman.

Gender Role Reversal and the (Re-)Writing of Myth

The gender politics of Cloudcuckooland are a matter of debate from the very foundation of the city, when the Athenian principals and the Chorus Leader debate which god will fulfil the role of the city's guardian (826–31). Peisetaerus seems to advocate for normative gender relations when Euelpides suggests Athena: 'How could a city be well ordered, where a god born a woman stands in full panoply while Cleisthenes holds a shuttle?' (καὶ πῶς ἂν ἔτι γένοιτ' ἂν εὔτακτος πόλις, | ὅπου θεὸς γυνὴ γεγονυῖα πανοπλίαν | ἕστηκ' ἔχουσα, Κλεισθένης δὲ κερκίδα; 829–31). A city in which gender roles are so clearly reversed from social reality, a city in which women engage in martial activities and men discharge the duties of weaving, cannot be εὔτακτος, well ordered; thus, Athena is rejected as the guardian deity of Cloudcuckooland.

This out-of-hand rejection and appeal to normative gender practices (women weaving, men arming for war) seems incongruous with the motivating force behind Cloudcuckooland: the rejection of Athenian norms. However, Peisetaerus's comment emphasizes not necessarily his adherence to gender norms as much as his rejection of the Greek pantheon and the power that it holds over the human realm. By dismissing Athena and all that accompanies her (including her implements of war and, by extension, the other Greek gods), he builds upon the conceit that the birds are the original

---

31 See Arrowsmith (1973, esp. 130): 'No other play of Aristophanes, not even *Lysistrata*, is so pervaded, so saturated by the language of desire. *Erōs, erastēs, epithumia, pothos* – over and over again the note of desire is struck, given constant visual dimension and the stress that only great poetry can confer.' See, however, Mahoney (2007, esp. 273): 'these words are not especially prominent in this play, in statistical terms, compared to other literary texts'; she discusses the prevalence of avian terminology expressed frequently by the Chorus, which sets the tone of the play and drives its plot.

gods (465–638), and he establishes the grounds upon which he can experience his own apotheosis at the end of the play, thereby supplanting such deities as Athena. Indeed, his participation in the objectification of Procne in front of her own husband violates Tereus's *oikos* and his social rights as a head of household;[32] such actions evince more strongly Peisetaerus's desire to subvert rather than uphold Athenian gender norms, such as the sacrosanctity of a husband–wife relationship.

The concept of gender role reversal, that is, the empowerment of women (often through speech) and the relative diminution of men (through physical and verbal emasculation) can be traced as a wider program in Aristophanes' plays later than the *Birds* (414 BCE), primarily in the 'women's plays', *Lysistrata*, *Women at the Thesmophoria* (both 411 BCE) and *Assemblywomen* (around 391–390 BCE), as many scholars have noted.[33] The numerous opportunities for female characters to vocalize political and social grievances and assume public roles exist solely because of the medium of delivery: 'women are rarely portrayed as public speakers in a political context, as orators or messengers, except in comedy, a genre that frequently inverts gender roles and linguistic genres'.[34] The societal reality of feminine silence and obscurity[35] renders plots like that of *Lysistrata*, in which women barricade the Acropolis and fight back against men, or *Women at the Thesmophoria*, in which women lambast Euripides for exposing their bad behavior, as fantastic and unrealistic.

This gender reversal that empowers women and gives them a voice in the 'women's plays' balances characters like Procne in *Birds* that are presented as objects who underline the social, patriarchal dominance of men: 'there is no mutuality, no interaction between two active agents, and there is not even sexuality. In each scene the female is an object gazed at, lusted after, and manipulated by a subject … She is totally dehumanized.'[36] Bella Zweig's summary applies to the mute nude women in *Lysistrata*, *Women at the Thesmophoria*, *Acharnians* and, indeed, *Birds*. However, the gender reversal in the later plays also throws into sharp relief what we see in *Birds*: a portrayal of a 'normative' man–woman relationship, with a vocal man and a silent woman. In the figure of Procne, we see a deliberate recasting of the power of the voice, from the expression of personal sentiments in *Tereus* to birdsong in *Birds*. Sophocles affords Procne a voice that she would

---

32 On which see Libatique (2018b, 134–5).
33 See, for example, Henderson (2010, 25–30); Compton-Engle (2005); Sulprizio (2007, 275–88); Rutherford (2015); McClure (1999, 205–59); Libatique (2018b, 140–2).
34 McClure (2001, 10).
35 See Henderson (2010, 22–5); Libatique (2018b, 98–100); Griffith (2001, 123–4); Blok (2001, 97); Zweig (1992, 76).
36 Zweig (1992, 87).

not have been allowed to express in contemporary Greek culture;[37] then, Aristophanes reverses Sophocles' gender reversal to depict a normative relationship according to Greek societal custom, perhaps as a nod to the contemporary socio-gender politics at play in 414 BCE.

With this comparison between the normative gender relationship in *Birds* and the subversions in the 'women's plays', we must keep in mind chronology: *Birds* was performed at the City Dionysia in 414 BCE, while *Lysistrata* and *Women at the Thesmophoria* were performed three years later in 411 and *Assemblywomen* was performed up to two decades later. At the time of the performance of *Birds*, the Sicilian Expedition was barely a year from launch, and so the mood at Athens would not have been nearly as dire as it would have been in 411, after the destruction of the Expedition. While scholarly readings of *Birds* vary widely in terms of Aristophanes' tone and the socio-political valence of its utopian plot,[38] it is undeniable that there is an optimistic bent[39] to the plot and its ending: Peisetaerus's apotheosis

---

[37] See McClure (2001, 5): 'It is quite remarkable, given the restricted role of women's public speech in classical Athens, that tragedy contains a larger number of speaking female characters than any other Greek literary genre.'

[38] See Hall (2020, 188-9) and Konstan (1997, 3-6) for succinct summaries of political versus apolitical readings of the *Birds* by scholars. I subscribe to the view of Henderson (1997, 136) that it is impossible to ignore the political undertones in the play: 'Some regard *Birds* as a detached escapist fantasy, a flight from the harsh realities of the actual polis to some sort of poetic fantasy world. But that cannot be right ... The resemblance of the plot to the sensational events of the preceding year, though not explicit, is close enough that no spectator could fail to see it, and this resemblance clearly suggests that among the play's agenda was satire of the lofty imperial ambitions engendered in the Athenians by contemporary rhetors, just as the name of the hero suggests satire of their persuasive rhetoric. For the spectators, then, Nephelokokkugia was not a distraction from Athens but a beguiling new way to contemplate it.' See also Dunbar (1998, 2-7); Sommerstein (1987, 1-6).

[39] Sommerstein (1987, 5) traces a demonstration of this optimistic spirit in the play's positive valuation of martial tropes: 'The prevailing spirit at Athens in the spring of 414 must still have been one of boundless optimism, and with this the spirit of our play harmonizes perfectly. It is symptomatic of this that every time an allusion is made in the play to current, recent, or projected military operations, the tone adopted is one of almost cheerful bellicosity. If the war in Sicily is hanging fire, it is because of the "shilly-shallying" of Nicias (639). A young man, full of fighting spirit in search of an outlet, is recommended to volunteer for service in the Thracian region (1360-71). And the terrible fate of Melos – an episode which was later to be seen by Athenians themselves as an indelible stain on their record as an imperial power – serves here as the theme for a joke (186). We cannot tell to what extent Aristophanes was himself affected by the public mood of the moment; but at any rate he did not this time feel it necessary or desirable to set himself in opposition to it.' See also Henderson (1997, 142-3): 'there is no expression of any desire for peace in this play and quite a lot of enthusiasm for aggression ... If anything, *Birds* suggests that the Athenians were showing not too much imperial ambition but too little, just as Alcibiades had argued against the cautious Nicias.'

and his assumption of Zeus's thunderbolt and Basileia as his queen. While there is no documentation of a deliberate shift on Aristophanes' part, the destruction of the Sicilian Expedition in 413 may have occasioned, at least in part, the transition from the optimism of *Birds* and the normative relationship portrayed between Tereus and Procne toward the topsy-turvy social orders of *Lysistrata* and *Women at the Thesmophoria*.

In *Lysistrata*, at least, there is an implication that Athenian women seemed to oppose the Expedition, when the Proboulos describes the women's lament for Adonis as the matter was brought to the Assembly (387–98):

ἆρ' ἐξέλαμψε τῶν γυναικῶν ἡ τρυφὴ
χὠ τυμπανισμὸς χοἰ πυκνοὶ Σαβάζιοι,
ὅ τ' Ἀδωνιασμὸς οὗτος οὑπὶ τῶν τεγῶν,
οὗ 'γώ ποτ' ὢν ἤκουον ἐν τἠκκλησίᾳ;
ἔλεγεν ὁ μὴ ὥρασι μὲν Δημόστρατος
πλεῖν εἰς Σικελίαν, ἡ γυνὴ δ' ὀρχουμένη
"αἰαῖ Ἄδωνιν" φησίν. ὁ δὲ Δημόστρατος
ἔλεγεν ὁπλίτας καταλέγειν Ζακυνθίων,
ἡ δ' ὑποπεπωκυῖ' ἡ γυνὴ 'πὶ τοῦ τέγους
"κόπτεσθ' Ἄδωνιν" φησίν. ὁ δ' ἐβιάζετο,
ὁ θεοῖσιν ἐχθρὸς καὶ μιαρὸς Χολοζύγης.
τοιαῦτ' ἀπ' αὐτῶν ἐστιν ἀκολαστάσματα.

Look, the wantonness of women has flared up, hasn't it, and the tum-tum of the drums and continual cries of 'Sabazios!' and that mourning for Adonis on the rooftops, which I heard once before when I was in the Assembly. Demostratos – bad luck to him! – said that we should sail to Sicily, but his wife was dancing and said '*Aiai*, Adonis!' Then Demostratos said that we should enroll Zacynthian hoplites, but she got drunk on the rooftop and said 'Beat your breast for Adonis!' He forced himself to go on, that god-hated, filthy Baron Bluster.[40] Such is the licentious behavior that you get from women!

The laments by Demostratos's wife for the youth Adonis imply a malaise about the proposition to send the city's youth to war. Indeed, the Proboulos casts the current occupation of the Acropolis in terms of 'the women's ill-omened cries that were heard in the assembly as it was deciding to send the flower of Attic youth into battle: as if the women were responsible for the outcome'.[41] This instance of hindsight (and the Proboulos's deliberate

---

40 'Baron Bluster' comes from Henderson (2000, 321).
41 Henderson (1987, 119 *ad* 390-7).

casting of the actions of women as ἀκολαστάσματα, licentious behavior, as opposed to the warnings or signs of discontent that they were) serves to justify the plot of the *Lysistrata*. The play's women, who are dismissed as licentious drunks (according to the Proboulos) or were forced to be silent as plans for the Expedition took shape,[42] attempt to correct the inefficacies and missteps of men. As Lysistrata herself says, after the decisions of men resulted in the male population's decimation, women could no longer maintain their silence (523–6):

> ὅτε δὴ δ' ὑμῶν ἐν ταῖσιν ὁδοῖς φανερῶς ἠκούομεν ἤδη·
> "οὐκ ἔστιν ἀνὴρ ἐν τῇ χώρᾳ." – "μὰ Δί' οὐ δῆτ' <ἔσθ'>," ἕτερός τις, –
> μετὰ ταῦθ' ἡμῖν εὐθὺς ἔδοξεν σῶσαι τὴν Ἑλλάδα κοινῇ
> ταῖσι γυναιξὶν συλλεχθείσαις. ποῖ γὰρ καὶ χρῆν ἀναμεῖναι;

> But when we heard you clearly in the streets, saying 'There's not a man left in the land', and someone else saying, 'By Zeus, no, there's not' – after this, it seemed right for us women to band together and save all of Greece. How long should we delay?

Birds was performed before such an occasion arose. While, again, we cannot say with certainty that Aristophanes advocated for the Expedition, several features of the play seem to imply that Aristophanes was on board: the portrayal of Tereus and Peisetaerus as strong agents of change, pushing respectively for a civilization of previously barbarous birds and the establishment of a utopian world order; the fruition of their goals; and domination over female characters like Procne, an 'Athenian' wife like Proboulos's.[43] Only with hindsight, at the time of the performance of *Lysistrata* after the Expedition came to its disastrous end, could Aristophanes present a scenario in which women gained the ability to say essentially that they were correct all along and take matters of state into their own hands.

Sophocles' *Tereus* and Aristophanes' *Birds*: Mythic Emulation

Dobrov aptly casts Aristophanes' *Birds* as Sophocles' *Tereus* 'refracted through the comic poet's metafictional prism',[44] but I would bend the

---

42 See, for example, Lysistrata's speech (with occasional interruptions) about the men's continual dismissals of their wives at 506–28.
43 See also Thuc. 6.24.3 on the Athenians' ἔρως for the Expedition; Aristophanes would not have been alone in an optimistic outlook at this time.
44 Dobrov (2001, 126).

metaphor further: Aristophanes does not simply distort the plot points of Sophocles' play but completely upends them by swinging various characters and elements from one extreme to the other. Tereus, Sophocles' illiterate, brutal barbarian, becomes Aristophanes' civilizing exemplum of leadership and good. Procne, Sophocles' empowered, vocal protagonist, becomes Aristophanes' mute, sexual object.

This engagement with Sophocles or, cast differently, this attempt to rewrite or re-appropriate the myth as Sophocles presented it manifests in other implicit ways. For example, the deliberate choice to present Procne as a songster (and little else) with whom the Chorus, Peisetaerus and Euelpides can play (ἵνα παίσωμεν μετ' ἐκείνης, 660) may operate on a metatheatrical level. The nightingale, as Aara Suksi has shown,[45] operates throughout the Greek tradition as a symbol of tragic poetry. Just as the personae in *Birds* play with the nightingale, so too does Aristophanes explicitly play with Sophocles' creation (see *Birds* 99–100), molding tragic details to build his new comic context.

The Athenian theater was a place where such emulations and engagements created excitement for an audience familiar with the mythic canon. Moreover, such rivalries were not limited to the tragic sphere of drama. As Dustin Dixon argues, 'it has long been acknowledged that tragedians, at least, altered traditional myths in order to intrigue and excite audiences ... the evidence indicates comedians did the same. Indeed, tragedians and comedians alike would be motivated to tell familiar stories in new ways in order to win the prestigious prizes at the dramatic competitions.'[46] The very nature of the competitive medium through which these plays were performed required innovation or, at the very least, differentiation if a dramatic work treated a theme or topic that another work had treated before it; else, a playwright would simply be copying another's work rather than creating his own or improving upon his predecessors and making an original claim for competitive supremacy.

Sophocles' *Tereus* appears, to judge from its fragments, to have afforded the character of Procne a capacity for emotive, expressive speech that would undoubtedly have cast her as sympathetic in an audience's eyes. Aristophanes' engagement with Sophocles' conception of the Tereus, Procne and Philomela myth then erases the agency that Sophocles created for Procne while casting Tereus as a generally positive exemplum, an arbiter of communication who wields power over the birds. Aristophanes' *Birds* not only cites but also actively refashions the details of Sophocles' work to fit his narrative, an avian transformation as a prelude to the establishment of a utopia. This engagement gives us insight into Aristophanes' modes of

---

45 Suksi (2001).
46 Dixon (2015, 16).

reception and his emulative participation in fashioning the Greek mythic web, the strands of which are constantly cut, lengthened, rearranged and dyed to fit new contexts.

Works Cited

Arrowsmith, William. 1973. 'Aristophanes' *Birds*: The Fantasy Politics of *Eros*'. *Arion* 1: 119–67.
Barker, Andrew. 2004. 'Transforming the Nightingale: Aspects of Athenian Musical Discourse in the Late Fifth Century'. In *Music and the Muses: The Culture of Mousike in the Classical Athenian City*, edited by Penelope Murray and Peter Wilson, 185–204. Oxford: Oxford University Press.
Blok, Josine H. 2001. 'Virtual Voices: Toward a Choreography of Women's Speech in Classical Athens'. In Lardinois and McClure 2001, 95–116.
Calder, William. 1974. 'Sophocles, *Tereus*: A Thracian Tragedy'. *Thracia* 2: 87–91.
Casanova, A. 2003. 'Osservazioni sui frammenti del *Tereo*'. In *Il dramma sofocleo: testo, lingua, interpretazione*, edited by G. Avezzù, 59–68. Stuttgart: Metzler.
Compton-Engle, Gwendolyn. 2005. 'Stolen Cloaks in Aristophanes' *Ecclesiazusae*'. *TAPA* 135: 163–76.
———. 2007. 'Procne's Beak in Aristophanes' *Birds*'. *SyllClass* 18: 113–28.
Coo, Lyndsay. 2013. 'A Tale of Two Sisters: Studies in Sophocles' *Tereus*'. *TAPA* 143: 349–84.
———. 2020. 'Greek Tragedy and the Theatre of Sisterhood'. In Finglass and Coo 2020, 40–61.
Curley, Daniel. 2003. 'Ovid's Tereus: Theater and Metatheater'. In *Shards from Kolonos: Studies in Sophoclean Fragments*, edited by Alan Sommerstein, 163-97. Bari: Levante.
de Klerk, Carina. 2020. 'The Politics of Diversity: A Quantitative Analysis of Aristophanes'. In Rosen and Foley 2020, 137–62.
Dixon, Dustin. 2015. 'Myth-Making in Greek and Roman Comedy'. PhD diss., Boston University. ProQuest (3714785).
Dobrov, Gregory, ed. 1997. *The City as Comedy: Society and Representation in Athenian Drama*. Chapel Hill: University of North Carolina Press.
———. 2001. *Figures of Play: Greek Drama and Metafictional Poetics*. Oxford: Oxford University Press.
Dova, Stamatia. 2020. 'Procne, Philomela, and the Voice of the *Peplos*'. *Arethusa* 53: 69–88.
Dunbar, Nan, ed. 1998. *Aristophanes: Birds*. Oxford: Oxford University Press.
Finglass, P. J. 2016. 'A New Fragment of Sophocles' *Tereus*'. *ZPE* 200: 61–85.
———. 2020. 'Suffering in Silence: Victims of Rape on the Tragic Stage'. In Finglass and Coo 2020, 87–102.
Finglass, P. J., and Lyndsay Coo, eds. 2020. *Female Characters in Fragmentary Greek Tragedy*. Cambridge: Cambridge University Press.
Fitzpatrick, David. 2001. 'Sophocles' *Tereus*'. *CQ* 51: 90–101.
Griffith, Mark. 2001. 'Antigone and Her Sister(s): Embodying Women in Greek Tragedy'. In Lardinois and McClure 2001, 117–36.

Haley, Maria. 2019. 'Teknophagy and Tragicomedy: The Mythic Burlesques of *Tereus* and *Thyestes*'. *Ramus* 27: 152–73.
Hall, Edith. 2020. 'Aristophanes' *Birds* as Satire on Athenian Opportunists in Thrace'. In Rosen and Foley 2020, 187–213.
Henderson, Jeffrey. 1987. *Aristophanes: Lysistrata*. Oxford: Oxford University Press.
———. 1997. 'Mass versus Elite and the Comic Heroism of Peisetairos'. In Dobrov 1997, 135–48.
———. 1998–2002. *Aristophanes*, 4 vols. Cambridge, MA: Harvard University Press.
———. 2010. *Three Plays by Aristophanes: Staging Women*. 3rd edn. New York and London: Routledge.
Hourmouziades, N. C. 1986. 'Sophocles' *Tereus*'. In *Studies in Honor of T. B. L. Webster*, vol. 1, edited by J. H. Betts, J. T. Hooker and J. R. Green, 134–42. Bristol: Bristol Classical Press.
Kiso, Akiko. 1984. *The Lost Sophocles*. New York: Vantage Press.
Konstan, David. 1997. 'The Greek Polis and Its Negations: Versions of Utopia in Aristophanes' *Birds*'. In Dobrov 1997, 3–22.
Lardinois, André, and Laura McClure, eds. 2001. *Making Silence Speak: Women's Voices in Greek Literature and Society*. Princeton: Princeton University Press.
Liapis, Vayos. 2006. 'Achilles Tatius as a Reader of Sophocles'. *CQ* 56: 220–38.
Libatique, Daniel. 2018a. 'The Speaker and Addressee of Sophocles' *Tereus* Fr. 588 Radt and the Context of Fr. 583'. *CQ* 68: 707–12.
———. 2018b. 'Tereus, Procne, and Philomela: Speech, Silence, and the Voice of Gender'. PhD diss., Boston University. ProQuest (10789680).
McClure, Laura. 1999. *Spoken Like a Woman: Speech and Gender in Athenian Drama*. Princeton: Princeton University Press.
———. 2001. 'Introduction'. In Lardinois and McClure 2001, 3–16.
Mahoney, Anne. 2007. 'Key Terms in *Birds*'. *CW* 100.3: 267–78.
Martin, Richard. 2021. 'Review of *Aristophanes and Politics: New Studies*, edited by Ralph M. Rosen and Helene P. Foley'. *BMCR* 2021.04.36.
Milo, Daniela. 2008. *Il Tereo di Sofocle*. Naples: M. D'Auria.
———. 2020. 'Passione, conoscenza e verità: seconde considerazioni sul *Tereo* di Sofocle'. *Vichiana* 57: 95–110.
Monella, Paolo. 2005. *Procne e Filomela: dal mito al simbolo letterario*. Bologna: Pàtron Editore.
Nooter, Sarah. 2019. 'Sounds of the Stage'. In *Sound and the Ancient Senses*, edited by Shane Butler and Sarah Nooter, 198–211. London and New York: Bloomsbury.
Privitera, Tiziana. 2007. *Terei puella: metamorfosi latine*. Pisa: ETS.
Radt, S. 1977. *Tragicorum Graecorum Fragmenta*, vol. 4. Göttingen: Vandenhoeck & Ruprecht.
Roche, Paul. 2005. *Aristophanes: The Complete Plays*. New York: New American Library.
Romer, F. E. 1983. 'When Is a Bird Not a Bird?' *TAPA* 113: 135–42.
Rosen, Ralph M., and Helene P. Foley, eds. 2020. *Aristophanes and Politics: New Studies*. Leiden and Boston: Brill.

Rutherford, Richard. 2015. '*Lysistrata* and Female Song'. *CQ* 65: 60–8.
Scattolin, Paolo. 2013. 'Le notizie sul Tereo di Sofocle nei papiri'. In *I papiri di Eschilo e di Sofocle: atti del Convegno internazionale di studi. Firenze, 14–15 giugno 2012*, edited by Guido Bastianini and Angelo Casanova, 119–41. Florence: Firenze University Press.
Segal, Charles. 1990. 'Violence and the Other: Greek, Female and Barbarian in Euripides' *Hecuba*'. *TAPA* 120: 109–31.
Slater, Niall W. 2018. 'What Language Did the Shuttle Speak? Voice and Vision in Sophocles' *Tereus*'. In *Frammenti sulla scena*, vol. 1: *Studi sul dramma antico frammentario*, edited by Luca Austa, 59–75. Alessandria: Edizioni dell'Orso.
Slattery, S. 2016. '5292. Sophocles' *Tereus*'. *The Oxyrhynchus Papyri*. Oxford.
Sommerstein, Alan. 1987. *The Comedies of Aristophanes*, vol. 6: *Birds*. Warminster: Aris and Phillips.
Sommerstein, Alan, David Fitzpatrick and Thomas Talboy, eds. 2006. *Sophocles: Selected Fragmentary Plays*, vol. 1. Oxford: Aris and Phillips.
Suksi, Aara. 2001. 'The Poet at Colonus: Nightingales in Sophocles'. *Mnemosyne* 54: 646–58.
Sulprizio, Chiara. 2007. 'Gender, Space and Warfare in the Early Plays of Aristophanes'. PhD diss., University of Southern California. ProQuest (3283577).
Suter, Ann. 2004. 'The Myth of Prokne and Philomela'. *NECJ* 31: 377–86.
Sutton, Dana F. 1984. *The Lost Sophocles*. Lanham, MD: University Press of America.
Taplin, Oliver. 1993. *Comic Angels and Other Approaches to Greek Drama Through Vase Paintings*. Oxford: Clarendon Press.
Telò, Mario. 2020. 'The Politics of *Dissensus* in Aristophanes' *Birds*'. In Rosen and Foley 2020, 214–47.
Welcker, F. G. 1839. *Die griechischen Tragödien mit Rücksicht auf den epischen Cyclus*. Bonn: E. Weber.
Zweig, Bella. 1992. 'The Mute Nude Female Characters in Aristophanes' Plays'. In *Pornography and Representation in Greece and Rome*, edited by Amy Richlin, 73–89. Oxford: Oxford University Press.

CHAPTER 3

Performing Ritual Sacrifice in Aristophanes' Peace *and* Birds

Mary C. English

In *Peace* (City Dionysia of 421 BCE) and again in *Birds* (City Dionysia of 414 BCE), Aristophanes crafts scenes where the comic heroes, Trygaeus and Peisetaerus, respectively, perform onstage sacrifices: Trygaeus is celebrating the restoration of the goddess Peace, and Peisetaerus is marking the establishment of Cloudcuckooland with a tribute to the new gods. Both characters lead out sacrificial victims, but they are thwarted from completing their ritual tasks because they suffer interruptions from a variety of intruders. Eventually, they consider it best to finish their sacrifices indoors. On the one hand, in these two scenes, Aristophanes almost seems to mock religious conventions by having Trygaeus and Peisetaerus use the prayers and instruments of sacrifice to further their comic agenda; yet, at the same time, he appears bound to maintain some sense of religious decorum by not having them complete their sacrifices onstage.[1] Perhaps this tension is an inherent element of satire or parody – where the humor derives from a careful balance of truth and comic exaggeration or where comic characters tease the audience with the possibility of violating social and religious norms – but Aristophanes seems only to stage this type of extended sacrifice scene at historical moments of civic assertiveness and

1 Arnott (1978 [1962], 54–5): 'As the practical objections [to sacrifice] can be met, the only possible restriction is religious taboo. It is unlikely that the priests would have countenanced an exact reproduction of their ritual in the theatre.' Sommerstein (2004b, 46–7) argues that the dramatic convention of 'no killing onstage' extended to animals and discusses why these scenes from *Peace* and *Birds* stop short of onstage sacrifice: 'Slaughter could not be simulated; a real animal would have to be really killed, not in order to please the god to whom it was ostensibly being offered but merely for the purpose of making a show. The complex, and partly obfuscatory, rituals that surrounded Greek animal sacrifice and especially its central act show how serious a matter the taking of a domestic beast's life was perceived to be, even though it was a necessity both for humans and for gods; it would have been unthinkable to do such a thing outside its true ritual context.' See Burkert (1983, 3–8) for the logistics of these sacrifices and the sources that document them.

political optimism. *Peace* coincides with the negotiations for the Peace of Nicias, and *Birds* was performed just under a year after the launching of the Sicilian Expedition when Athens still held hope that the deployment of troops to that region would benefit the polis. If we compare Trygaeus's and Peisetaerus's aborted sacrifices to the other moments in the extant comedies where Aristophanes stages the reenactment of Athenian religious rituals,[2] or at least implied reenactment,[3] we notice that, in *Peace* and *Birds*, Aristophanes takes greater liberties with religious norms although he is careful never to endorse behavior too 'subversive' to the religious identity of the polis or too threatening to the core beliefs of Athens.

Comic Playwrights and 'Slander' Legislation

In considering these scenes, we may be able to profit from discussions amongst scholars of comedy as to whether or not the comic poets were bound by civic rules for public speech and whether the criticism that they lobbed against specific individuals was subject to the codes of behavior that we see prevalent in the Athenian courts of law. In his article 'Attic Old Comedy, Frank Speech and Democracy', Jeffrey Henderson convincingly argues that, while comic playwrights enjoyed the freedoms of *isēgoria* (the right of citizens to offer advice) and *parrhēsia* (the right of citizens to frank criticism), they were careful to limit their 'outspokenness' so that it did not hinder any specific member of the *dēmos* from full participation. In other words, comic playwrights were subject to the same slander laws as everyone else (perhaps even more so given the decrees of Morychides, in effect from 440/39 to 437/6 BCE, and of Syracosius, the latter of which may have limited comic references to those implicated in the scandal over the mock celebration of the Mysteries that occurred just before the Sicilian Expedition).[4]

---

2 Consider Lysistrata's makeshift oath to secure the allegiance of women in Athens and the Peloponnese in her struggle to end wartime oppression (*Lys.* 181–239). At lines 185–6, she calls for a shield and some sacrificial parts over which she and the other women can swear their allegiance. A few lines later, she decides the oath would be better sworn over a cup of wine. Sommerstein (1990, *ad* 186) argues that Lysistrata's request for the sacrificial parts is never fulfilled because the women choose a more convivial way of conducting the oath.
3 Consider Carion's speech at *Wealth* 649–747 where he describes the events at the shrine of Asclepius and the restoration of Wealth's sight.
4 Henderson (1998, 255–60). Henderson's article draws different conclusions on this topic from Halliwell (1991), who suggests that the dramatic festivals allowed the playwrights certain liberties of speech. For a summary of the evidence for the decree of Morychides and its implications for Athenian playwrights, see Marshall (2000, 231–3); for discussions on the decree of Syracosius, see Sommerstein (1986) and Atkinson (1992, esp. 61–4); and for a discussion of whether or not comic playwrights were subject to Athenian legislation, see Sommerstein (2004a and 2004c).

More importantly, Henderson uses these conclusions to assert that comedy was an integral part of the democratic system and warns against a common notion that the insults of comic heroes were innocuous and apolitical. He cautions us not to exempt the comic poets from the social norms of the polis and not to conclude that their verses were above legal and cultural scrutiny. Just because it was 'festive', Henderson argues, does not mean that Old Comedy stood apart from Athenian life: 'The close historical synchrony of democracy and political comedy, as festive competition and as genre, cannot be coincidental. For poets and spectators alike, drama was not an escape or a time-out from democratic life but a form of participation in it.'[5] Thus, the balance between comic outrage and civic responsibility was a delicate one for the playwrights to maintain. On the one hand, comedy was licensed to push the boundaries of social norms, to showcase common citizens executing outrageous acts and to offer fantastic solutions to common problems; on the other hand, it strove to give legitimate advice to the polis for the betterment of the community.[6] As Henderson argues, the poets of Old Comedy upheld, perhaps even championed, the concepts of *isēgoria* and *parrhēsia*, and they were well aware of the subtleties of these principles.

Perhaps comic playwrights were just as sensitive to matters of *asebeia*.[7] After all, we have evidence (albeit a tad bit spurious) that Aeschylus was put on trial for profaning the Mysteries (probably in his drama *Eleusinioi*) and that the charges against him were dismissed only because in the courtroom Aeschylus's brother revealed the wounds he had suffered while serving in the battle of Marathon.[8] Comic poets also, it seems, did not shy away from charging individuals mentioned in their plays with accusations of *asebeia*. In fr. 53, Lysias, as part of his defense of Phanias, alleges that the poet Cinesias committed acts of *asebeia* and that these offenses were common knowledge because the comic playwrights regularly mocked him onstage for his outrageous behavior.[9] In *Peace* and *Birds*, then, Aristophanes must

---

5 Henderson (1998, 266–7).
6 *Frogs* 1008–10: Αἰσχύλος: ἀπόκριναί μοι, τίνος οὕνεκα χρὴ θαυμάζειν ἄνδρα ποιητήν; Εὐριπίδης: δεξιότητος καὶ νουθεσίας, ὅτι βελτίους τε ποιοῦμεν τοὺς ἀνθρώπους ἐν ταῖς πόλεσιν. (Aeschylus: Answer me – why should we admire a dramatic poet? Euripides: For cleverness and sound advice, and because we make the people in the cities better.)
7 Sommerstein (2004a, 206) provides a good working definition of the 'law of impiety' (*asebeia*): 'The law of impiety (*asebeia*) was available against any actions or words that threatened directly or indirectly to endanger good relations between the Athenian people and the gods, and is well known to have been in very active use in the late fifth and early fourth centuries.' Sommerstein's note directs us to MacDowell (1978, 197–202), Bauman (1990, 37–42, 62–8, 105–27) and Todd (1993, 307–15).
8 Arist. *NE* 1111a8–10 and Aelian *VH* 5.19. See also Sommerstein (2004b, 42 n. 2) and (1996, 25–6).
9 Sommerstein (2004a, 220 n. 41). See also Campbell (1993, 50–5).

consider both the norms surrounding the ritual sacrifice that is 'performed' in the play and the rules, implicit or explicit, of the ritual performance of the play itself, which seemed to have a *nomos* against murder onstage. Despite the fact that the execution of their sacrifices is often flawed to say the least, Trygaeus and Peisetaerus approach their tasks with a sincerity that affords Aristophanes the license almost, but not quite, to violate these layered ritual norms for comic effect and to interject good-natured jokes about Athenian religious practices into the comic banter of his characters.

A Closer Look at the Sacrifice Scenes in *Peace* and *Birds*

Trygaeus begins his sacrifice when he orders a household slave to fetch a sheep (*Peace* 937). He has already considered and rejected the more modest offering of pots of boiled vegetables (923–4) as well as a more bountiful ox (925–6) or sow (927–8). Trygaeus agrees to provide the altar on which to execute the sacrifice (938).[10] Sommerstein and Olson suggest that Trygaeus accidentally stumbles upon the stage altar (942) and abandons his plan to provide his own portable platform for the sacrifice (942).[11] This staging would heighten the threat of *asebeia* – a professional actor officiates as a priest at a real altar over what appears to be an actual sacrifice. A more conservative reading has the altar appear when the slave exits and returns with the other equipment needed for the sacrifice – the basket (κανοῦν), the barley grains (ὀλαί), the wreath for the head of the sheep (στέμμα), the fire (πῦρ), the lustral basin (χέρνιψ) and the knife (μάχαιρα) for cutting the hair from the victim's head (948–9).[12] The slave probably leads out the sheep after another song from the Chorus at lines 950–5. Trygaeus then orders his slave to take the basket and the lustral water and circle the altar (956–7). He dips his brand into the water and shakes it over the sacrificial victim and the altar (959),[13] and he waits for the sheep

---

10 Tordoff (2011, 187–90) notes that the performance of this sacrifice helps solidify peace and reestablish order for the polis, in part by driving away the smells of dirt and excrement from the beginning of the play and replacing them with the savory odors of the sacrificial meal.
11 Sommerstein (1985, *ad* 942) and Olson (1998, *ad* 942). The presence of a permanent altar in the orchestra or closer to the *skēnē* is debated. Arnott (1978 [1962], 43–53) and Dearden (1976, 46–8) argue in favor of the altar; Rehm (1988, 264–74) provides excellent counterevidence.
12 Sommerstein (1985, 95 and *ad* 948–9) counters the earlier argument of Bonanno (1969) that lines 948–9 be assigned to the slave; I agree that it makes better sense that the slave has forgotten the animal and that he and Trygaeus exit and return with the sheep to correct the oversight. Olson (1998, *ad* 948–9) also assigns lines 948–9 to Trygaeus.
13 Olson (1998, *ad* 959). The manuscripts confuse δᾳδίον (diminutive of δαίς) and δαλίον; however, there was probably very little difference in the physical appearance of these two items.

to nod its head in consent of the sacrifice (960). Then, both Trygaeus and the slave wash their hands with the water from the basin (961). The slave showers the audience with barley grains that become the foundation for a sexual joke as to what 'husbands will give to their wives in the evening' (966-7).[14] The slave then douses the audience (or the Chorus) in lustral water instead of just sprinkling them with it (969).[15] Trygaeus probably cuts the animal's hair before he begins the prayer to the goddess Peace at line 974, holds the hairs in his hand as he recites the prayer and throws the shorn locks into the fire when he has finished.[16] Finally, Trygaeus orders the slave to slaughter the sheep (1017-18), but before that can be accomplished, the slave observes that Peace does not take delight in slaughter (1019-20). Trygaeus concurs and suggests that they kill the sheep inside, bring out the thigh bones and save some of the sheep for the choregus (1020-2). The slave in turn takes the knife and leads the sheep into the wings.[17]

In *Birds*, Peisetaerus exhibits similar adherence to ritual procedure. At line 850, he orders one of the household slaves to retrieve his basket (κανοῦν) and some lustral water (χέρνιψ) so that he can make a sacrifice to the gods.[18] After the Chorus finishes its song at lines 851-8, Peisetaerus and the officiating priest lead onstage not a sheep, but a small, and presumably

---

14 Sommerstein (1985, 97; *ad* 962; and *ad* 964-7): Trygaeus here refers to the ὀλαί as κρίθαι, technically processed grain, because of its phallic connotations. See Henderson (1991, 119-20) and *Birds* 505-6. Without such a substitution, the slave's comment at line 966 about the men giving the women some 'barley' would not make sense. This scene also parodies other comedies where the characters toss nuts and fruits at the characters: *Wasps* 58-9 and *Wealth* 797-9. See also Olson (1998, *ad* 960 and *ad* 961-2) for tossing barley and other small food items at the audience.
15 Sommerstein (1985, 97) and Olson (1998, *ad* 969).
16 Sommerstein (1985, 101 and *ad* 973), where he suggests that Trygaeus follows the appropriate procedure for such a sacrifice. For the cutting of hair as the last act before the actual slaughter, see Hom. *Od*. 3.444-6 and *Od*. 14.422-4; Eur. *El*. 810-14. See also Olson (1998, *ad* 973).
17 Onstage slaughter would also involve practical improbabilities: killing livestock, even in ritual contexts, required the expertise of a trained butcher (μάγειρος). For more on butchers, see Olson (1998, *ad* 1017-18); for more on the details of the sacrifice described here and the reference to the feast sponsored by the choregus, see Olson (1998, *ad* 1020-2).
18 When they enter at the beginning of the play, Peisetaerus and Euelpides are carrying a ritual basket, a pot and some myrtle branches. It is implied that the basket contains the requisite items for the sacrifice that must take place upon the founding of a new city. See Sommerstein (1987, *ad* 43) and Dunbar (1997, *ad* 43). Cf. Hamilton (1985, 238-9), who argues instead that these items are for neither sympotic nor sacrificial purposes. He proposes that items from the bird kingdom replace the objects mentioned in lines 42-3.

cheaper, he-goat.[19] The goat likely has a wreath adorning his head.[20] The procession approaches the altar. After the priest's tedious and erroneous invocation, Peisetaerus dismisses the man, usurps his role as religious officiant and vows to sacrifice the victim by himself (894). He most likely washes his hands with the lustral water during the choral song that immediately follows.[21] However, before Peisetaerus can begin his sacrifice, he is interrupted by the arrival of a poet seeking admission to Cloudcuckooland (904). After dismissing the poet, Peisetaerus is interrupted four more times, by an oracle-monger, by the astronomer Meton, by an *episkopos* and, finally, by a decree-seller. After much comic madness, Peisetaerus finally decides that it would be better to sacrifice the goat inside (1056–7).

In these scenes, Aristophanes teases his audience with the threat of *asebeia* – will Trygaeus and Peisetaerus actually perform their sacrifices to untraditional gods onstage? Probably not, but they do come close, and Aristophanes at the last minute upholds the dramatic convention of 'no death onstage' and saves his actors from committing public acts of impiety.[22] To heighten this tension, Aristophanes also shows Trygaeus and Peisetaerus disrupting their ritual duty and resorting to brute force to chase away the interlopers. When Trygaeus reappears onstage with the offal and begins to prepare Peace's celebratory banquet, the oracle-monger Hierocles enters and demands his share of the offerings. Trygaeus ignores his interruptions, and, when Hierocles tries to steal the offals, Trygaeus beats him with the firewood and strips him of his sheepskins (1117–26). Peisetaerus too beats an oracle-monger with his oracle book (989–90); he strikes the astronomer Meton (1017–20); he assaults the *episkopos* (1029–31); and, finally, he beats

19 Peisetaerus's words at 891–2 further substantiate the small size of the animal, and the Chorus also observes the lack of meat on the he-goat as they invite only one of the gods to the ceremony (898–902). For a full discussion of the anticlimactic nature of this substitution, see Sommerstein (1987, *ad* 856).
20 Dunbar (1997, *ad* 893): 'here the priest could have taken it [the wreath] from the κανοῦν brought to him at 863, which the audience would expect also to hold the ritual barley-grains and knife ... If he [the bird-priest] has already put it over the goat's horns, he probably leaves it behind when he runs off or, if he grabs it and runs, the basket may have contained a replacement, since we should expect the goat to be wreathed when Peis. is about to take a knife to it at 959.' In the same note, Dunbar lists two other (less likely) uses for the στέμματα of this scene: as a headband for the priest or as a decoration for a staff that might have been in his possession. See also Sommerstein (1987, *ad* 893).
21 Sommerstein (1987, 113).
22 Sommerstein (2004b, 42 n. 3) notes that Aristophanes often taunts the audience with the possible violation of convention only to circumvent such a violation at the last minute. He gives the example of *Thesm.* 626–33, where the women test Euripides' Relative by asking him about last year's ritual. The Relative in turn does not reveal the 'secrets' of the Thesmophoria but merely cites conventional male beliefs – that women gather for the Thesmophoria to indulge in excessive drinking.

back the decree-seller while fending off a second attack from the *episkopos* (1043–55).

Although this behavior is hardly admirable in characters who have assumed the role of officiating priests, the adversaries of Trygaeus and Peisetaerus are also enemies of Peace and opposed to the ideals of Cloudcuckooland. And if we believe that Trygaeus is the hero that saved the polis from the deleterious effects of War[23] and if we champion Peisetaerus as the sophistic magic-maker who outwitted the Olympian gods and constructed a new and better polis in direct response to his frustrations with Athens,[24] are not the violent outbursts of these characters and their bold onstage sacrifices more laudatory than subversive? In other words, what could be interpreted as violating the codes of reverent behavior is in actuality noble, but comically misguided, conduct that renders these comic heroes victors over their enemies and champions of their new and improved cities.

Evidence (or Lack Thereof) from the Comic Fragments

I believe that Aristophanes chose to interject this type of humor into plays performed during times of high political optimism and before popular opinion began to associate the defeat of the Sicilian Expedition with the mutilation of the herms; and that Aristophanes and his contemporaries had to gauge the religious climate of the community before they staged scenes that could potentially offend their audiences.[25] Unfortunately, there is little evidence in the fragments of Old Comedy to support or deny this claim. Many Old Comic playwrights other than Aristophanes seemed interested in the comic potential of 'sacrifice': Crates (*floruit* c. 454–424 BCE) composed *Beasts*, in which animals, perhaps targeted as victims for sacrifice, take control of mortal affairs and refuse to be eaten;[26] Cratinus wrote

---

23 For a discussion of Peace as a reflection of a growing desire in Athens for the establishment of an official cult of Peace, see Athanassaki (2018).
24 For a 'critical and hopeful' reading of *Birds* and the comic hero Peisetaerus, see Henderson (1997).
25 Mikalson (1983, 10) cautions us about drawing conclusions about average Athenians and their religious attitudes by an 'over'-literal interpretation of Aristophanes' heroes: 'We should be very reluctant to accept the caricatures of Aristophanes as average Athenians. I use Aristophanes, like other literary and philosophic writers of the period, only to illuminate religious beliefs and attitudes established by more reliable evidence. Aristophanes is valuable for this purpose, but excessive reliance upon him could lead only to a very distorted picture.' That said, we need to balance that caution against the possibility that Aristophanes' comedies may provide some insight, albeit small, into shifting attitudes toward Athenian popular religion in the 420s and 410s, for which see Raaflaub (1998, esp. 40–1).
26 Storey (2011a, 214–9). See Wilkins (2000, 348): 'The dismayed response of speaker B in fr. 19 appears to indicate that all meat-eating is now banned. The mention of meat,

Runaways, a comedy dated to the 440s BCE, fr. 66 of which refers to Lampon as an ax-collector or sacrificer (ἀγερσικύβηλις), a beggar-priest (ἀγύρτης) and an ax-wielder (κυβηλιστής);²⁷ Eupolis *(floruit* c. 429–415 BCE) wrote *Goats*, another comedy with an animal chorus;²⁸ Metagenes wrote *Sacrifice-Lover* in the last decade of 400s;²⁹ Plato Comicus *(floruit* c. 420–380s BCE) wrote *Women Returning from the Rites* with possible religious parody;³⁰ and Cephisodorus *(floruit* c. 400 BCE) wrote *Pig*.³¹ It is unclear from the fragments of these plays whether the comic poets crafted staged sacrifices or whether they just used the concept of sacrifice, or references to it, as a backdrop for the action of the play. This distinction seems important to navigating the boundaries of *asebeia*.

A few fragments from Aristophanes, however, may lend some support to my argument. At the Lenaea of 414, just months before the production of *Birds*, Aristophanes seems to have staged in his *Amphiaraus* a scene at a healing shrine where a husband and wife submit to an incubation and cure. Three fragments indicate stage properties and suggest that some scenes at the shrine were reenacted onstage: fr. 17 refers to a hen knocking over a wine-cup; fr. 18 includes a command for someone to fetch a linen cushion and pillow; and fr. 25 mentions 'this meat'.³² In contrast, at the end of his career amidst a startlingly different political climate from that which existed in Athens at the outset of the Sicilian Expedition, Aristophanes returns in *Wealth* to the comic potential of activities at such shrines. He has Carion describe in vivid detail to Chremylus's wife the restoration of Wealth's sight at the shrine of Asclepius (649–747). As Sommerstein notes, Aristophanes here adapts the tragic convention of the messenger speech to suit his comic purposes.³³ He presents to his audience an 'imagined' dramatic scene so as not to violate the mysteries of this cult. At least that has been the prevailing

---

rissoles and black puddings bought in the agora implies that the ban extended to meat from all sources including sacrifice. If the sacrificial order was brought into question and human beings and animals now lived as equals, the polis of the play was reordered in a form that Aristophanes carefully avoided in *Birds* and that appears not, on present evidence at least, to have concerned Archippus in *Fishes*.'

27 Storey (2011a, 296–301). See Bowie (2000, 328).
28 Storey (2011b, 54–63). See Wilkins (2000, 348): 'Was the issue of the sacrifice and eating of goats raised in the play? The question is impossible to answer, but our study of potentially edible choruses allows this much to be said. It would be surprising if the sacrificial order was disturbed in this play, since, with the possible exception of Crates, the comic poets appear to have avoided so radical a step.'
29 Storey (2011b, 362–5). Cf. *Wasps* 82, where the term 'sacrifice-lover' is thrown out as one of Philocleon's rumored addictions.
30 Storey (2011c, 96–9).
31 Storey (2011a, 188–91).
32 Henderson (2008, 118–29).
33 Sommerstein (2001, *ad* 647).

interpretation of this episode. But what if Aristophanes was basing his artistic choices on a more subtle reading of the religious attitudes of his audience and choosing 'safer' and 'riskier' stagings depending upon what he perceived the polis would tolerate?[34]

Conclusion

The extent to which Aristophanes pushed at the boundaries of *asebeia* seems to have depended upon the political climate at the time of the production.[35] Aristophanes staged *Peace* when negotiations for the Peace of Nicias provided Athens with some hope that their ten-year civil strife was at last coming to an end. Trygaeus's bold sacrifice to the goddess Peace, staged at the City Dionysia in front of Athens' allies, is a brazen statement from the comic poet to his audience about the necessity of peace and the prosperity that it would bring. Likewise, Peisetaerus embodies the fierce optimism that Athens felt in the early days of the Sicilian Expedition, and his sacrifice to the new gods of Cloudcuckooland affirms not only his new identity but also his new autonomous polis, one distinct from the Olympian gods and one set in opposition to the ills that afflict Athens. We should read these scenes as a gauge of shifting attitudes toward Athenian popular religion and begin to look beyond the procedures of sacrifice that Aristophanes documents therein to the culture that allowed such scenes to be staged. The sanctity of religious ritual seems to have taken precedence over the comic potential of the material, and thus Aristophanes, it seems, took some risk in staging direct parody of ritual sacrifice.

---

34 This insight into fifth-century attitudes toward the comic potential of ritual sacrifice can also prompt discussion of the parody of religious practice in contemporary American theater and television comedy. *All in the Family*, Season 6, Episode 22 provides a perfect example of the type of humor found in these scenes from *Peace* and *Birds*: Archie Bunker, concerned that his daughter Gloria's rejection of Christianity and her adoption of her husband's atheistic ways might jeopardize his grandson's moral future, kidnaps the child, brings him to the church and baptizes the infant himself. Although Christian doctrine allows the average worshipper to baptize individuals in the event of emergencies, Archie certainly has stretched the limits of this notion. We are carried along in the scene because, to some extent, we accept that our comic hero Archie is truly worried that his grandson's parents have put him in moral danger.

35 Henderson (2013) argues that the comic poets were aware of political shifts and adjusted their comic arsenal accordingly: 'So the most straightforward explanation for the eclipse of political comedy after 403 looks to be the same as for similar eclipses earlier: a shift in leadership back to the wealthy and to rightist policies – which, for whatever reason, were unappealing targets for the political poets ... It is in times of demotic self-assertion or counter-revolution that we find political comedy' (258).

Works Cited

Arnott, Peter. 1978 [1962]. *Greek Scenic Conventions in the Fifth Century* B.C. Westport, CT: Greenwood Press.

Athanassaki, Lucia. 2018. 'The Cult of Peace on the Athenian Stage During the Peloponnesian War: From Euripides's *Cresphontes* to Aristophanes's *Peace* and Beyond'. *ICS* 43: 1–24.

Atkinson, J. E. 1992. 'Curbing the Comedians: Cleon Versus Aristophanes and Syracosius' Decree'. *CQ* 42: 56–64.

Bauman, R. 1990. *Political Trials in Ancient Greece*. London: Routledge.

Boedeker, D., and K. Raaflaub, eds. 1998. *Democracy, Empire, and the Arts in Fifth-Century Athens*. Cambridge, MA: Harvard University Press.

Bonanno, M. G. 1969. 'Note alla Pace di Aristofane'. *Museum Criticum* 4: 44–9.

Bowie, Angus. 2000. 'Myth and Ritual in the Rivals of Aristophanes'. In Harvey and Wilkins 2000, 317–39.

Burkert, Walter. 1983. *Homo Necans: The Anthropology of Ancient Greek Sacrificial Ritual and Myth*. Berkeley: University of California Press.

Campbell, David A. 1993. *Greek Lyric*, vol. 5: *The New School of Poetry and Anonymous Songs and Hymns*. Cambridge, MA: Harvard University Press.

Dearden, C. W. 1976. *The Stage of Aristophanes*. London: Athlone Press.

Dunbar, Nan. 1997. *Aristophanes: Birds*. Oxford: Oxford University Press.

Halliwell, Stephen. 1991. 'Comic Satire and Freedom of Speech in Classical Athens'. *JHS* 111: 48–70.

Hamilton, R. 1985. 'The Well-Equipped Traveller: *Birds* 42'. *GRBS* 26: 235–39.

Harvey, David, and John Wilkins, eds. 2000. *The Rivals of Aristophanes: Studies in Athenian Old Comedy*. London: Duckworth and the Classical Press of Wales.

Henderson, Jeffrey. 1991. *The Maculate Muse: Obscene Language in Attic Comedy*. Oxford: Oxford University Press.

———. 1997. 'Mass Versus Elite and the Comic Heroism of Peisetairos'. In *The City as Comedy: Society and Representation in Athenian Drama*, edited by G. Dobrov, 135–48. Chapel Hill: University of North Carolina Press.

———. 1998. 'Attic Old Comedy, Frank Speech and Democracy'. In Boedeker and Raaflaub 1998, 255–73.

———. 2008. *Aristophanes: Fragments*. Cambridge, MA: Harvard University Press.

———. 2013. 'A Brief History of Athenian Political Comedy (c. 440–c. 300)'. *TAPA* 143: 249–62.

MacDowell, Douglas M. 1978. *The Law in Classical Athens*. Ithaca, NY: Cornell University Press.

Marshall, C. W. 2000. '*Alcestis* and the Problem of Prosatyric Drama'. *CJ* 95: 229–38.

Mikalson, Jon. 1983. *Athenian Popular Religion*. Chapel Hill: University of North Carolina Press.

Olson, S. Douglas. 1998. *Aristophanes: Peace*. Oxford: Oxford University Press.

Raaflaub, Kurt. 1998. 'The Transformation of Athens in the Fifth Century'. Boedeker and Raaflaub 1998, 15–40.

Rehm, Rush. 1988. 'The Staging of Suppliant Plays'. *GRBS* 29: 263–307.

Sommerstein, Alan H. 1985. *The Comedies of Aristophanes*, vol. 5: *Peace*. Warminster: Aris and Phillips.

———. 1986. 'Decree of Syrakosios'. *CQ* 36: 101–8.

———. 1987. *The Comedies of Aristophanes*, vol. 6: *Birds*. Warminster: Aris and Phillips.

———. 1990. *The Comedies of Aristophanes*, vol. 7: *Lysistrata*. Warminster: Aris and Phillips.

———. 1996. *Aeschylean Tragedy*. Bari: Levante Editori.

———. 2001. *The Comedies of Aristophanes*, vol. 11: *Wealth*. Warminster: Aris and Phillips.

———. 2004a. 'Comedy and the Unspeakable'. In *Law, Rhetoric and Comedy in Classical Athens*, edited by D. L. Cairns and R. A. Knox, 205–22. London: Classical Press of Wales.

———. 2004b. 'Violence in Greek Drama'. *Ordia Prima* 3: 41–56.

———. 2004c. 'Harassing the Satirist: The Alleged Attempts to Prosecute Aristophanes'. In *Free Speech in Classical Antiquity*, edited by Ineke Sluiter and Ralph Rosen, 145–74. Leiden: Brill.

Storey, Ian C. 2011a. *Fragments of Old Comedy*, vol. 1: *Alcaeus to Diocles*. Cambridge, MA: Harvard University Press.

———. 2011b. *Fragments of Old Comedy*, vol. 2: *Diopeithes to Pherecrates*. Cambridge, MA: Harvard University Press.

———. 2011c. *Fragments of Old Comedy*, vol. 3: *Philonicus to Xenophon, Adespota*. Cambridge, MA: Harvard University Press.

Todd, S. C. 1993. *The Shape of Athenian Law*. Oxford: Oxford University Press.

Tordoff, R. L. S. 2011. 'Excrement, Sacrifice, Commensality: The Osphresiology of Aristophanes' *Peace*. *Arethusa* 44: 167–98.

Wilkins, John. 2000. 'Edible Choruses'. In Harvey and Wilkins 2000, 341–54.

CHAPTER 4

Political Ambition and Poetry in Aristophanes' Birds *and Plato's Aristophanes*

I-Kai Jeng

Aristophanes' *Birds* is unusual because although it comments generally on contemporaneous political affairs, the play is distant enough from particular events that the play's political stance is not easy to discern. In this chapter, I follow some commentators in thinking that *Birds* is concerned with more general matters than actual, specific events.[1] Perhaps, given the optimistic mood in Athens at the dawn of the Sicilian Expedition, Aristophanes felt little need to criticize the city's foreign policy. Instead, the Expedition becomes an occasion to reflect on the ineradicable human longing for greatness. I shall argue that *Birds* convincingly portrays a successful development of political ambition, while simultaneously showing what Aristophanes' poetry can do to temper it. In this sense, *Birds* is a useful point of departure for examining Plato's Aristophanes in the *Symposium*, because in the latter, the character explicitly presents his teaching about Eros (I call it 'teaching' because he expects it to be taught: διδάσκαλοι, *Symp.* 189d4) as philosophical.[2] The fictional Aristophanes urges the symposiasts not to take his myth of spherical humans as an elaborate way of making fun of Pausanias and Agathon's love affair, as if his speech were one of his comedies (193b6–c5). Instead, he is talking about human nature in general (τὴν ἀνθρωπίνην φύσιν, 189d5–6; ἁπάντων, 193c2). The parallel runs even deeper because, as I shall argue, Plato's Aristophanes also understands political ambition as problematic and also attempts to moderate it through his poetic art. Moreover, certain puzzling features about the myth can be illuminated in light of the play.

1 Konstan (1995, 30–2) assesses the literature that attempts to extract a political commentary and argues that the play interrogates configurations of nature and culture; Slater (1997) thinks it examines not policies but the nature of the city. Hall (2020) challenges the orthodox view that *Birds* reacts to the Sicilian Expedition, arguing that it alludes to troublemakers in Thrace instead.
2 Translations of the *Symposium* are my own. I quote from Henderson's (1999) translation of *Birds*, unless otherwise noted.

That *Birds* can guide us to a better understanding of a Platonic passage will be shown in the second part of this chapter.

Political Ambition in *Birds*

Birds examines the human longing for greatness. This longing for greatness seems to be the meaning of the change of plan by Peisetaerus and Euelpides. Aristophanes designs the plot so that there is a contrast between two impulses, the impulse away from politics (initially they leave Athens to find a place that is ἀπράγμων, 44) and the fundamentally restive impulse (the plan to found a city in the sky is referred to as a πρᾶγμα at 198, 321, 460).³ While restiveness is depicted as a special trait of Athenians, *Birds* does not appear to be commenting on Athenian temperament alone, as this would not explain the difference between Peisetaerus and Euelpides: the latter disappears soon after Cloudcuckooland is founded (845–6). Their difference suggests a more general comment on human affairs instead of only Athenian ones: the energetic, proactive and restless types have more influence on human affairs.

The utopian city in *Birds* claims to pursue freedom and justice. The principle of freedom is stated by the birds in their first parabasis and can be parsed into four dimensions: first, the realization of desire. Cloudcuckooland is where one can do whatever one wants (see βούλεται, 753). Related to this is the second feature: liberation from the shackles of νόμος, law or custom. When the birds dream of their new city, they do not contrast human laws and bird laws, but their city rather seems to lack laws entirely: 'Whatever's shameful here, for people controlled by custom (νόμῳ), it's all considered admirable among us birds' (755–6). They do not think of the new city as having laws at all. But this is not the lawlessness that tends to disorder and anarchy, but one that spontaneously engenders order and variety. When the Hoopoe first convenes the birds, they each come from their own habitat, where they nourish themselves sufficiently. Here νόμοι show up as pasturage.⁴ As each bird is allotted (νέμεσθε, 231; νομὸν ἔχει, 239) a place, there is no war amongst them.⁵ Birds in their pre-political state exemplify the harmony of νόμος ('custom') and φύσις ('nature'), to the point that their natural habitats are described in terms of νόμος or its cognates. They seem to think that this harmony will continue in the new city. But, since the ability to do what one wants requires not only the lack of external restraints

---

3   Later, Peisetaerus criticizes the birds for not being πολυπράγμων (471).
4   Words with the νεμ- root show up several times in the Hoopoe's first bird-calling song: 209 (σύννομε), 210, 231, 239. See also 678.
5   This is, of course, a fiction. In real life, birds do attack each other. As Ambler (2012, 191) observes, Tereus might be deliberately avoiding calling birds of prey to show up, even though some hawks eventually arrive.

but also the ability to realize it, freedom thirdly requires power. On the one hand, power is understood physically, as the wings that enable one to move anywhere swiftly (785–800). On the other hand, the physical power of birds cannot appear splendid without the political power that makes it shine (see λιπαρόν, 826; 1709–12). It is only when the city backs up what its citizens do that freedom becomes real. Finally, the freedom thus conceived implies a certain equality. In the human world, inequality seems largely due to νόμος. It is why strong youths must obey weak elders (757–9), and why some people are hirelings or slaves, others employers or masters (760–7). Equality in bird town will give hirelings and slaves splendor in variegated types of plumage. The utopia in *Birds* thus appears to practice democracy domestically: everyone is equally free to pursue what they wish.

So far it is already clear that, even while *Birds* is sparse with allusions to contemporaneous political affairs, it remains a political play. The significance of this becomes even more strongly felt when freedom in Cloudcuckooland is contrasted with its justice. The birds, as providing a bird's-eye view, do not notice that these four dimensions of freedom are not harmonious with one another. Equality requires restrictions on freedom. One cannot do what causes inequality; political power requires imposing law and order, and therefore there must be νόμος of some kind. These conflicts require adjudicating, and successful negotiation between them requires some notion of what is fair or right or just. Here Peisetaerus's difference from the birds emerges: while he aims to pursue maximal freedom, he also keeps an eye on the conflicting tendencies within it. So, while the birds invite immigrants (753–68), Peisetaerus does not treat visitors with the welcoming attitude one might expect from the birds' parabasis. He chases away the oracle-collector, for example, because the latter, in claiming to have the power to interpret divine authority (970), potentially challenges Peisetaerus's own authority and the communal unity embodied in him. The power to announce oracles must belong to Peisetaerus alone (983–5, 987–8) so that the political order is stable. Later in the scene, Peisetaerus also refuses Meton's division of the city into a powerful center with roads connected to the outer parts (1005–9), presumably because it risks creating inequality between avian districts.

But the most conspicuous difference between Peisetaerus and the birds shows up in his treatment of the father-beater (1337–71). This episode is significant since his difference from the birds becomes readily noticeable to the Athenian audience. The birds had claimed that father-beating was allowed in their city (757–9), and now a would-be father-beater wants to live in Cloudcuckooland in order to do what he wants. However, Peisetaerus engages in two strategies to convince the father-beater not to strangle his father. Though the birds had implied that their new city would be free from law, Peisetaerus first cites a law, 'an ancient one that's written on the Tablets of the Storks' (νόμος | παλαιὸς ἐν ταῖς τῶν πελαργῶν κύρβεσιν, 1353–4). Not only is the father-beater prohibited from murdering his father, he has an obligation to take care of him in his old age.⁶ The father-beater is disappointed. Then, Peisetaerus acknowledges the young man's aggressive tendency (1368), offers some sympathy (1362–3) and puts his aggression to good use: he convinces him, with the help of imagination (1366), to fight in Thrace and earn a living for himself (1369).

Some commentators detect a sinister reading of the play here. The Chorus is like the *dēmos* duped by the tyrant, whose actions only aggrandize himself against the birds' aspiration for the new city.⁷ But one should not forget that Peisetaerus serves as the brains and the birds the brawn (636–7). The division of labor makes it unsurprising that the birds only see the attractive side of the city and state its aspirations in unqualified fashion, while Peisetaerus shows how realistically the city's motto can be applied by doing the less savory works of politics. The father-beater is the only person whose request for wings is granted. To the extent that the father-beater can satisfy his natural, aggressive tendencies, Peisetaerus is not aggrandizing himself but carrying out what the birds claimed in the parabasis: to harmonize between νόμος and human natures as far as possible. The father-beater receiving 'orphan wings' (1361) is not unlike the birds' advertisement that a tattooed hireling will become a dappled francolin (760–1): in both cases, natural impulses are not suppressed but rechanneled. Father-beating is therefore only allowed insofar as Peisetaerus successfully sublimates the father-beating urge into fighting barbarians instead.

The general thrust of Peisetaerus's actions shows a concern with justice.⁸ The parasitical nature of the oracle-collector, decree-seller and informer makes their presence in the city undesirable, as they take without giving in return.⁹ The threat of the rape of Iris (1253–6), a difficult episode to interpret, must at least reflect a concern with justice. Peisetaerus claims that her trespassing of the city walls is unjust (ἀδικεῖς, 1221) and death would be an extremely just punishment (δικαιότατα, 1222). And while the birds seem to neglect the need for justice in their own city, in their dealings with outsiders they remain concerned with it. Once Peisetaerus convinces them that kingship over the world is rightfully (ὀρθῶς, 478) theirs (465–538), they begin to think that their attack against gods will be just (δίκαιος, 632). After the city is founded, they ask humans to kill or arrest tyrants and bird-catchers

---

6 The double emphasis of the archaic character of this law in παλαιός ('ancient') and κυρβείς ('tablets') reinforces the connection between respecting elders and respecting tradition. See Konstan (1995, 178 n. 40).
7 Hubbard (1997).
8 See Heath (1997, 231).
9 See Henderson (1997, 142): 'Nephelokokkugia has none of the annoyances that plague the Athenians, and none are allowed in.'

while maintaining a beneficial order, as befits superior beings (1072–83). Unlike Peisetaerus, the birds care about justice not as a necessity reluctantly accepted for the sake of preserving freedom, but rather as an end in itself: wrongdoers ought to be punished. Even imagining their righteous revenge on bird-catchers and bird-sellers brings the birds joy (1084–7).

Cloudcuckooland is therefore not a city that endorses unconditional hedonism. Humans wish to be a part of a community not simply because they are vulnerable without it, but also because they wish to live the right way of life, and only as a community can the demands of what is right or just be carried out. This is perhaps the more profound reason why restlessness guides human affairs more than the desire to be ἀπράγμων: because one longs for public acknowledgment of the right kind of life. This also explains why the birds do not show signs of disillusionment when Peisetaerus's actions appear to be at odds with what they expected in the parabasis. It is not because the birds are foolish or that Peisetaerus's total power has made it impossible for them to speak out, but because Peisetaerus is actually doing what they want: making them just and powerful rulers of the world. Under Peisetaerus's leadership, their power and untrammeled view of human behavior allows for an administration of the world more just than the rule of Olympian gods.

The ambiguity of Peisetaerus as 'tyrant' (τύραννος) can be read from this point of view. In the second parabasis, the term is used negatively, approaching the meaning 'anti-democratic' (1074). Near the end of the play, however, a messenger introduces Peisetaerus's marriage procession by referring to him as a τύραννος (1708), which, while referring to the usurping of Zeus's rule, also carries the splendor attending the wise use of absolute power.[10] Through the double blame and praise of τύραννοι, the play gestures toward the idea that there is no end to the threat of tyranny, because humans restlessly pursue greater and greater things, unless there is a single tyrant that destroys all tyrants. While a τύραννος is generally unjust, justice cannot be realized without one.[11]

The plot of *Birds* in turn suggests, as Henderson has shown, that the best way to realize freedom and justice is a wise or clever leader with mass appeal. On his reading, Peisetaerus is an unusual Aristophanic hero because he is a hybrid social type and shares more in common with the Athenian

10 As Henderson (2003) notes, both the negative and positive valuation are understandable within Athenian democracy; while 'by the 420s, tyranny was, in the popular mind, the opposite of democracy' (170), such an ideology was seen by Aristophanes as detrimental to the city, making the city unable to choose the aristocratic elites as their leaders (163–4).
11 Even the roasting of the anti-democratic birds, long an episode hotly debated for Aristophanes' intended meaning, ought perhaps to be understood from this point of view. See the similar view of Henderson (1997, 144–5).

intellectual elite than with the 'man of the people' rustic.[12] Henderson sees the play as portraying what would happen to Athens should the people be more trusting of the elite, and as a result, Peisetaerus takes on recognizably Alcibiadean traits.[13] I would carry this further and claim that Aristophanes sees Cloudcuckooland as the best possible outcome for political ambition in general, and not simply for Athenian politics in particular. Stated in Platonic terms, democracy and tyranny, the two worst types of regimes (*Rep.* 555b–569c), produce the best city when they are suitably combined.

Again, against commentators who detect a critique of the Sicilian Expedition behind the success of Peisetaerus, Henderson also argues that the ending of *Birds* is not ironic: it critiques neither Peisetaerus nor whatever foreign policy Athens was pursuing.[14] He points out that 'irony ... as a wholesale device seems so alien to Old Comedy', and reading *Birds* as such a critique requires reading the whole play ironically.[15] Moreover, in response to the observation that Peisetaerus is impious in usurping Zeus, Henderson notes that both tragedies and comedies have criticized gods and challenged their authority.[16] This makes Peisetaerus's apotheosis much less repulsive than one imagines it to be. This response can be buttressed by my reading: defiance of gods is the logical outcome of wishing to be the master of oneself and one's community.

There are, however, signs that Aristophanes in the end prefers political moderation instead of what *Birds* portrays. The ambiguity of τύραννος has already been mentioned: even if a wise and benevolent tyrant is not impossible, the Athenians have an ostensible distaste for tyranny. Moreover, the disappearance of Euelpides soon after Cloudcuckooland is founded suggests his awareness that Peisetaerus is about to build a second Athens in the air. He therefore departs after he gets his wings.[17] The two sides of human nature, one that enjoys more the thrill of pursuing peace than peace itself, and the other that truly desires the simple, quiet and easy life as such, can

---

12 Henderson (1997, 138–9).
13 Henderson (1997, 139–40, 142–5; 2003, 162, 171–3). Henderson's reading makes better sense of two points in the plot. First, the natural enmity (371) between birds and humans can be interpreted as the hostility between the common people and the elite class. Second, it provides a ready explanation for why the Olympian gods appear to practice democracy (1570–1) and have Athenian inheritance laws (1641–69). It is not because, as some think, the contrast between Cloudcuckooland and the gods alludes to the differences between Sparta and Athens, but because it alludes to the difference between people with and without a wise ruler.
14 See Konstan (1995, 30–1) for an overview.
15 Henderson (1997, 142).
16 Henderson (1997, 143–4).
17 In seeing Euelpides' disappearance as significant, I follow Strauss (1966, 194) and Ambler (2012, 205–6), who further suggests that Euelpides and Peisetaerus represent two basic possibilities of life in an imperial city. See also Hubbard (1997, 45 n. 63).

only join forces for the briefest of moments before inevitably diverging, because, for all the freedom enjoyed by the citizens of Cloudcuckooland, one loses the freedom to be ἀπράγμων. Peisetaerus uses his wings to rule; Euelpides might use his to live the carefree life described by the Hoopoe (155–61; see also 40–1). In addition, Cloudcuckooland does not welcome all poetry. The treatment of the poet, who sings in a Pindaric style, and of Cinesias, who composes fashionable dithyrambs, reveals Peisetaerus's overall attitude toward poetry. While Aristophanes clearly makes fun of the elaborate and empty language in the new dithyrambic style, both he and Cinesias take pride in innovation (1376), and their creativity is related to the clouds. The clouds are Cinesias's source of inspiration (1384); Aristophanes creates a great city in the clouds through his poetry. Aristophanic poetry founds the city but perhaps cannot exist in it, as Peisetaerus needs to monopolize the myth of archaic bird rule, and poets competing to see who is more innovative would threaten that. Finally, as the Iris episode indicates, there is a certain irrationality, insanity even, in the urge to be one's own master: the political impulse in humans appears to require the absurdity that immortals die (1222–4). The risky nature of the enterprise undertaken in *Birds*, the suppression of peacefulness and certain innovative poetry, and the inherent madness of human restlessness, altogether imply a preference for restraint.

Admittedly, these moments of the play are rather fleeting and less conspicuous than the celebration of Peisetaerus's action. Seemingly paradoxically, Aristophanes intends to temper Athenian restlessness by discharging it through comedy. In dealing with the sycophant, Peisetaerus states that speech is what gives wings to humans (1437–49). As a number of commentators have noted, this applies to Aristophanes' own poetry as well. What drives the plot is the power of words to create and shape reality.[18] On the level of narration, Peisetaerus comes up with a myth on the spot that convinces the birds that they once ruled the world. Without the sense of lost glory and present wretchedness and injustice, the birds never would have united to revolt. An expression such as ἐς κόρακας ἐλθεῖν (28), which idiomatically means 'go to hell' but literally 'go to the crows', brings the protagonists to birds. The dwelling place of the birds, the vault or pole of the heavens (πόλος), becomes where a polis (πόλις) ought to be (178–84).

The power of language constitutes a significant part of the play's reflection on politics. To begin with, political actions also require this power of speech to shape reality. A ruler is a ruler only if there are enough people who accept being ruled, that is, only if an adequate number of them more or less follow the ruler's orders. In this respect, when Peisetaerus orders the wall built and the birds immediately get the work done, he is also 'giving wings' to

---

18 Whitman (1964, 167–99).

birds. Both poetry and politics are effective through this wing-giving power of words. A ruler's commands are recognized as coming from a superior and bringing social cohesion. Similarly, in the episode of the father-beater, Peisetaerus asks the young man to deem or imagine (νομίσας, 1366) that a crest is a cockscomb. νόμος is rooted in make-believe: it becomes real when a group of people think so. Rulers and poets both make fantasy real through speech. Peisetaerus himself notes their kinship when he reacts to news about the wall being finished by saying, ἴσα γὰρ ἀληθῶς φαίνεταί μοι ψεύδεσιν ('To tell the truth, it sounds like a mighty tall tale!', 1167), juxtaposing ἀληθῶς ('the truth') and ψεύδεσιν ('tall tale', or literally 'lies'). This reads like a comment on Hesiod's *Theogony* 27 and 80–103, according to which the Muses not only know how to speak lies like the truth, but also are guardians of kings and poets. The power to create reality through words and thereby disarm conflict or soothe agony is common to both political leaders and poets.[19]

Moreover, if the political already has something fantastical about it, the fantastical can conversely be (felt as) real. *Birds* indeed treats its fantasy as part of reality. Consider the fact that this is one of the plays where Aristophanes does not make the Chorus speak in his name in the parabasis.[20] When choruses or characters address the audience in comedy, they sometimes do so not as their character, but as the actor or on behalf of the poet. In *Birds*, however, when this happens with the Chorus, they do not depart from their roles as birds (753–68, 785–96, 1072–87, 1102–16); one exception is 445–7, but even there the Chorus Leader seems to be speaking simultaneously as the performer and as the leader of birds, swearing to abide by the truce. It is unlike, for example, *Peace* 173–4, where the illusion is truly dropped and the actor speaks as concerned for himself. In *Birds* 1072–87, it even appears that the dramatic illusion is extended, as if an imperial city is now onstage, dictating the laws in Athens.[21]

These features lead me to think that *Birds* evaluates certain political methods positively without recommending them in practice. And it does this precisely through, not in spite of, the positive evaluation of it. In contemporary times, we sometimes observe that when a joke critiques or reveals some injustice, the enjoyment of that joke can be mistakenly felt as a correction of that injustice itself. Although, on a rational level, one is aware that the joke is no substitute for real work addressing the injustice, on the level of experience, being able to laugh at the person or system

---

19 See also Slater (1997, esp. 79–85), who notes several puns that serve to describe both the founding of a city in the play and the poet's production of theater onstage.
20 Strauss (1966) seems to suggest that Aristophanes either need not appear because he fully agrees with Peisetaerus's way of maintaining political order, or that the plot of *Birds* is so shocking that he had to distance himself from it.
21 See Slater (1997, 83–4).

responsible for the problems is easy enough for one to 'feel good about oneself' and forget the work that is supposed to follow. A joke critiquing society then risks not changing it for the better precisely because the joke worked. I suggest that Aristophanes understood this about laughter: the fictional realization of a human longing is designed to be mistakenly felt as actually satisfying that longing, in a kind of comic catharsis. Peisetaerus's desire comes true and Cloudcuckooland becomes real through the power of words. This is Aristophanes' song, his νόμος, and it also makes something unreal real. In contrast to his other plays, *Birds* reinforces the illusion to a greater extent by the absence of Aristophanes' own voice and by its very length.[22] Aristophanes shows that what Socrates accuses the poets of doing – confusing the real with the illusory, the false – can indeed be done to curb human passions instead of unleashing and legitimating them.

Aristophanes' Speech in Plato's *Symposium*

Birds was produced one year after the Sicilian Expedition began, and the dramatic date of the *Symposium* is shortly before the Expedition. Eros (ἔρως) is the theme of the *Symposium*, and the term and its cognates show up in significant ways in *Birds*. The importance of eros in the play has been convincingly argued for by Arrowsmith.[23] In addition, many historical figures suspected of mutilating the herms and profaning the Mysteries appear in the *Symposium*. In other words, Plato's dialogue occurs against a background in which a connection between the desire to rule the world and indifference to gods is lurking. This historical background, although barely alluded to in either work, nevertheless appears as fertile ground for exploring human longing and its attitude toward the divine.

It seems likely that Plato had *Birds* in mind when composing the speech for his Aristophanes given the points of comparison I shall discuss below.[24] But I intend my comparison to be heuristic instead of historical, because the two texts illuminate each other when read side by side. On my reading, eros names the source of human restlessness in both *Birds* and Aristophanes' speech in the *Symposium*. At the extreme, it manifests itself as the impulse to become god (see *Symp.* 180b3). Eros is therefore ambiguous with respect to piety. And Plato's Aristophanes tells a myth about love

---

22 Dunbar (1998, 9) remarks that *Birds* 'is likely to have been exceptionally long for Old Comedy in general'.
23 Arrowsmith (1973).
24 Dover (1966) argues that the myth of spherical humans cut in half is inspired not by any particular Aristophanic comedy but by the genre of fable. He further suggests that Plato quite appropriately makes Aristophanes the spokesperson for the popular view of eros in order to criticize it later.

in order to rechannel and limit this impulse to pursuing romantic love.²⁵ This parallels the apotheosis of Peisetaerus, which arguably touches upon the same theme.

The Platonic Aristophanes' speech and *Birds* at first glance appear to say opposite things. Plato adapts some of the play's narrative features but reverses the elements therein. Consider the following. Both the birds (*Birds* 691–704) and the spherical humans in the *Symposium* myth have cosmic origins (190b1–3), which separate them from the Olympian gods. In both texts, gods need humans (specifically their sacrifices) more than humans need gods (*Birds* 190–2, 1231–3, 1266–8, 1518–24; *Symp.* 190c4–5). And in both texts, the gods suffer from cluelessness – in *Birds* from beginning to end and in the *Symposium* at least in the beginning (see ἠπόρουν, 190c2–3). And now for the reversals. *Birds* adopts the motif of the gigantomachy or titanomachy but the birds defeat the gods; the Platonic Aristophanes also adopts the motif, but the god-defiant spherical humans lose as before.²⁶ Moreover, the difference between the spherical humans and us is that our current shape (and thus our nature, both of which are expressed by φύσις in Aristophanes' myth; see 189d6, 191a5) is molded by Olympian gods (190d6–191a5, 191b6–7). *Birds* celebrates human striving insofar as it achieves wise and total political rule; Plato's Aristophanes celebrates the repose that human eros can find in private love and sexual satisfaction. The *Birds* praises dethroning the Olympian gods; Plato's Aristophanes asks us to revere Eros and the Olympian gods, making piety (εὐσέβεια) a necessary condition for happiness (193d3–5; also 189c5–7 and 193a8). Indeed, the main proposal the Platonic Aristophanes makes is that each of us has a lost other half, and only instituting a new cult of Eros (189c5–7) gives us hope of finding our soulmate.

Do the two Aristophaneses state opposing views then? I would argue that the opposing messages can, in fact, be reconciled: both concern how to regulate, moderate or tame human restlessness. Plato's Aristophanes, like the radical poet of the *Birds*, wishes to curb the transgressive inclinations of humans. Promoting piety that acknowledges the existence of things outside of human control and dependence on higher powers is one way to do that.

Certain puzzling features in the Platonic Aristophanes' myth make better sense in light of *Birds*. For example, in the myth, eros is said to

---

25 I agree with many commentators that Plato's Aristophanes presents a pessimistic or tragic view of eros; see, for example, Saxonhouse (1985), Nussbaum (2001 [1986], 171–6), Hyland (2008, 38–41), Obdrzalek (2017). I also agree that, like the historical Aristophanes, his speech expresses a politically conservative taste; see Dover (1966, 47–8) and Hyland (2008, 39–40). For a different view, see Hooper (2013).

26 For the use of the motif in *Birds*, see Dunbar (1998, 7–9); Plato's Aristophanes compares spherical humans to the giants Otos and Ephialtos at 190b7.

emerge only after spherical humans are cut in half. This appears to suggest that the desire of the spherical humans to revolt against gods is not eros. And at 190b5-c1, Aristophanes speaks of them 'attempting to ascend to the heavens' (190b8), not as if they are in love with the heavens. By contrast, *Birds* imparts an erotic motif to the revolt against gods. When Peisetaerus and Euelpides are asked by the Hoopoe what kind of life they desire (127; see also ἐρῶ, 136; ἐρᾷς 143), they describe reversals of customs.[27] Euelpides, for example, wants to live in a place where he is reproached by the father for not kissing or fondling the son (139-42). He desires what is prohibited by custom. Later, the Hoopoe tells the birds that the two old men are lovers (ἐραστά, 324; ἔρως, 411) of the birds' way of life. And the birds themselves, after they decide to follow Peisetaerus's lead and found a city, proclaim themselves to be the offspring of Eros (703-4). Even Tereus could not have played the crucial intermediary between the protagonists and the birds had he not followed his illicit desire for his sister-in-law and committed a crime.[28] Founding Cloudcuckooland and 'recovering' the lost avian superiority from the gods, therefore, have their origin in eros.

Since, as mentioned above, the birds occupy the role of giants in the gigantomachy myth, the fact that their revolt against gods is energized and charged by eros makes one wonder if the revolt of spherical humans against the gods is not an instance of human eros as well. There are reasons to think that this is actually the case. First, Pausanias had mentioned that being ambitious, or more literally having 'big thoughts' (φρονήματα μεγάλα, 182c2) is the mark of male lovers. Aristophanes alludes to this when he describes spherical humans attacking the gods because they 'had big thoughts' (τὰ φρονήματα μεγάλα εἶχον, 190b6). Second, eros, according to Plato, is a dissatisfaction with one's present state and a concurrent striving toward what one does not have (200a5-b3). The spherical humans are portrayed as self-sufficient and perfect: they are powerful (ἰσχύν, ῥώμην, 190b5), have cosmic origin (190b1-3), were complete in shape (ὅλον ... τὸ εἶδος, 189e5) and do not need the other sexes for reproduction (191b7-c2). But despite all this, they are still unsatisfied: they want even more. They remind us of Peisetaerus and Euelpides at the beginning of *Birds*. The two old men live in a great city – they even attest to its greatness (36-8, 123) – but still want something else. If eros is indeed the desire to have the whole for oneself (192e10-193a1), then the revolt of the spherical humans is much more erotic than any urge to unite with one's other half, because the two halves they want to bridge are heaven (τὸν οὐρανόν, 190b8) and earth

---

27 Cf. Konstan (1995, 34).
28 It is also possible, as Dobrov (2001, 105-32) suggests, that appropriation of Sophocles' tragedy is a 'battle between genres and poetics'.

(γῆν, 191c1).²⁹ These observations suggest that the Platonic Aristophanes, just like *Birds*, understands human nature as radically erotic: whether spherical or not, they restlessly strive for more.

If spherical humans indeed revolted out of eros, why does Aristophanes refrain from saying so? Because, I think, when he does so, a lesser but safer satisfaction of eros appears as the most desirable, so that one forgets the politically and religiously dangerous longing. *Birds* attempts to temper human restlessness by satisfying its highest longing fantastically; the Platonic Aristophanes does this by making a lower version of that longing – the longing for romantic union – appear as the highest happiness available to humans.³⁰ Scholars debate whether Aristophanes' account of love as 'desire for an original unity' is the correct or a defective understanding of love.³¹ But perhaps to judge it in terms of right or wrong is a category mistake: the real standard is whether this view awakens beneficial or harmful desires. What the Platonic Aristophanes does is precisely to make fantasy appear real through the power of words. Peisetaerus invents a past glory that makes the birds long to recover it. In the *Symposium*, Hephaestus makes the result of the lovers' embrace the purpose of that embrace (192d8–e3). What he proposes to do to the lovers' bodies (to weld them together), Aristophanes does to our souls: he invents a myth about these spherical humans to encourage us to seek sexual union and forget the restlessness that would lead people to seek divine status.³²

Birds illuminates Aristophanes' myth in a second way. Similar to *Birds*, where the protagonist's desire for rest ends up creating a second Athens in the sky, Plato's Aristophanes seems to tacitly acknowledge that his attempt might not succeed in making humans forget political ambitions. If romantic love or sexual union is a 'doctor' (189d1) and a 'healing' (191d3) for human nature, complete recovery is not guaranteed. Midway through his speech, he makes a passing remark that those whose original nature was male-male humans tend to engage in politics (192a2–7). This remark is usually understood as an ironic echo of Aristophanes' mockery

---

29 The birds state that Eros was contained in a wind-egg (*Birds* 695–6); when Zeus punished spherical humans, they were cut in half like eggs divided in half by a string (*Symposium* 190e1). If Plato is alluding to the passage, then the allusion suggests that eros was to some extent already in spherical humans, but this urge, like wind-eggs, turns out to be futile.

30 I call this 'lower' because it is private instead of public, and because it is more easily satisfied than the political urge to master everything.

31 Bloom (1993, 484–5) and Nussbaum (2001 [1986], 171–6) consider the account true to general human experience, while Nichols (2004) and Rowe (1998, 157–60) argue that it fails to tell the whole story about love.

32 Hyland (2008, 40).

of politicians as εὐρύπρωκτοι in his plays.³³ However, Plato could have chosen other Aristophanic tropes to give the speech an Aristophanic flavor: why choose this one in particular? If indeed, as I have just suggested, eros exists in spherical humans as well as political ambition, then this comment reveals how Plato's Aristophanes assesses his own project: despite his efforts, not everyone will forget their original desire. For some people, the private bliss of romantic love is not an appealing enough substitute. Like Peisetaerus, they will continue to pursue public glory won through mastery over others.

The comparison to *Birds* also discloses a feature of Aristophanes' speech not often commented upon, namely relaxing the sexual norms of society. Similar to Peisetaerus, Plato's Aristophanes also negotiates between freedom and law. The taming of political eros compels a relative permissiveness of private, romantic eros. Therefore there must be more tolerance of homosexual practices than there already was in ancient society. Traditionally, the pederastic relationship was asymmetrical, a view represented by Phaedrus and Pausanias in the dialogue. But Aristophanes' myth makes it mutual, and even grounds such love in nature: since split human beings love each other, the παιδικά is no longer only ἐρώμενος but ἐρῶν as well. Also, since it was frowned upon when the παιδικά continued a pederastic relationship after his beard had begun to grow, Aristophanes implicitly urges a relaxation of such moral policing. He claims that pederastic lovers and beloveds marry women later in life because 'they are compelled by law' (192b2), and he later urges people to let them follow their natural preferences (193c7–8). There is a difference between the two texts in this regard: in *Birds*, the people enjoy the increase of their private freedom through the expansion of political power; in the *Symposium*, the increase in private freedom is designed to curb 'big thoughts'.

Fourth and finally, despite the difference in strategy, both texts show the same understanding of the poet's role in shaping society. The notion that 'humans are given wings by speech', as argued above, means that making people mistake fantasy for something real can have salutary effects. And the art that accomplishes this is the comic art or poetry in general. Plato's Aristophanes does the same thing. The lovers cannot articulate why they wish to be together (192d3–5); like Peisetaerus's insistence that Iris must die, their romantic urge is also irrational. What Aristophanes' myth does is to articulate the lovers' experience so that their experience appears grounded in reality. Lovers often feel they are fated to meet each other, or 'I'm so comfortable around you, it's as if we had known each other long ago.' The myth cancels the 'as if' by inventing a past and a lost soulmate. And the intended effect of creating such

---

33 E.g. Dover (1966, 45).

an illusion both in *Birds* and here is the same: to make the listener rest content in the illusion as reality. Poetry is the art that reconciles human nature with the world.

Conclusion

My interpretation began from Henderson's insight that *Birds* is not ironic and extends it to show that the play depicts a kind of best-case scenario for the restless element in human nature and that the play, nevertheless, refrains from urging its adoption as a matter of actual policy. Moreover, the fantasy approach, which highlights the power of language to create reality, not only can be incorporated into a political reading of the play, but also shows Aristophanes reflecting on the role that his own poetry plays in human affairs.

Aristophanes' myth in Plato's *Symposium* contains a similar message and can be heuristically interpreted when one treats it as a creative, philosophical paraphrase of *Birds*. It is well known that Plato disagreed with Aristophanes and the poets. He did not think that high-minded people would fall for Aristophanes' exhortation to love, nor that the good life should involve persisting illusions, nor that human restlessness is deep down irrational. But while he let Socrates and philosophy have the last say, he also acknowledged that the quarrel between poetry and philosophy remained open. After Socrates criticized Aristophanes' view of eros, Aristophanes wanted to respond, but Alcibiades, that paradigmatic model of restlessness – and, as Henderson noticed, a real-life Peisetaerus – barged in and praised Socrates instead (212c4–d5). Although Aristophanes was silenced, Alcibiades' speech does not clearly grant victory to Socrates. As his encomium unfolds, the reader cannot help but wonder if Socrates' failure to turn Alcibiades toward philosophy fully does not make the young man a living proof that the promise of philosophy is not as attractive as the charms of Aristophanic poetry.

Works Cited

Ambler, W. 2012. 'Tyranny in Aristophanes' *Birds*'. *Review of Politics* 74: 185–206.
Arrowsmith, William. 1973. 'Aristophanes' *Birds*: The Fantasy Politics of Eros'. *Arion* 1: 119–67.
Bloom, Allan. 1993. 'The Ladder of Love'. In *Love and Friendship*, 429–546. New York: Simon & Schuster.
Dobrov, Gregory W., ed. 1997. *The City as Comedy: Society and Representation in Athenian Drama*. Chapel Hill: University of North Carolina Press.
———. 2001. *Figures of Play: Greek Drama and Metafictional Poetics*. Oxford: Oxford University Press.
Dover, K. J. 1966. 'Aristophanes' Speech in Plato's *Symposium*'. *JHS* 86: 41–50.

Dunbar, Nan. 1998. *Aristophanes: Birds*. Student edn. Oxford: Oxford University Press.
Hall, Edith. 2020. 'Aristophanes' Birds as Satire on Athenian Opportunists in Thrace'. In *Aristophanes and Politics: New Studies*, edited by Ralph M. Rosen and Helene P. Foley, 187–213. Boston: Brill.
Heath, M. 1997. 'Aristophanes and the Discourse of Politics'. In Dobrov 1997, 230–49.
Henderson, Jeffrey. 1990. 'The Dēmos and the Comic Competition'. In *Nothing to Do with Dionysos? Athenian Drama in Its Social Context*, edited by John J. Winkler and Froma I. Zeitlin, 271–313. Princeton: Princeton University Press.
———. 1997. 'Mass Versus Elite and the Comic Heroism of Peisetaerus'. In Dobrov 1997, 135–48.
———. 1999. *Aristophanes: The Birds*. Indianapolis: Focus Publishing.
———. 2003. 'Demos, Demagogue, Tyrant in Old Attic Comedy'. In *Popular Tyranny*, edited by Kathryn Morgan, 155–180. Austin: University of Texas Press.
Hooper, Anthony. 2013. 'The Greatest Hope of All: Aristophanes on Human Nature in Plato's *Symposium*'. *CQ* 63.2: 567–79.
Hubbard, T. K. 1997. 'Utopianism and the Sophistic City in Aristophanes'. In Dobrov 1997, 23–50.
Hyland, Drew. 2008. *Plato and the Question of Beauty*. Bloomington: Indiana University Press.
Konstan, David. 1995. *Greek Comedy and Ideology*. Oxford: Oxford University Press.
Nichols, Mary P. 2004. 'Socrates' Contest with the Poets in Plato's *Symposium*'. *Political Theory* 32.2: 186–206.
Nussbaum, Martha. 2001 [1986]. *The Fragility of Goodness*. Revised edn. Cambridge: Cambridge University Press.
Obdrzalek, Suzanne. 2017. 'Aristophanic Tragedy'. In *Plato's Symposium: A Critical Guide*, edited by Pierre Destrée and Zina Giannopoulou, 70–87. Cambridge: Cambridge University Press.
Rowe, C. 1998. *Plato: Symposium*. Warminster: Aris and Phillips.
Saxonhouse, Arlene. 1985. 'The Net of Hephaestus: Aristophanes' Speech in Plato's *Symposium*'. *Interpretation* 13.1: 15–32.
Slater, N. W. 1997. 'Performing the City in *Birds*'. In Dobrov 1997, 75–94.
Strauss, L. 1966. *Socrates and Aristophanes*. Chicago: University of Chicago Press.
Whitman, Cedric H. 1964. *Aristophanes and the Comic Hero*. Cambridge, MA: Harvard University Press.

CHAPTER 5

Sophocles and Happy Endings
Anne Mahoney

When I ask my first-year undergraduates about tragedy, they all know what it is: the plot type in which bad things happen, and half the cast is dead by the end of the play.[1] They might cite *Hamlet* or *Romeo and Juliet* as examples. Comedy is the other kind of plot, the lighter drama that makes you laugh and that has a happy ending, often with a wedding, such as *As You Like It*. The undergraduates find fifth-century plays like *Oedipus the King* or *Birds* comfortable because those plays conform to the students' expectations. But then they meet Euripides' *Helen*. What's that? Nothing bad happens, the villain is thwarted, and the main characters live happily ever after. How can this be a tragedy?

Some specialists, too, find *Helen* an odd play. It's easy to dismiss it, along with *Iphigenia Among the Taurians* and *Ion*, as just Euripides being Euripides, an experiment, outside the 'real' boundaries of tragedy. After all, these are preserved among the alphabetic plays, not the selection, so they must be second-rate, mustn't they? While it's unlikely that anyone thinks the alphabetic plays actually are inferior, it's clear that the alphabetic plays include all the problem plays, while such recognizably tragic plays as *Medea*, *Hippolytus* and *Trojan Women* belong to the selection. That is, the happy-ending plays were not part of the Byzantine canon.

But perhaps our idea of tragedy is narrower than that of the fifth-century Athenian audience. There are other plays with happy endings, and not just by Euripides; in fact, at least a quarter of the extant complete tragedies arguably have happy endings. Aeschylus's *Eumenides* ends in

---

1 It is a pleasure to celebrate Jeff's illustrious career. Back in my day, he offered two off-hand bits of advice to his graduate students. First, for those of us interested in drama, he recommended paying attention to fragments, as there's still much good work to be done there. Then, he suggested that in our leisure reading, we take up lighter classical scholarship, not just light fiction. It was in the course of following that congenial advice that I took up the book by de Romilly (2000) that inspires the present study.

triumph for democracy: 'truth, justice, and the Athenian Way', if you like.[2] Among Sophocles' extant plays, *Philoctetes* ends with the desired resolution; Philoctetes goes to Troy, although not entirely willingly, and Odysseus is restrained from making any more mischief. *Oedipus at Colonus*, too, ends happily, at least for Oedipus and for Theseus, though the shadow of the battle for Thebes hangs over Antigone. Even *Ajax*, despite the suicide of Ajax himself, ends with reconciliation. *Tyro*, now fragmentary, may have been even closer to the type we see in Euripides' alphabetic plays, as it seems to have ended with a recognition scene similar to the one in *Ion*: mother and sons are reunited and all ends happily. Apparently this plot type was not so far outside the bounds of tragedy as the surviving plays lead us to think.[3]

So what is tragedy, for the fifth century? In his excellent commentary on *Helen*, William Allan rejects terms such as 'romantic tragedy' and says the distinction between tragedy and comedy is primarily that the characters in a tragedy must suffer. While it is true that the characters in our plays do suffer – for example, Menelaus in *Helen* is menaced with death and Helen herself is effectively a captive – this by itself does not make a good definition: any engaging plot needs to have some sort of conflict, some character who has a problem. Lysistrata, for example, and the other women of the Greek-speaking world are suffering the effects of a major war. Another definition sometimes proposed, ultimately going back to Plautus's *Amphitruo* in which Mercury calls the play a *tragicomoedia* (59), is that tragedy involves high-status characters like kings and queens, while comedy is about ordinary people. This is in fact true of all extant Athenian tragedies and comedies, but plays like *Amphitruo* and its Greek forebears are comedies involving high-ranking characters, human and divine. And the birth of Heracles was also treated in tragedies – the very same plot as

---

2 Discussing the non-tragic aspects of this play, Oliver Taplin (1996, 198) calls its ending 'a procession which is closer to the endings of Aristophanes than to anything else in tragedy that we know of'; see also the response by Bernard Gredley (1996).
3 Milagros Quijada Sagredo (2011, 36–46) gives a brisk overview of the extensive scholarship on genre within tragedy and of the categories Plato and Aristotle had in mind. Donald Mastronarde (1999–2000, 27) problematizes the entire idea of genre for fifth-century literature, noting that 'an audience recognizes a tragedy by its place in the festival program' as well as by its formal characteristics; Mastronarde (1999–2000, 33–4) concludes that 'as a poetic form devoted almost exclusively to heroic myth and arising within the tradition of hexameter epic, high-style choral lyric, and Stesichorean lyric (whether choral or not), tragedy had continuously available to it the full range of heroic narratives, including story-patterns of both positive and negative outcome, and allowing tones and overtones of various sorts (including terror, pity, regret, admiration, celebration)'. On such questions of tragic and comic conventions, see also Henderson (2013b) and (2013c).

in Plautus.⁴ Thus a play with high-status characters is not necessarily a tragedy, though it may be true that a play whose main characters are of low status is always a comedy.

Jacqueline de Romilly has argued, in her book *Héros tragiques, héros lyriques*, that the modern idea of tragedy as a plot type is mainly due to the Romans, and perhaps particularly Seneca. She distinguishes tragic heroes and tragic plots, like Oedipus or Electra, from what she calls lyric heroes and their stories, which often involve supernatural monsters or love stories. A paradigmatic example of a lyric plot is the story of Perseus, who rides a winged horse, kills a Gorgon, saves Andromeda from a sea monster, and falls in love with her. This was the theme of several fifth-century tragedies, now all lost, and also of several early Roman tragedies. Seneca, however, does not use this story. So de Romilly suggests that at some point between Euripides and Seneca, stories like this stopped being 'tragic'. By the time the later Roman and early Byzantine scholars were selecting plays to comment on for their students, the lyric plots and the disaster-averted plots had fallen out of favor, and so they left them aside. On this hypothesis, then, it is not an accident that *Helen*, *Iphigeneia Among the Taurians* and *Ion* come to us from the alphabetic group, and that *Tyro* is fragmentary.

If de Romilly is correct, then there may have been little difference between tragedy and comedy in the fifth century. The plot types could overlap, high-status characters could be prominent in either type, and any play might have a happy ending. Presumably the fundamental distinction was formal: tragedies were performed in the tragic competition, comedies in the comic competition; comedies had a larger chorus; comedies were freer in the use of resolution in the iambic trimeter of dialogue, and in their choice of linguistic registers; tragedies used a stylized Doric dialect in songs while comedies usually stuck to plain Attic. But if that is the entire distinction, why does Plato, several decades later, make Socrates, Aristophanes and Agathon argue about whether the same person could write plays of both kinds? (*Symposium* 223d: Socrates claims these are the same skill, but the dramatists apparently disagree.) Plato certainly recognizes a difference between two kinds of drama, but it may not have to do with their plots.⁵

---

4   We know of plays called *Alcmene* by Euripides, Ion of Chios, and possibly others, and an *Amphitryo* by Sophocles. As Christensen (2000, 50) points out, 'we can assume that in both Attic and southern Italian theatre there were many more dramatic treatments of the Zeus–Alkmene–Amphitryon story'.
5   It is tantalizing to look at early modern theater from this point of view. Some authors specialized in one genre, others did not. In France, Jean Racine (1639–99) and Pierre Corneille (1606–84) primarily wrote tragedies, while Molière (1622–73) wrote only comedies. But in England a generation or so before, William Shakespeare (1564–1616) wrote both. Racine's one comedy, *Les Plaideurs* (1668), based loosely on Aristophanes' *Wasps*, was successful. Corneille's first play was also a comedy, but he, too, quickly turned

Can we narrow down the time of the plot restriction? Aristotle in *Poetics* treats two plays as particularly good examples of tragedy. One, as everyone knows, is *Oedipus the King* (1452a22), but the other is *Iphigenia Among the Taurians* (coupled with *Oedipus* at 1455a18), a happy-ending play. Thus, although Aristotle is fond of the bad-things-happen plots and though he even says ἡ μὲν οὖν κατὰ τὴν τέχνην καλλίστη τραγῳδία ἐκ ταύτης τῆς συστάσεώς ἐστι ('the best and most characteristic tragedy has this plot type' 1453a22), he also likes the 'disaster-averted' plots and even says a bit further on that this kind is the ideal plot (1454a4, giving *IT* as an example). Quijada Sagredo observes that 'la concepción sobre el género de Aristóteles es a este respecto mucho más flexible que la rígida ortodoxia posterior'.[6] For Aristotle, then, in the later fourth century, plays like *IT* are still perfectly acceptable tragedies. So is *Tyro*, which he mentions briefly for its recognition using a boat (οἷον ἐν τῇ Τυροῖ διὰ τῆς σκάφης, 1454b25).

The early Roman tragedians also have happy-ending plays. They use the plots de Romilly calls 'lyric', and occasionally also plots with recognition and a happy ending. These plots are much less common in their works than de Romilly's 'tragic' type, though. For example, Ennius, Livius Andronicus and Accius each wrote an *Andromeda*, a lyric plot. Naevius wrote an *Iphigenia* using the same plot as Euripides' *Iphigenia Among the Taurians*. The *Atalanta* of Pacuvius and the *Agamemnonidae* of Accius may also have a recognition leading to a happy ending. Ennius is a bit different: although he has plays with recognition scenes, they are not the happy-ending type. *Alexander* culminates in the recognition of Alexander/Paris by his birth family at Troy, though this is not a happy recognition, as his sister Cassandra explains how he will bring destruction on the city. Similarly, the recognition in Ennius's *Melanippa*, as in Euripides' version, does not lead to reconciliation: when Melanippe's father realizes that the children are her sons, he kills them and imprisons her. Still, Ennius does have some happy endings, as in his *Eumenides* modeled on Aeschylus's play of the same name.

By the time we get to Cicero, the picture has changed. Cicero regularly quotes Roman tragedy in his speeches, and both Greek and Roman in his philosophical writings (in his own beautiful verse translations), but the tragedies he quotes are all tragic in the modern sense: *Medea*, *Thyestes*, *Atreus* and so on. He does not quote from any of the 'lyric' plays or other happy-ending plays named above, whether from Latin authors or

---

to the more prestigious genre. Corneille used the 'lyric' plot type; Racine did not. In the Netherlands, Joost van den Vondel (1587–1679) just wrote tragedies, but in Spain Pedro Calderón de la Barca (1600–81) wrote both. On the other hand, by the sixteenth century tragedies and comedies were clearly different plot types: an early modern tragedy might have a 'lyric' plot but will not have a happy ending.

6 Quijada Sagredo (2011, 45).

from Greek. Petra Schierl argues that Cicero's choices 'mirror at least to some extent the canonizing processes at work in the late Republic'.[7] In other words, it is possible that happy-ending plays are becoming less popular. Perhaps, then, the restriction of tragedy to the bad-things-happen plot type emerges earlier than Seneca.

We have little evidence for plays from Cicero's own day, or in general between the early poets and Seneca. There are a few names of tragedians in the Augustan period, and very few fragments: we know of a *Thyestes* by L. Varius Rufus, which Albrecht calls one of 'the classic tragedies of the Romans';[8] *Atalanta*, *Peliades* and another *Thyestes* by Gracchus;[9] *Medea* by Ovid; and *Ajax* by the young Augustus. The historian C. Asinius Pollio also wrote tragedies, but we have no titles or fragments. Of these plays, *Peliades*, about Medea and the daughters of Pelias, is probably a lyric plot, but the others are clearly de Romilly's 'tragic' type, and it seems likely that none of them has a happy ending.

For the Romans, then, certainly by the time of Seneca and probably as early as Cicero, 'tragedy' has something close to its modern sense. For fifth-century Athenians, though, tragedy is a form rather than a plot type, and tragedies can have happy endings. This much is well known. I suggest, though, that there are several different types of happy endings. One is de Romilly's 'lyric' type, with a hero saving a damsel in distress from a fabulous monster. Another is the 'romantic' or 'melodramatic' type, such as *Iphigenia Among the Taurians*, with the return of a long-lost family member, recognized just in time to avert disaster. In the third type, a story comes to a peaceful conclusion without the *coups de théâtre* of the lyric or romantic plays. Among the plays of Sophocles, *Philoctetes* and *Oedipus at Colonus* belong to this type, and a case might also be made for *Ajax*. Aeschylus's *Eumenides* and Euripides' *Suppliants* are also in the group.[10] We may call this the 'serene' type. Thus, the distinction between tragedies that are tragic in the modern sense and those that are not, while familiar and correct, can be refined. In fact, we can identify four kinds of tragic plots: the tragic type, in which bad things happen; the lyric type, in which a hero fights a supernatural monster or wins the hand of a princess, often both, and the play may end happily; the recognition type, in which a long-lost family member is recognized just before a disaster would have happened; and the

7   Schierl (2015, 47).
8   Albrecht (1997, 97, 107).
9   This is the Gracchus mentioned by Ovid (*Pont.* 4.16.31), alongside Varius, probably a Sempronius Gracchus and likely the one who had been the lover of Julia, daughter of Augustus (*New Pauly s.v.* 'Gracchus').
10 Aeschylus may have closed other trilogies with happy-ending plays as well (*Danaids* for example), but this was not an invariable rule for him: for example, *Seven Against Thebes* does not end happily.

serene type, in which a happy ending, or at least a tranquil one, does not depend on recognition, though it may involve divine intervention. All four of these plot types were available to fifth-century Athenian tragedians, and to early Roman ones, and although the playwrights had their own preferences, Aeschylus, Sophocles and Euripides all used at least one of the three 'non-tragic' plot types.

Glenn Moodie notes helpfully that 'Sophocles appears to have played a larger role than has traditionally been thought in the creation of this dramatic style', referring to the recognition-and-happy-ending plot form.[11] Sophocles and Euripides presumably influenced each other in choosing and developing dramatic plots. But the serene type seems more characteristic of Sophocles than of Euripides. Among the extant plays of Euripides, *Suppliants* is the only one with the serene plot type, though some of the fragmentary ones, like *Philoctetes*, may have used it.

I will analyze *Tyro* and *Oedipus at Colonus* as examples of how Sophocles uses the 'non-tragic' plot types. In both plays, the characters are of high status, and in both plays the sympathetic characters suffer, but in each one the impending disaster is averted and the story comes to a happy ending. *Tyro*, with its recognition, probably belongs to the romantic type, and *Oedipus at Colonus* to the serene type.

The extant fragments of *Tyro* do not give us much idea of the plot, but the story is known from Apollodorus and other sources.[12] Tyro, daughter of Salmoneus son of Aeolus, falls in love with the river god Enipeus. Poseidon, meanwhile, loves her and takes the form of Enipeus in order to seduce her. She becomes pregnant with twin sons, which angers her father and her stepmother (or foster mother) Sidero, and so she exposes the boys. As always in such stories, the children are rescued. They are Pelias and Neleus, known from other stories as uncle of Jason and father of Nestor. Meanwhile, Sidero continues to treat Tyro badly. When Pelias and Neleus grow up, they come to their mother's rescue and attempt to kill Sidero. She takes refuge at an altar of Hera, but Pelias kills her there (thus making an enemy of Hera). Finally, Pelias and Neleus tell Tyro who they are, and all ends well. Aristotle mentions the recognition 'using the cradle' (διὰ τῆς σκάφης, *Poetics* 1454b25), presumably the one in which Tyro exposed her sons at their birth, much like the cradle in *Ion*. The word may also refer to a small boat, and so Tyro may have floated the children on water, maybe even on the river Enipeus itself.

11 Moodie (2003, 137).
12 Robert (1916) summarizes what is known about Tyro's story from literary and visual sources. Apollodorus (1.9) tells the story. Before Sophocles, the main surviving source is *Odyssey* 11.235ff.; Hesiod also mentions Tyro (frr. 30, 31 MW). Later writers also use or allude to the story, including Men. *Epit.* 325ff., Strabo 8.3, Luc. *Ver. Hist.* 2.3 and *Dial. Mar.* 13, *Anth. Gr.* 3.9, Diod. Sic. 4.68 and Philostr. in *Athenian* 1.47 and *Lemnian* 2.8.

Sophocles wrote two plays called *Tyro*, and sources place the recognition scene in the second one. A scholion on *Birds* 275 tells us that Aristophanes has taken this line from the second play, so we know that the second play was before 414. Lloyd-Jones observes that 'what is recorded about Tyro does not appear to provide material for more than one tragedy', and concludes that the second play is just a revision of the first.[13] Moodie, on the other hand, says this is an unnecessary assumption and the two plays more likely treat different parts of the myth, though he does not speculate about what their two plots might have been.[14] Clark also argues for two separate plots, with the first play showing Tyro's encounter with Poseidon 'and its consequences for an orphaned girl, hitherto a virgin, growing up in her uncle's house', and the second showing her rescue by her now-grown sons.[15] She places the longest fragment (659) into the first play: Tyro laments that her hair has been cut off by Sidero as a punishment for her sleeping with Poseidon.[16] Carrara, following Hoffman, puts one of the *Tyro* plays at the Lenaea of 419/18, based on a fragmentary victory list from that festival.[17]

The fragments we have amount to some three dozen lines. As Moodie observes, 'fragments, unless they are of considerable length, are often of little help in shedding light on the plot',[18] and that is certainly true here. The longest (fr. 659), quoted by Aelian, is Tyro's lament for her shorn hair. In another (fr. 658), someone describes Sidero as a fighter for whom the name 'Iron Lady' is entirely suitable. Tyro, 'Ms Cheese', gets her fairness from having been raised on milk (fr. 648). Fiona McHardy notes the 'fairy-tale nature of the names' and shows that the interaction between Sidero and Tyro is typical of women's violence toward other women in tragedy.[19] Tyro is a new woman in Sidero's house, and Sidero wants to assert power over her. Cutting Tyro's hair 'is an act of dominance that signifies control'.[20] Sidero may be punishing her for unchastity (with Poseidon) or may be jealous of her as a potential sexual rival, particularly if Sophocles has followed the version of the story in which Sidero is not Tyro's father's second wife, but her uncle's wife. Moreover, as McHardy points out, 'the prominence of female violence in plotlines where a woman has been raped by a god or by a victorious warrior indicates that susceptibility to violent treatment by a woman is associated with women who are already in a vulnerable position, having previously been sexually assaulted and treated violently by a man

---

13 Lloyd-Jones (1996, 313).
14 Moodie (2003, 120–1).
15 Clark (2003, 80); this reconstruction goes back at least to Carl Robert (1916, 300–1).
16 Clark (2003, 91).
17 Carrara (2012, 321–2).
18 Moodie (2003, 132).
19 McHardy (2020, 30).
20 McHardy (2020, 33).

or god'.[21] That is, Sidero, like women in other plays, shows no sympathy for Tyro, gives her no support and instead punishes her for her beauty.

The fragments tell us nothing about the scene in which Tyro recognizes her sons Neleus and Pelias, except that the recognition token is a cradle (σκάφη). A line from a papyrus is clearly spoken by one of the sons, if it belongs to this play at all (fr. 649 f, P.Hibeh 10 ll. 52–3):

]ας ἀρωγὸν πατέρα λίσσομα[ι μολεῖν
ἄν]ακτα πόντου μητρί

I entreat my father, lord of the sea, to come as a helper for my mother.

Whether Poseidon actually appears in the play is unclear. Moodie summarizes the arguments and decides he could have appeared *ex machina* at the end to confirm that he is the father of Neleus and Pelias, though it is also possible that some other god appeared in his place, or that there was no final divine appearance at all.[22]

If the two *Tyro* plays have different plots, only the second, the recognition play, would have a happy ending. The first, *Tyro keiromene* as Clark calls it, presumably ends with Tyro humiliated and miserable; this plot is tragic in the modern sense. But the second *Tyro* ends with a reunion of mother and sons, much like Euripides' *Ion*, and with Sidero's punishment for her treatment of Tyro. This plot has seemed to many scholars more like one of Euripides' plays than like the complete plays of Sophocles. Moodie cautiously admits 'the possibility that Sophocles, like Euripides, wrote happy-ending tragedies';[23] clearly Sophocles did use this plot structure at least once. But the recognition plot and the lyric-hero plot are not the only kinds of happy-ending tragedies.

Oedipus at Colonus is a different kind of happy-ending play, the type I am calling 'serene', neither de Romilly's 'lyric' type nor the recognition-and-reconciliation type. It takes place many years after the events of *Oedipus the King*. Oedipus has left Thebes and has been wandering, an exile, accompanied only by Antigone. He arrives in Colonus in Attica and immediately recognizes that this is where he must stay (45–6). The local residents are skeptical at first, particularly when he attempts to enter the sacred grove of the Eumenides (125–37) and when they find out his name (220–6). They summon Theseus, who allows Oedipus to stay (634–7).[24]

---

21 McHardy (2020, 38–9).
22 Moodie (2003, 130–1).
23 Moodie (2003, 138).
24 Whether Theseus actually grants Oedipus Athenian citizenship depends on the reading of line 637: the manuscripts have ἔμπαλιν, but many editors, including Lloyd-Jones and Wilson (1990), accept Musgrave's ἔμπολιν. Wilson (1997) is an extended study of the

There is a prophecy that, once Oedipus is dead, his body will be a blessing to the land where it lies (389–90, 576–8). Creon has heard this and is also aware that his nephews, Oedipus's sons, are about to wage their war over Thebes (399–400). He therefore comes to Colonus to convince Oedipus to return to Thebes – or to coerce him. Theseus sends Creon away (1038). Polynices, who has also heard the prophecy, arrives next, hoping to convince his father to support him, but Oedipus angrily refuses, repeating his curse on his sons (1348–96). Then, prompted by a rumble of thunder (1461), Oedipus goes into the Eumenides' grove, with Theseus. A messenger comes to tell the Chorus that Oedipus is gone, and only Theseus has seen exactly what happened. Antigone and Ismene are heartbroken, but Theseus tells them there is no need for mourning (1751).[25]

For Oedipus, this is a happy ending. He has earned divine favor and a peaceful resting place. The play leaves open the possibility that he has not actually died but been taken away by the gods.[26] He will be a source of blessings on Attica. Theseus, too, has a happy ending: he has brought a crisis to a favorable conclusion, keeping Athens out of the imminent war in Thebes. While the audience knows that Polynices and Eteocles are about to fight, and to die at each other's hands, the end of the play is more concerned with the fate of Oedipus. Antigone does plan to go directly to Thebes, hoping to avert the war, and Theseus says he will support her, but the last words, from the Chorus, are an admonition against grief.

Certainly *Oedipus at Colonus* is not as light a play as Euripides' *Helen*, but it ends peacefully, and nothing bad has happened. Creon's attempt to kidnap Antigone and Ismene is foiled, and the war for Thebes is still in the future. Moreover, the play fits some of the proposed definitions of 'tragedy'. The characters are of high status, kings and princes. Oedipus suffers during the action, until his final release from all suffering; so does Antigone. And the main character dies, or disappears, during the action. Nonetheless, this play does not seem tragic in the same way as *Antigone* or the earlier *Oedipus* play. The suffering here is almost redemptive: Oedipus has spent

> implications of the choice; he retains the manuscript reading and argues that Oedipus is granted *xenia* rather than citizenship.

25 At a first reading, the play may seem episodic: a scene with the Chorus, a scene with Ismene, a scene with Theseus and so on. I have argued elsewhere (2013) that part of the unity of the play comes from a musical motif audible in the first half, culminating in the 'Colonus Ode' (668–719).

26 Lee Breuer's *The Gospel at Colonus* makes the ending of the play downright joyful. Antigone and Ismene are less prominent in the final scene, and the Chorus sing 'Lift him up!' (1989, 49; cf. 1567 in Sophocles) as if Oedipus is being raised to heaven. The final hymn is even more definite: 'Now let the weeping cease. Let no one mourn again. The love of God will bring you peace. There is no end' (1989, 53, corresponding to 1777–9 of the Greek). Oedipus here is equated to a martyr or, perhaps, to Christ. While that is anachronistic, I find it quite true to the spirit of the play.

years of his life atoning for having killed his father and married his mother and is now, finally, freed of guilt.

No one else in the play seems to see it this way, though. For Polynices and Creon (and perhaps also for the Colonian elders in the Chorus), Oedipus has become a relic, an object to fight over; neither his son nor his brother-in-law seems to care about the living Oedipus, so long as they can have his tomb as a cult place. For Ismene and especially for Antigone, Oedipus is an object to care for, and Antigone is more concerned with her own loss than with her father's transfiguration. If the audience is focusing on Antigone, the end of the play may appear grim; if the focus remains on Oedipus and Theseus, the ending is tranquil.

Sophocles used the 'serene' plot type in *Philoctetes* as well, another play in which nothing bad happens, even though the characters are not all happy at the end. Heracles has had to appear and order the mortal characters to do the right thing: Philoctetes must go to Troy. *Ajax*, too, ends with reconciliation between Teucer and Odysseus and with acquiescence from Agamemnon. Although we are not permitted to forget the death of Ajax, since Tecmessa remains onstage visibly mourning throughout the long debate in the second half of the play, we see the rest of the characters return to a civil relationship. I would not go so far as to call the ending of *Ajax* happy, but it is not as grim as *Oedipus the King*, *Antigone* or other more obviously 'tragic' tragedies. It is a sort of hybrid between the tragic type and the serene type.

We see, then, that Sophocles used all the various plot types, just as Euripides and other authors did. The 'tragic' type, though probably the most popular even in the fifth century, had not become an invariable rule for tragedies. This restriction seems to have happened in Rome, probably around the time of Cicero or just before, earlier than de Romilly suggests. In the fifth century, the 'lyric', 'romantic' or 'recognition' and 'serene' tragic plot types were not unusual experiments but standard, mainstream structures available to any playwright and acceptable to any audience.[27]

Works Cited

Albrecht, Michael von. 1997. *A History of Roman Literature from Livius Andronicus to Boethius*. Leiden: Brill.

---

27 This conclusion is similar to one Henderson himself reached for comedy. As he put it, 'Comedy had no uniform style in the fifth century': the plot type based on current events and satire of well-known Athenians was not universal (1990, 293). His 2013 Presidential Address to the SCS (then the APA) studies the question in more detail, observing that the standard model that distinguishes periods of comedy by plot types, political for Old Comedy and domestic for New, does not really fit the evidence, particularly when fragments are taken into account; see Henderson (2013a).

Allan, William. 2008. *Euripides: Helen*. Cambridge: Cambridge University Press.
Boyle, A. J. 2006. *An Introduction to Roman Tragedy*. London: Routledge.
Breuer, Lee. 2003. *The Gospel at Colonus*, libretto. Alexandria, VA: Alexander Street Press.
Carrara, Laura. 2012. 'Il numero dei drammi satireschi sofoclei: Sofocle alle Lenee ed i drammi "prosatirici"'. *Annali della Scuola Normale Superiore di Pisa* (Classe di Lettere e Filosofia) 5.4.2: 315–32.
Christenson, David. 2000. *Plautus: Amphitruo*. Cambridge: Cambridge University Press.
Clark, Amy C. 2003. '*Tyro keiromene*'. In Sommerstein 2003, 79–116.
Gredley, Bernard. 1996. 'Comedy and Tragedy – Inevitable Distinctions: Response to Taplin'. In Silk 1996, 203–16.
Henderson, Jeffrey. 1990. 'The *Dēmos* and the Comic Competition'. In *Nothing to Do with Dionysos?*, edited by John J. Winkler and Froma I. Zeitlin, 271–313. Princeton: Princeton University Press.
———. 2013a. 'A Brief History of Athenian Political Comedy (c. 440–c. 300)'. *TAPA* 143: 249–62.
———. 2013b. 'Comedy and Tragedy: Generic Interactions'. In Roisman 2013, 238–42.
———. 2013c. 'Comic Scenes in Greek Tragedy'. In Roisman 2013, 245–8.
Lloyd-Jones, H. 1996. *Sophocles: Fragments*. Cambridge, MA: Harvard University Press.
Lloyd-Jones, H., and N. G. Wilson. 1990. *Sophoclis Fabulae*. Oxford: Oxford University Press.
Lucas, D. W. 1968. *Aristotle: Poetics*. Oxford: Oxford University Press.
McHardy, Fiona. 2020. 'Female Violence Toward Women and Girls in Greek Tragedy'. In *Female Characters in Fragmentary Greek Tragedy*, edited by P. J. Finglass and Lindsay Coo, 19–39. Cambridge: Cambridge University Press.
Mahoney, Anne. 2013. 'A Musical Motif in Sophocles' *Oedipus at Colonus*'. *NECJ* 40: 169–90.
Mastronarde, Donald J. 1999–2000. 'Euripidean Tragedy and Genre: The Terminology and Its Problems'. *ICS* 24/5: 23–39.
Moodie, Glenn. 2003. 'Sophocles' *Tyro* and Late Euripidean Tragedy'. In Sommerstein 2003, 117–38.
Quijada Sagredo, Milagros. 2011. *Estudios sobre Tragedia Griega: Eurípides, el teatro griego de finales del siglo V a.C. y su influencia posterior*. Madrid: Ediciones Clásicas.
Robert, C. 1916. 'Tyro'. *Hermes* 51: 273–302.
Roisman, Hanna M., ed. 2013. *The Encyclopedia of Greek Tragedy*, vol. 1. Malden, MA: Wiley-Blackwell.
Romilly, Jacqueline de. 2000. *Héros tragiques, héros lyriques*. Saint-Clément-de-Rivière: Fata Morgana.
Schierl, Petra. 2015. 'Roman Tragedy – Ciceronian Tragedy? Cicero's Influence on Our Perception of Roman Tragedy'. In *Brill's Companion to Roman Tragedy*, edited by George W. M. Harrison, 45–62. Leiden: Brill.
Silk, Michael, ed. 1996. *Tragedy and the Tragic*. Oxford: Oxford University Press.

Sommerstein, Alan H., ed. 2003. *Shards from Kolonos: Studies in Sophoclean Fragments*. Bari: Levante.

Taplin, Oliver. 1996. 'Comedy and the Tragic'. In Silk 1996, 188–202.

Webster, T. B. L. 1970. *Sophocles: Philoctetes*. Cambridge: Cambridge University Press.

Wilson, Joseph P. 1997. *The Hero and the City: An Interpretation of Sophocles' Oedipus at Colonus*. Ann Arbor: University of Michigan Press.

CHAPTER 6

Heroism in the Middle in Sophocles' Philoctetes

Emily Austin

The Sophoclean Philoctetes articulates a unique and personal type of heroism.[1] As a person without a community, he cannot be a Homeric hero. The heroic activities of sacking Troy and winning *kleos*, or glory, are unavailable to him. Further, many conditions are thrust upon him against his will: isolation, sickness, desertion on an island. To sack Troy and win *kleos* is a form of active heroism and is out of Philoctetes' reach. The second set of conditions is passive: Philoctetes suffers things that are done to him, against his will, and he can do nothing that would remedy these horrendous conditions. But in the course of Sophocles' play it becomes clear that Philoctetes, despite his enormous sufferings and inhibited actions, is not simply a sufferer. When Neoptolemus comes to him, Philoctetes' desperate need for an alleviation of sufferings is complemented by pride in his own achievement. In order to better articulate this hero's sense of heroism, I will employ in this essay the framework of the Greek middle voice. In doing so, I am not suggesting that the grammatical category of the middle voice is identical to Philoctetes' personal view of his heroism.[2] But using these grammatical categories gives us a way of thinking how Philoctetes both is and is not a passive sufferer, and both is and is not an Iliadic hero capable of action.

---

1 During my time at Boston University, I was a direct recipient of Jeff Henderson's prodigious expertise on virtually any topic in antiquity. I felt this breadth most keenly (and gratefully) when I was preparing for my History of Greek Literature exams and sought Jeff's guidance. I offer this contribution with gratitude for Jeff's generous mentorship, and in the spirit of viewing old categories with new eyes.
2 In fact, Philoctetes' suffering and action are perhaps the conceptual inverse of the Greek middle voice; his 'middle heroism' is not the indirect-reflexive effect of actions he initiates as an agent, but rather his agent-like involvement in that which he undergoes. On the Greek middle voice, see Barber (1975), Rijksbaron (2002, 134–63), Allan (2003).

What I call 'heroism in the middle', in the story of Philoctetes, is a third way between suffering and action.³

Heroism

Sophocles' *Philoctetes* concerns itself deeply with ideas about heroism and action. The play engages such questions at the most basic level through its setting at the end of the Trojan War. Its characters are Homeric heroes; the play will end with Philoctetes agreeing to return to Troy and aid in its final sack. The *Philoctetes* constantly reminds us that the men onstage have been defined by the long war at Troy. The heroism of fighting a war is, so to speak, the play's backdrop. Iliadic heroism, however, is not merely a framing background for the play's action. Rather, the heroism won at Troy forms a counterpoint to the heroism articulated by Philoctetes. Philoctetes constantly separates himself from the leaders of the Greek army, and in so doing, he separates himself from the heroism of fighting at Troy. This separation between Philoctetes and the other Greeks takes the form of various ethical debates throughout the play. How should one act in a world in which a wounded and deserted man wishes to return home, but an army of men, who had abandoned him, need him now to return to their fighting?

Odysseus's opening conversation with Neoptolemus frames their expedition to Philoctetes' island as temporarily turning themselves over to shamefulness (83–5):

νῦν δ' εἰς <u>ἀναιδὲς</u> ἡμέρας μέρος βραχὺ
δός μοι σεαυτόν, κᾆτα τὸν λοιπὸν χρόνον
κέκλησο πάντων <u>εὐσεβέστατος</u> βροτῶν.

But now, for a brief portion of the day,
give yourself over to <u>shamefulness</u>, and then for all time
be called the <u>most pious</u> of all humankind.

Neoptolemus at first rejects the deceitful approach, preferring to carry Philoctetes off against his will (90–1). He declares, 'I would rather, my

---

3 This interpretation of Philoctetes' heroism differs sharply from Cook's brilliant analysis of Odysseus. Cook (1999, 153) focuses on the active and passive dimensions of heroism that shape the complex matrix of Odysseus's identity: 'inflicting pain and suffering it, hating and being hated, impetuosity and self-restraint, fame and concealment, death and survival, eating and fasting'. For Cook, Odysseus repeatedly asserts his warrior identity, that of the traditional 'Man of Pain' who both causes and experiences pain, over the 'Trickster' identity (likewise both active and passive) that had been crucial to Odysseus's survival and return home.

lord, <u>act well</u> and fail, rather than conquer by <u>acting basely</u>' (βούλομαι δ', ἄναξ, <u>καλῶς | δρῶν</u> ἐξαμαρτεῖν μᾶλλον ἢ νικᾶν <u>κακῶς</u>, 94–5). The dichotomy between acting nobly and acting basely is thus central to the play from the first.

After Odysseus persuades Neoptolemus to attempt the deception, these ethically charged descriptions recur in Philoctetes' first conversation with the young hero. Philoctetes speaks highly of Neoptolemus's father throughout their first encounter, calling Neoptolemus the 'son of a father most dear' (ὦ φιλτάτου παῖ πατρός, 242) and comparing Achilles to Apollo in his nobility (εὐγενής, 336). Those who are dead or inactive at Troy are called 'good' (ἀγαθός of Nestor, 421; χρηστός of Ajax, Antilochus, Patroclus and the like, 437) while the living are 'base' (πονηρός of Odysseus, the sons of Atreus and the like, 437; ἀνάξιος of Thersites, 439; cf. κακός, 446). Lest we miss the point that Troy is synonymous with the baseness of the Greek leaders, Neoptolemus reflects Philoctetes' judgment in his final summation, 'From now on, I will be careful to keep far away from <u>Troy and the sons of Atreus</u>' (τὸ λοιπὸν ἤδη τηλόθεν <u>τό τ' Ἴλιον | καὶ τοὺς Ἀτρείδας</u> εἰσορῶν φυλάξομαι, 454–5). Those who continue to fight at Troy are, in this dialogue's typology, base, wicked and unworthy.

Yet even as Philoctetes identifies Troy with the survival of wicked heroes, he begs Neoptolemus to live up to his ancestry in terms of Iliadic excellence. When Neoptolemus pretends to be leaving, Philoctetes supplicates him in terms of 'the good' or 'the worthy' (τὸ χρηστόν) which, notably, he calls 'glorious' (εὐκλεές). Despite the disgust Neoptolemus and the other sailors will feel because of his disease, Philoctetes exhorts the young hero (475–9):

ὅμως δὲ τλῆθι· τοῖσι γενναίοισί τοι
τό τ' αἰσχρὸν ἐχθρὸν καὶ τὸ χρηστὸν <u>εὐκλεές</u>.
σοὶ δ', ἐκλιπόντι τοῦτ', ὄνειδος οὐ καλόν,
δράσαντι δ', ὦ παῖ, <u>πλεῖστον εὐκλείας γέρας</u>,
ἐὰν μόλω 'γὼ ζῶν πρὸς Οἰταίαν χθόνα.

Nevertheless, endure; since, you know, to noble men
shamefulness is hateful, and goodness is <u>glorious</u>.
And for you, if you forsake this, there will be ignoble shame,
but if you do it, o child! you will have the <u>greatest prize of noble glory</u>,
if I go alive to the land of Oitia.

Philoctetes uses Iliadic terms for publicly recognized excellence – 'prize' (γέρας) and *kleos* – but he applies them to what might well turn out to be a private endeavor: doing what is honorable, being 'good' (χρηστός) by bringing Philoctetes home instead of abandoning him to this life of pain and loneliness.[4]

This Iliadic language for heroism continues when Philoctetes later grants Neoptolemus permission to touch his bow (662–70):

ὅσιά τε φωνεῖς ἔστι τ', ὦ τέκνον, θέμις,
ὅς γ' ἡλίου τόδ' εἰσορᾶν ἐμοὶ φάος
μόνος δέδωκας, ὃς χθόν' Οἰταίαν ἰδεῖν,
ὃς πατέρα πρέσβυν, ὃς φίλους, ὃς τῶν ἐμῶν
ἐχθρῶν μ' ἔνερθεν ὄντ' ἀνέστησας πέρα.
θάρσει, παρέσται ταῦτά σοι καὶ θιγγάνειν
καὶ δόντι δοῦναι κἀξεπεύξασθαι βροτῶν
ἀρετῆς ἕκατι τῶνδ' ἐπιψαῦσαι μόνῳ·
εὐεργετῶν γὰρ καὐτὸς αὔτ' ἐκτησάμην.

What you speak of is holy, child, and it is lawful,
you who alone have granted to me to look upon this light of the sun,
who grant me to see the land of Oitia,
and my elderly father, and my friends, you who, when I
was beneath my evils, raised me up beyond them.
Take courage, these things are in your power both to touch (the bow)
and to return it to the giver, and <u>to boast</u> among mortals
that <u>you alone handled these weapons on account of your excellence</u>.
For I too came to possess these <u>by acting nobly</u>.

The ethically charged discourse makes use of Iliadic language again – 'boast' (εὔχομαι, see 668), 'excellence' (ἀρετή, see 669) – and reframes it to Philoctetes' purposes. Whereas the other Greeks abandoned Philoctetes to live with his diseased foot unaccompanied, and thereby showed themselves to be base, Philoctetes invites Neoptolemus to the *kleos* of acting nobly, which is rooted in his excellence, and which will be his boast. The backdrop of fighting at Troy – glory and excellence from battle, conducted by unworthy leaders – is to be disparaged, but the values of glory and excellence, in Philoctetes' appeals, can be given new content. One can act heroically by acting well (see δράσαντι δ', ὦ παῖ, πλεῖστον εὐκλείας γέρας, 478; and εὐεργετῶν, 670).

---

4 Beye (1970, 72) aptly notes that, by the end of the play, Philoctetes creates a 'noble figure in Neoptolemus' by insistently figuring the young warrior in nobly heroic terms. See also Kyriakou (2012, 151–6) on Philoctetes' effective use of Neoptolemus's loyalty to his father.

Suffering

At the same time, in the play's discourse, suffering pervades our view of Philoctetes. Philoctetes' situation is marked by passivity, by what has happened to him. Philoctetes has been abandoned by the Greeks (257, 265, 268–9 etc.). He is afflicted by a horrendous wound (258–9, 265–7 etc.). He has been cut off from society, stranded on a deserted island (280–3, 301–3 etc.). This character is not an Iliadic hero. In fact, he is barely a man.[5] He is surviving, but one might say that this is passive survival, without action.[6]

The play often describes the ongoing, persisting nature of Philoctetes' sufferings. He cries, 'then you have heard no report of my evils, none at all? – the evils because of which I have been continually perishing?' (οὐδὲ τῶν ἐμῶν κακῶν κλέος | ἤσθου ποτ' οὐδέν, οἷς ἐγὼ διωλλύμην; 251–2) – note the imperfect tense of the verb διωλλύμην. The Chorus likewise describes his ongoing dying in the imperfect, with a kind of horrified wonder: '[I've never heard of] any man likewise perishing in things equal to this so worthlessly' (ἀλλ' ἴσος ἐν ἴσοις ἀνήρ, | ὤλλυθ' ὧδ' ἀναξίως, 684–5).[7] In another passage, Philoctetes summarizes his ten years of survival with a present-tense ἀπόλλυμαι: 'But I, wretched, am perishing for the tenth year now, in hunger and in evils, consuming this devouring sickness' (ἀλλ' ἀπόλλυμαι τάλας | ἔτος τόδ' ἤδη δέκατον ἐν λιμῷ τε καὶ | κακοῖσι βόσκων τὴν ἀδηφάγον νόσον, 311–13). The present-tense ἀπόλλυμαι suggests that Philoctetes still identifies with his suffering condition: 'I am continually perishing.' This man is a sufferer, not a doer.

The sense of passivity in Philoctetes' suffering emerges even more strongly in moments when he is about to be abandoned once again. When Neoptolemus first pretends to be leaving, Philoctetes begs to be brought along, describing himself as 'a powerless sufferer, a lame man' (καίπερ ὢν | ἀκράτωρ ὁ τλήμων, χωλός, 485–6). This characterization of himself connects Philoctetes' suffering to an inability to act. Later in the play, suffering and loss of power are intensified when Philoctetes loses his bow. Neoptolemus, still holding Philoctetes' bow, reveals that he intends to bring Philoctetes back to Troy. At this devastating revelation, Philoctetes recedes into hopeless declarations – 'in taking away my bow, you rob me of life' (ἀπεστέρηκας τὸν βίον τὰ τόξ' ἑλών, 931) – and calls himself a 'corpse' or a 'shadow of smoke' (945–7):

---

5 See Christensen (2020, 75–8).
6 Poe (1974, 37) says as much; see also Poe's (1974, 13–37) elucidation of Philoctetes' forced passivity.
7 The Chorus marvels explicitly in this stanza that Philoctetes has been utterly alone (μόνος, 689).

ὡς ἄνδρ' ἑλὼν ἰσχυρὸν ἐκ βίας μ' ἄγει.
κοὐκ οἶδ' ἐναίρων νεκρόν, ἢ καπνοῦ σκιάν,
εἴδωλον ἄλλως.

He takes me by force as if he captures a powerful man,
and he does not know that he is slaying a corpse, or a shadow of smoke,
a shade only.

Philoctetes, without his bow, sees himself as a dead man, or less than a man; a shadow without substance. The sense of passivity is so extreme that he is neither alive nor human.

Philoctetes' powerlessness as a sufferer is again linked to the loss of his bow when Odysseus reveals himself toward the end of the play. After Odysseus leaves with Neoptolemus – who still carries Philoctetes' bow – Philoctetes laments his dashed hopes with the language of passive suffering. He repeatedly calls himself a sufferer (πανάθλιον, 1026; ἀνδρὸς ἀθλίου, 1038; ἄθλιος ... ἀνήρ, 1214). He describes Odysseus actively laughing while he is grieved, emphasizing the contrast between action and suffering with an antithesis (μέν ... δέ): 'You, on the one hand, laugh and live, while I am grieved' (σὺ μὲν γέγηθας ζῶν, ἐγὼ δ' ἀλγύνομαι, 1021). He elaborates on that which grieves him: 'I am grieved – in this especially, that I live with many evils, a wretch' (ἐγὼ δ' ἀλγύνομαι | τοῦτ' αὔθ' ὅτι ζῶ σὺν κακοῖς πολλοῖς τάλας, 1021-2). The emphatic 'wretch' (τάλας) echoes characterizations of Philoctetes throughout the play, but now the sense of passivity is more intense. Without his bow and without the friend he thought he had made in Neoptolemus, there is absolutely nothing he can do (1101-10):

ὦ τλάμων τλάμων ἄρ' ἐγὼ
καὶ μόχθῳ λωβατός, ὃς ἤ-
δη μετ' οὐδενὸς ὕστερον
ἀνδρῶν εἰσοπίσω τάλας
ναίων ἐνθάδ' ὀλοῦμαι,
αἰαῖ αἰαῖ,
οὐ φορβὰν ἔτι προσφέρων,
οὐ πτανῶν ἀπ' ἐμῶν ὅπλων
κραταιαῖς μετὰ χερσὶν ἴσχων·

Oh, I am suffering, I am a suffering man
and one treated shamefully by hardship, I who now will perish,
a wretch, dwelling from now on in this place without a single human person,
aiai, aiai!

No longer will I bring in food,
not by my winged arrows
with strong hands
holding ...

The cry grows in helplessness: the double τλάμων ('suffering', 1101) expands with μόχθῳ λωβατός ('one treated shamefully by hardship', 1102). Hardship causes suffering and outrage; Philoctetes is the passive recipient of both. After predicting his lonely death (note again the verb, ὀλοῦμαι, 1104), Philoctetes fixes his cry on the disabling loss of his bow. οὔ ... οὔ, he repeats the negative, twice bemoaning what is no longer possible for him, hunting for food. And he leaves unnamed the key instrument, his bow, lingering on the participle ἴσχων ('holding') drawing our attention to the activity that he can no longer undertake.

More than Suffering: Heroism in the Middle

In light of these two features of the play's discourse – the theme of Iliadic heroism, which we might call heroism 'in the active voice', and that of undergoing suffering, which we might call heroism (insofar as Philoctetes is a Greek hero by tradition) 'in the passive voice' – Philoctetes' notions of a special, personal type of heroism stand out. He is not fighting wars, not winning glory on the battlefield, but that does not mean, in Philoctetes' presentation of his survival, that he is a passive hero, a sufferer only. Philoctetes certainly endures things he has not chosen. But interwoven with his cries and assertions of unique suffering is a thread of pride. Philoctetes conceives of his survival as a kind of achievement, especially when he contrasts himself with the Greek leaders at Troy. In enduring what he has suffered, Philoctetes achieves a unique form of excellence. This excellence through endurance is something in between doing and experiencing; we could call it heroism 'in the middle'.

There is no single verb or noun that describes this kind of 'middle-voice' heroism. In many of the passages where I see heroism in the middle, the verb is the same as in passages depicting more passive suffering: 'endure' (τλάω). But these 'middle-voice' passages evoke a sense of achievement, often contrasting with the omissions of the other Greek leaders. The content of Philoctetes' 'accomplishment' is horrid: he survived living with a diseased foot, for ten years, utterly alone.[8] But he repeatedly associates his

---

8 Compare his description of himself immediately after the Greek leaders abandoned him: he awoke finding 'no man at all in the place, no one who might assist me, no one who could take part in my illness with me, when I am wearied by it' (ἄνδρα δ' οὐδέν' ἔντοπον, | οὐχ ὅστις ἀρκέσειεν οὐδ' ὅστις νόσου | κάμνοντι συλλάβοιτο, 280–2).

endurance with a form of excellence, being noble, unlike those leaders who abandoned him. After Philoctetes wakes up from the slumber induced by overwhelming agony, he praises Neoptolemus for remaining with him during his anguish. He speaks with a kind of wonder (869-71):

οὐ γάρ ποτ', ὦ παῖ, τοῦτ' ἂν ἐξηύχησ' ἐγώ,
τλῆναί σ' ἐλεινῶς ὧδε τἀμὰ πήματα
μεῖναι παρόντα καὶ ξυνωφελοῦντά μοι.

For never would I have boasted of this, o child,
that you would endure my pains in this way, full of pity,
enduring to remain present and to help me.

Neoptolemus's endurance includes things he has done. He has remained at Philoctetes' side, and he has joined with Philoctetes (ξυνωφελοῦντα) in helping him. This active endurance contrasts sharply with the Atreids' desertion (872-6):

οὔκουν Ἀτρεῖδαι τοῦτ' ἔτλησαν εὐφόρως
οὕτως ἐνεγκεῖν, ἀγαθοὶ στρατηλάται.
ἀλλ' εὐγενὴς γὰρ ἡ φύσις κἀξ εὐγενῶν,
ὦ τέκνον, ἡ σή, πάντα ταῦτ' ἐν εὐχερεῖ
ἔθου, βοῆς τε καὶ δυσοσμίας γέμων.

The sons of Atreus certainly did not endure to bear this
as something easily borne, those excellent generals.
But since your nature is noble and of noble lineage,
o child, you can handle all these things without disgust,
although you are laden with shouting and a foul smell.

The contrast between the generals' disgust and Neoptolemus's spirit of endurance applies even more to Philoctetes himself. Not just once, but for ten years Philoctetes has carried the heavy load (γέμων, 876) of his illness. The triple reference to bearing (ἔτλησαν εὐφόρως | οὕτως ἐνεγκεῖν, 872-3) reinforces the weakness of the generals. By contrast, Neoptolemus has shown himself able to associate with Philoctetes' illness, without squeamishness (πάντα ταῦτ' ἐν εὐχερεῖ | ἔθου, 875-6). In praising Neoptolemus's endurance as a form of activity, one avoided by others, Philoctetes also describes his own ability to carry his dreadful burden as a form of accomplishment.[9]

---

9 Cf. the wonder of the Chorus (θαῦμά μ' ἔχει, 686) at Philoctetes' holding on to life, alone (μόνος ... βιοτὰν κατέσχεν, 688-90). The inversion of agency between the Chorus,

In the first section of this paper, we observed the connection between bearing Philoctetes as cargo and the glory of τὸ χρηστὸν, of 'goodness': 'Nevertheless endure! since for noble men, you know, shamefulness is hateful and goodness is glorious' (ὅμως δὲ τλῆθι· τοῖσι γενναίοισί τοι | τό τ' αἰσχρὸν ἐχθρὸν καὶ τὸ χρηστὸν εὐκλεές, 475–6). In this passage too, τλάω denotes more than mere suffering. The content of this endurance is a 'doing' that stands opposed to the 'non-doing' of leaving Philoctetes behind: 'For you, <u>if you forsake this</u>, will have ignoble shame, but <u>if you do it</u>, oh child, you will have the greatest prize of glory' (σοὶ δ', <u>ἐκλιπόντι</u> τοῦτ', ὄνειδος οὐ καλόν, | <u>δράσαντι</u> δ', ὦ παῖ, πλεῖστον εὐκλείας γέρας, 477–8). Philoctetes exhorts Neoptolemus to courage: the toil of bringing him home will last but a single day (ἴθ'· ἡμέρας τοι μόχθος οὐχ ὅλης μιᾶς, 480), so he should dare to undertake it (τόλμησον, 481). That which is being endured is something to be taken on, something to be dared.

The most spectacular declaration of Philoctetes' private notion of 'middle-voice' heroism comes at the end of his first conversation with Neoptolemus, when he and Neoptolemus have agreed to leave the island together. Philoctetes bursts forth with a cry of gratitude, followed by an invitation to see his cave (530–8):

ὦ φίλτατον μὲν ἦμαρ, ἥδιστος δ' ἀνήρ,
φίλοι δὲ ναῦται, πῶς ἂν ὑμῖν ἐμφανὴς
ἔργῳ γενοίμην, ὥς μ' ἔθεσθε προσφιλῆ.
ἴωμεν, ὦ παῖ, προσκύσαντε τὴν ἔσω
ἄοικον εἰσοίκησιν, ὥς με καὶ μάθῃς
ἀφ' ὧν διέζων ὥς τ' ἔφυν εὐκάρδιος.[10]
<u>οἶμαι γὰρ οὐδ' ἂν ὄμμασιν μόνον θέαν</u>
<u>ἄλλον λαβόντα πλὴν ἐμοῦ τλῆναι τάδε·</u>
<u>ἐγὼ δ' ἀνάγκῃ προὔμαθον στέργειν κακά.</u>

Oh, most beloved day, and sweetest man,
and beloved sailors, how might I make clear to you,
with deeds, how you have made me a friend.
Let us go, child, after we show our respect to the place within,
my home that is no home, so that also you may know me,
and from what I have survived, and how I am by nature stout-hearted.
<u>For I think that no other man except me could endure these things,</u>

---

held by wonder, and Philoctetes, holding on to life, further underscores the (horrible!) accomplishment highlighted in the stanza.
10 Schein (2013, *ad* 535–8) calls εὐκάρδιος (535) 'a rare and elevated word', one that 'suggests Phil.'s consciousness of his distinctive heroic nature'. Schein (2013, *ad* 536–8) similarly claims that those following lines explain εὐκάρδιος and 'indicate Phil.'s sense of his own, special heroism'.

<u>not even taking in with his eyes the sight of them alone;</u>
<u>but I have gradually learned through necessity to embrace evils.</u>

This final line, 'I have learned through necessity to embrace evils', is a striking declaration of achievement in endurance. Philoctetes wants to show Neoptolemus the means by which he survived (ἀφ' ὧν διέζων, 535), so that Neoptolemus can know that he, Philoctetes, is 'strong-hearted' (εὐκάρδιος, 535). He then further articulates the uniqueness of his survival: he has endured things (τλῆναι τάδε, 537) which no other man could even look upon. But the final line goes beyond endurance to articulating a form of accomplishment, something he has learned to do: 'but I, out of necessity, have learned over time to embrace my evils' (ἐγὼ δ' ἀνάγκῃ προὔμαθον στέργειν κακά, 538). This line encapsulates Philoctetes' heroism 'in the middle'. Philoctetes has not chosen to live in this way; he has been forced to (ἀνάγκῃ, 538). But neither has he suffered only. He has learned to acquiesce to, even to love, his evils (προὔμαθον στέργειν κακά).

I have translated στέργειν three ways in the paragraph above: to embrace, to acquiesce to, to love. I am not suggesting that Philoctetes feels affection for his degrading sufferings. This is clearly untrue. But neutral translations, like 'tolerate'[11] or 'endure', could mislead. They remove from this passage the striking assertion of accomplishment, of something Philoctetes has learned to do. The verb's negative object, 'evils', could make one think στέργειν must express something closer to 'endure' in this line. Yet in most parallel passages in Greek tragedy where the object of στέργειν is something repellent to the subject, a translation along the lines of 'embrace' or 'willingly accept' works well.[12] More definitively for this passage, the active connotation of 'embrace' better accounts for the import of προὔμαθον. Philoctetes has learned over time to do something. The line conveys the passive aspect of

---

11 Pape (1954 s.v. στέργειν) offers *ertragen* ('to tolerate') for a parallel usage at Eur. *Or.* 1023. He offers *zufrieden sein mit* ('be satisfied with') for the passage from *Philoctetes*.

12 Schein (2013, ad 536-8) offers the translation 'embrace'. For some parallel examples from elsewhere in tragedy: the object of στέργειν is 'evils' (κακά) in Euripides' *Phoenician Women* (1685). When Antigone resolves to give up marriage and go into exile with her father Oedipus so that he will not be alone, Oedipus urges her to remain, declaring: 'Remain, with good fortune; and my evils I will <u>embrace</u>' (μέν' εὐτυχοῦσα· τἄμ' ἐγὼ <u>στέρξω</u> κακά, 1685). See also Kratos's opening speech in Aeschylus's *Prometheus Bound*: 'For such a transgression, then, it is necessary that he pay the penalty to the gods, so that he may learn to <u>willingly accept</u> the tyranny of Zeus and cease from his human-loving ways' (τοιᾶσδέ τοι | ἁμαρτίας σφε δεῖ θεοῖς δοῦναι δίκην, | ὡς ἂν διδαχθῆι τὴν Διὸς τυραννίδα | <u>στέργειν</u>, φιλανθρώπου δὲ παύεσθαι τρόπου, 8–10). Interestingly, David Grene (see Grene and Lattimore 1960, 65) keeps his translation of στέργειν open in this passage: 'that he may learn to *endure and like* the sovereignty of Zeus and quit his man-loving disposition'. For other examples, compare Aesch. *Ag.* 1570, Eur. *Or.* 1023, Eur. *El.* 407, Eur. *Hipp.* 458.

his sufferings, the violent compulsion (ἀνάγκη), but also his sense of personal involvement in the heroic endurance of these sufferings. Philoctetes claims his unique survival of loneliness and illness as an achievement that outstrips anything the Greek leaders have done at Troy. This combination of suffering and accomplishment gives us a clear expression of what I am calling heroism 'in the middle voice'.

Philoctetes' personal sense of heroism is thematized in his bow.[13] We saw above how the loss of his bow coincides with the hero's greatest expressions of passivity and suffering. By contrast, the bow's possession enables him to carry out deeds of survival and to protect himself from potential enemies – as he does at 1299, when, bow in hand, he drives away Odysseus with a threat. The bow, and his use of it, transforms his endurance of suffering from something wholly passive to something marked by achievement.

Philoctetes' bow also links his sufferings with the toils of Heracles, who gave the bow to him.[14] A key word in this link is πόνοι. At 507–8, the Chorus speaks of Philoctetes' 'many toils hard to bear' (πολλῶν ... δυσοίστων πόνων). During Philoctetes' bout of pain, Neoptolemus uses the same word to describe his evident distress: 'you, wretched indeed <u>because of all of these toils</u>' (δύστηνε δῆτα <u>διὰ πόνων πάντων</u> φανείς, 760). 'Toil' (πόνος) also describes the effort involved in living with Philoctetes' illness, which we have established as a kind of accomplishment: Neoptolemus says that the sailors will not shy away from the toil of picking him up (τοῦ πόνου γὰρ οὐκ ὄκνος, 887), and Philoctetes counters that there will be sufficient toil on ship in living with him (πόνος ... συνναίειν ἐμοί, 892). The connection between Philoctetes' sufferings and the labors of Heracles becomes explicit when Heracles interrupts the final action of the play. The god describes how he toiled and passed through labors (ὅσους πονήσας καὶ διεξελθὼν πόνους, 1419), and then he tells Philoctetes, 'you also had to suffer this, know it well' (καὶ σοί, σάφ' ἴσθι, τοῦτ' ὀφείλεται παθεῖν, 1421). The bow participates in this link between Heracles' labors, which were aided by the bow, and Philoctetes' survival of suffering, aided by the same bow. The two are linked in their sufferings and in the resources with which they met those sufferings.

In some ways, Heracles' final speech moves us away from heroism in the middle. The god explicitly links Philoctetes' suffering to Iliadic *kleos*,

13 For Harsh (1960, 412), the bow of Heracles is a fourth 'actor' in the play, which 'symbolizes intelligence *brought into action* to guarantee man's domination of the earth' (emphasis mine). Harsh (1960, 414) continues that none of the human actors matches the heroic ideals of the bow 'until both Philoctetes and Neoptolemus consciously and deliberately do so at the appearance of [the bow's] master' at the play's end.
14 Some of the most compelling scholarship on this play concerns the role of *philia* and reciprocity. See Gil (1980), Segal (1981, 292–361), Blundell (1989, 184–285), Newman (1991), White (1985). See also Rose (1992, 266–330).

claiming, 'you had to suffer this to make your life glorious through these toils' (τοῦτ' ὀφείλεται παθεῖν, | ἐκ τῶν πόνων τῶνδ' εὐκλεᾶ θέσθαι βίον, 1421-2). Indeed, part of the dissatisfaction so often felt in this ending is that Heracles forces a return to Troy and to the kind of heroism that will come with that city's sack.[15] But the words of Heracles also pick up an earlier claim of the Chorus: 'But now he has met the son of noble men and will become happy and great from going through (ἐκ) those things' (νῦν δ' ἀνδρῶν ἀγαθῶν παιδὸς ὑπαντήσας | εὐδαίμων ἀνύσει καὶ μέγας ἐκ κείνων, 719-20). The ἐκ is astonishing. Not 'in spite of' or 'after', but (to use Schein's translation once again) 'out of and because of'.[16] Heracles' reference to a life made glorious because of toils (ἐκ τῶν πόνων τῶνδ' εὐκλεᾶ θέσθαι βίον) similarly locates the origin of his life's *kleos* in his sufferings. Even as we are moving to Troy and to the glory of sacking the city, we are reminded that Philoctetes' achievement on the island – surviving alone for ten years – has created a new discourse on suffering and heroism. In that discourse, passive suffering and active heroism have blended together in Philoctetes' personal sense of heroic action. He learned to survive his illness and his desertion on the island; he has accomplished the activity, so to speak, of endurance.

Conclusion

The 'Spirit of Aristophanes' emerges in this volume in many guises. One such guise is the effort, modeled so well in Jeffrey Henderson's teaching and scholarship, to engage with and question received categories. This essay has traced the major ways characters in Sophocles' *Philoctetes* talk about heroism, using a framework of the grammatical 'middle voice' as a way to move beyond an active–passive binary in how we view suffering and action on the Athenian tragic stage. The discourse about heroism in the *Philoctetes* centers on an ethical battle over how Neoptolemus should behave – whether he should aid Odysseus and thereby serve the heroic project of sacking Troy, or whether he should aid Philoctetes and live up to a new standard of heroism by nobly enduring proximity to Philoctetes' disease. But in the midst of this ethical battle, the play also stages a defiant rewriting of Philoctetes' own sufferings. In between the cries and horror of what he has endured, Philoctetes also asserts a form of unmatched excellence. When he articulates to Neoptolemus the personal qualities of goodness and nobility required for living and enduring loneliness and disease, he also asserts the uniqueness of his survival, unparalleled by any accomplishments at Troy.

15 Poe (1974, 48 n. 89) makes the point forcefully: 'The *ex machina* ending ... provide[s] a kind of inevitable climax of the play's bleak pessimism'; see also Linforth (1956), Kott (1974, 162–85), Craik (1979, 21–2).
16 Schein (2013, *ad* 720).

And this entire picture of personal heroism is something other than what is captured in the categories 'active' and 'passive'. Philoctetes' ten years of survival have forged in him a kind of heroism 'in the middle voice'.[17]

Works Cited

Allan, Rutger. 2003. *The Middle Voice in Ancient Greek: A Study in Polysemy*. Amsterdam: J. C. Gieben.

Barber, E. J. W. 1975. 'Voice – Beyond the Passive'. *Proceedings of the First Annual Meeting of the Berkeley Linguistics Society*, 16–24.

Beye, Charles. 1970. 'Sophocles' *Philoctetes* and the Homeric Embassy'. *TAPA* 101: 63–75.

Blundell, M. W. 1989. *Helping Friends and Harming Enemies: A Study in Sophocles and Greek Ethics*. Cambridge: Cambridge University Press.

Christensen, Joel. 2020. *The Many-Minded Man: The Odyssey, Psychology, and the Therapy of Epic*. Cornell: Cornell University Press.

Cook, Edwin. 1999. '"Active" and "Passive" Heroics in the *Odyssey*'. *CW* 93: 149–57.

Craik, Elizabeth M. 1979. 'Philoktetes: Sophoklean Melodrama'. *L'Antiquité Classique* 48: 15–29.

Gil, C. 1980. 'Bow, Oracle, and Epiphany in Sophocles' *Philoctetes*'. *G&R* 27: 137–46.

Grene, D., and R. Lattimore, eds. 1960. *Greek Tragedies*, vol. 1. Chicago: University of Chicago Press.

Harsh, P. W. 1960. 'The Role of the Bow in the *Philoctetes* of Sophocles'. *AJP* 81: 408–14.

Kott, J. 1974. *The Eating of the Gods: An Interpretation of Greek Tragedy*, translated by B. Taborski and E. Czerwinski. London: E. Methuen.

Kyriakou, Poulcheria. 2012. 'Philoctetes'. In *Brill's Companion to Sophocles*, edited by Andreas Markantonatos, 149–66. Leiden: Brill.

Linforth, I. M. 1956. *Philoctetes the Play and the Man*. Berkeley: University of California Press.

Newman, Robert J. 1991. 'Heroic Resolution: A Note on Sophocles, *Philoctetes* 1405–1406'. *CJ* 86: 305–10.

Pape, W. 1954. *Griechisch-Deutsches Handwörterbuch*, vol. 2: Λ-Ω, edited by M. Sengesbusch. Akademische Druck- und Verlagsanstalt: Graz.

Poe, Joe Park. 1974. *Heroism and Divine Justice in Sophocles' Philoctetes*. Mnemosyne Supplement 34. Leiden: Brill.

---

17 With gratitude to Rachel Fisher for her suggestions and insights. She perceptively notes that this type of heroism is also 'middle voice' insofar as Philoctetes has achieved it 'for himself' or 'in his own interest'. In other words, he does not contribute to the acquisition of prizes to be divided up, nor does he have any hope of 'being sung' until someone else shows up on this island (and even then, the focus is on returning home). His endurance of suffering was an achievement done with reference to himself (this idea from a personal correspondence with Rachel Fisher in 2021).

Rijksbaron, Albert. 2002. *The Syntax and Semantics of the Verb in Classical Greek*. J. C. Gieben: Amsterdam.

Rose, P. W. 1992. *Sons of the Gods, Children of the Earth: Ideology and Literary Form in Ancient Greece*. Ithaca, NY: Cornell University Press.

Schein, Seth. 2013. *Sophocles: Philoctetes*. Cambridge: Cambridge University Press.

Segal, C. 1981. *Tragedy and Civilization: An Interpretation of Sophocles*. Cambridge, MA: Harvard University Press.

White, J. B. 1985. 'Persuasion and Community in Sophocles' *Philoctetes*'. In *Heracles' Bow: Essays on the Rhetoric and Poetics of the Law*, 3–27. Madison: University of Wisconsin Press.

CHAPTER 7

διδαγμάτων ἥδιστον: Storytelling and the Origin of Religion in the Sisyphus Fragment (43 Fr. 19 TrGF)
Andrew Ford

The phrase that will serve as the focal point of this study also provides an apt keynote for honoring the humane and generous teaching of Jeffrey Henderson, διδασκάλων ἥδιστος. When I entered the Yale graduate program, Jeff was finishing up his groundbreaking *Maculate Muse*, a work that bridged a then entrenched divide between traditional philologists and those wanting Classics to adopt new methods to discuss new aspects of ancient society. To talk with him at that time was both highly instructive – his example showed how fruitful a close and painstaking study of diction could be for opening up new areas of research – and also a pleasure: no one was more encouraging or happier to put at his students' disposal his learning, his tricks of the trade and his general good humor. In particular, I gratefully recall a casual conversation with the young Assistant Professor (in company with his wry comic partner, Alan Nussbaum) that guided me to a dissertation topic that focused my interests in Greek literary criticism. The present thank offering aims to apply those interests to a fascinating and much debated text in an area of Jeff's expertise, classical Greek drama.

The text is a fragment of forty connected trimeters with a summarizing couplet appended in which a speaker speculates about the origin of religion. Our sources, Sextus Empiricus (*Math.* 9.24) and Aetius (*Plac.* 1.7.2 = [Plut.] *Mor.* 880e–f), do not tell us the name of the play the speech comes from or whether that play was a tragedy or satyr-play; and they disagree about its author: it is attributed to Critias by Sextus and to Euripides by Aetius (who helpfully informs us that the speaker was Sisyphus). In the body of the speech Sisyphus recounts how, in an early stage of human civilization, an unnamed wise man persuaded people that there were all-knowing and powerful divinities in the sky who observed everything that humans did, said and even thought; in this way he ensured that people would obey the laws even in their secret actions for fear of retribution from above. Blending strands of the most advanced thinking of the day about theology, cosmology and the evolution of civilization,[1] the origin story is rigorously non-mythological: the speaker allows that the discourse about the gods was a lie (ψευδεῖ … λόγῳ, 26) and yet in the same breath calls it 'the sweetest of teachings' (διδαγμάτων ἥδιστον, 25). Pinning down the tone of the latter expression has proved difficult: a number of editors find it inapt in context and have proposed to emend; others leave the phrase as is but give it an ironic reading, either as a sarcastic dig at the imposition of religion or at the demagoguery of the would-be sage ('Nice teaching, that'); yet others read it as expressing unqualified approval ('What a useful falsehood the invention of religion was!').

These different interpretations reflect a larger disagreement among scholars about the tone of the fragment as a whole. Because the speech is spoken by the arch criminal of myth, an assailant of the gods and a cunning trickster who would cheat death itself, it is tempting to read it as a withering exposure of the emptiness of religion, showing that it is rooted in a cynical and manipulative lie.[2] On the other hand, Sisyphus's declamation is clearly in the popular sophistic mode of explaining cultural history without the gods by identifying for any social practice a human 'first inventor' (πρῶτος εὑρετής), and these accounts tended to be optimistic and progressive;[3] from this perspective, the speech is not cynical but acknowledges the positive effects of religious belief as a useful fiction that fostered social cooperation and progress.[4] In this paper I propose to bring new evidence to bear on the debate by arguing that the text, in addition to reflecting sophisticated theological, cosmological and political thought, also engages with current thinking about pleasure and persuasion in fifth-century rhetoric and poetics. Considering how similar deceptive tales are described in texts ranging from Pindar to Aristotle will suggest that διδαγμάτων ἥδιστον refers to Sisyphus's artful use of storytelling techniques to win credibility, specifically by appealing to a predilection people have to take pleasure in shocking stories. This interpretation not only adds context for interpreting a puzzling epithet but also suggests that we read the fragment as a whole

---

1 On the philosophical background see Billings (2021, ch. 1 (84–90 on the Sisyphus fragment)) and Kahn (1997). It is a pleasure to recall discussing the Sisyphus fragment with Josh Billings on a long, rainy car ride through western Pennsylvania in 2016.
2 Kahn (1997, 259), for example, calls the fragment 'the most extreme expression of this atmosphere of moral cynicism, documented in the Antiphon fragments and caricatured in the *Clouds*'.
3 Kleingünther (1933). For a collection of translated texts on these themes see Guthrie (1969, 79–84) and, for their reflection in drama, Billings (2016, esp. 320–45).
4 For example, Bett (2002, 252): 'religion may be a fiction, but it is a fiction possessing great utility … [I]t is vitally important that we have nomoi, and that they have some authoritative backing, even if this is based on a fiction'. For religion as a useful invention here, see O'Sullivan (2012).

as a scientific and neutral account of the origin of religion rather than a cynical and contemptuous one. Sisyphus in this scene is only being rational in the best modern way, whatever fate may have befallen him in the rest of the play.

The first step in taking the measure of διδαγμάτων ἥδιστον is being specific about its referent, and this requires recognizing two shifts in the argument – both marked by mid-verse transitions with enjambment[5] and ring-composition – which analyses sometimes ignore: first comes a compact statement of the problem of early lawlessness (1–11a); its solution in the invention of religion takes up the rest of the fragment (11b–42), but that part itself is divided into two distinct topics: a theological discourse on the nature of divinity (11b–24a) followed by a cosmological account of where the gods live (24b–40); it is this latter part that contains the focal phrase.

Part 1 begins, as often in this genre of discourse, in fairy-tale mode: 'once upon a time' (ἦν χρόνος ὅτε, 1), early in their evolution from savagery to civilization, human beings (ἄνθρωποι, 5) developed laws so that good deeds would be rewarded and evil deeds punished (1–8); the legal penalties, however, turned out to be ineffective because evildoing that went unobserved remained unpunished (9–11a). Sisyphus transitions to the solution in mid-line, zeroing in on a specific time and a specific individual (11b–13):

τηνικαῦτά μοι δοκεῖ
<πρῶτον> πυκνός τις καὶ σοφὸς γνώμην ἀνήρ
<θεῶν> δέος θνητοῖσιν ἐξευρεῖν

12 <πρῶτον> Enger: <ἄγαν> Steffen   13 θεῶν Wecklein: γνῶναι Sextus | δέος Petit: δὲ or ὅς δέοση Sextus

Then it was, I think, that someone, a wise and intelligent man, first[6] invented fear of the gods for mortals

---

5 The text's enjambments have been taken as 'Sophoclean' and so as evidence against Euripidean authorship: Davies (1989, 21–2); Pechstein (1998, 294). My analysis steers clear of authorship, both because championing one candidate over the other often seems to compromise interpretation and because I think we know too little about Critias's proclivities as a dramatist to settle the question.
6 How Sextus is emended is often consequential for the cynical/optimistic debate: Steffen's ἄγαν ('too wise') provides the missing metrical x – in 12, but pre-emptively skews the text toward the cynical by suggesting that the sage is 'too clever by half'; see Collard and Cropp (2008, 675 n. 4). Enger's πρῶτον ('for the first time') makes no such presumption, but it is admittedly unnecessary beside ἐξευρεῖν; I have printed it because, if πρῶτον is accepted, it lends support to the ring-composition with 40–1. By contrast, Wecklein's θεῶν in 13 is necessary to specify δέος; Sextus's γνῶναι would be a misplaced gloss on or a variant for γνώμην in the previous line.

How this exceptionally wise individual[7] persuaded his fellows to fear the gods is the main theme of the fragment and is marked off as a unit when these introductory verses are recapitulated in a couplet that Sextus says 'followed soon after' line 40:

(ὀλίγα προσδιελθὼν ἐπιφέρει)
    οὕτω δὲ πρῶτον οἴομαι πεῖσαί τινα
    θνητοὺς νομίζειν δαιμόνων εἶναι γένος

(and going on a little, he adds)
    In this way, I think, someone first[8] persuaded mortals to
    believe in a race of divine powers

The heart of the speech, then, is the teaching about the gods that extends from verse 11b up to this point, including what was in the short lacuna before 41. Within this unit, however, another mid-line change of topic combined with ring-composition divides the teaching into two distinct sets of claims: the first is theological, a sophisticated but not very startling discourse on the nature of these divinities (δαίμονες) in 16–24a;[9] the second turns to cosmology and locates these observant gods in the heavens. This second set of claims is introduced with the phrase διδαγμάτων ἥδιστον (24b–36):

                τούσδε τοὺς λόγους λέγων
διδαγμάτων ἥδιστον εἰσηγήσατο
ψευδεῖ τυφλώσας τὴν ἀλήθειαν λόγῳ·
ναίειν δ' ἔφασκε τοὺς θεοὺς ἐνταῦθ' ἵνα

---

7 Neither πυκνός nor σοφὸς γνώμην carries an obvious suggestion of trickiness or deceptiveness. Again (as in the previous note), the fragment's overall interpretation depends on whether πυκνός is taken to mean tricky and manipulative or merely smart and perhaps shrewd. As applied to the mind, πυκνός (epic πυκινός) may refer both to preceptive intelligence (as when events on the field at Troy 'did not escape the πυκινός mind' of Zeus (οὐ λῆθε Διὸς πυκινὸν νόον, Il. 15.461; compare 14.294) and to shrewdness, craft, cunning associated with trickery (for example, εἰδὼς παντοίους τε δόλους καὶ μήδεα πυκνά, Il. 2.202, etc.; cf. 2.55, 4.392). The latter sense is clearly ascendant when Pindar applies it to Sisyphus (Σίσυφος πυκνότατος παλάμαις, Ol. 13.52), but I agree with Bett (2002, 252) that our fragment shows 'no sign of irony in the description of the inventor of religion as wise'.
8 The ring-composition is more obvious if πρῶτον is read in 12; see n. 6 above.
9 The sage's all-seeing gods meting out justice have roots in Hesiod's Zeus (Works and Days 252–69) and Xenophanes' 'one god' (B 23–6, A 1 DK = D16–20 Laks-Most); the idea that the gods perceive all that is said and done and even what is plotted in secret is attributed to Socrates by Xenophon (πάντα μὲν ἡγεῖτο θεοὺς εἰδέναι, τά τε λεγόμενα καὶ πραττόμενα καὶ τὰ σιγῇ βουλευόμενα, Mem. 1.1.19).

μάλιστ' ἂν ἐξέπληξεν ἀνθρώπους ἄγων,
ὅθεν περ ἔγνω τοὺς φόβους ὄντας βροτοῖς
καὶ τὰς πονήσεις τῷ ταλαιπώρῳ βίῳ,
ἐκ τῆς ὕπερθε περιφορᾶς, ἵν' ἀστραπὰς
κατεῖδον οὔσας, δεινὰ δὲ κτυπήματα
βροντῆς τό τ' ἀστερωπὸν οὐρανοῦ σέλας –
Χρόνου καλὸν ποίκιλμα, τέκτονος σοφοῦ,
ὅθεν τε λαμπρὸς ἀστέρος στείχει μύδρος
ὅ θ' ὑγρὸς εἰς γῆν ὄμβρος ἐκπορεύεται.

25 ἥδιστον Sextus: μέγιστον F. W. Schmidt: κράτιστον Mutschmann: κύδιστον Haupt, Diggle: κέρδιστον Nauck 26 τυφλώσας Aetius: καλύψας Sextus 27 ναίειν Pierson: αἰεὶ Sextus 28 μάλιστ' ἂν Toup: μάλιστα Sextus | ἄγων Sextus: λέγων Grotius 30 πονήσεις Sextus: ὀνήσεις Musgrave 32 κατεῖδον Snell: κατεῖδεν Sextus 33 σέλας Chrysippus: δέμας Sextus 35 ἄστερος Sextus: ἡλίου Nauck

In telling this story he introduced a very pleasing piece of teaching, using a false tale to blind (those he taught)[10] as regards the true state of affairs: he maintained that the gods dwelt in a place where, if he put them there, he would most astound men, the place from which he knew that terrors come to men and travails for their wretched lives, from the vault above where they observed there was lightning, the terrifying crash of thunder and the flashing of the star-eyed sky – the beautiful embroidery of Time, that wise architect, the place from which a glowing metal lump of a star approaches and (from which) wet stormwater sets out on its way to earth.

Again, ring-composition marks off the cosmological discussion as a separate component in the invention of religion: in the recapitulation of this argument (following at 37–40, quoted and analyzed below), καλῶς picks up ἥδιστον in the introduction, and ἐν πρέποντι χωρίῳ, harkening back to ναίειν ... ἐνταῦθ' (27), epitomizes the intervening matter. Sisyphus dwells on this cosmological teaching, treating it at twice the length of the theology, because it is essential to the sage's plan: to extinguish lawbreaking it is not enough to persuade people that gods exist and know all they do and think; it needs settling them in the heavens, a 'fitting' location (40) to curb secret

10 The syntax of Aetius's τυφλώσας in 26 makes it the *lectio difficilior* (τὴν ἀλήθειαν is accusative of respect and not the verb's direct object, which must be inferred from διδαγμάτων); Sextus's καλύψας looks like a simplifying gloss. To say that the sage 'blinded' his hearers is not to depict him as malevolent, but to highlight the influence that a single wise man can exert over a mass of people; as Pindar put it: τυφλὸν δ' ἔχει | ἦτορ ὅμιλος ἀνδρῶν ὁ πλεῖστος (*Nem*. 7.23–4; cf. fr. 52h.18 M).

lawbreaking because it suggests that the menace and trouble that come from the skies are the gods' way of showing their displeasure.

Having seen that διδαγμάτων ἥδιστον refers specifically to the gods' location in the heavens, we can return to the question of why this teaching should be called particularly pleasing. Because a teaching designed to rouse people's fears (see δέος, 13; δεῖμα, 14) hardly seems pleasant, many scholars read ἥδιστον ironically: O'Sullivan and Collard translate 'most pleasant (?)' and comment, 'if correct, may be sardonic (as perhaps is "beautifully" in 38)';[11] Davies approved of the epithet as adding 'the pungent paradox of a pleasant lie'.[12] A good number of scholars have proposed to change ἥδιστον, for example, into 'most important' (μέγιστον), 'most powerful' or 'excellent' (κράτιστον), 'most glorious' (κύδιστον), or 'most profitable' (κέρδιστον); none of these proposals is compelling, and most of them assume that the phrase is no less ironic or cynical than the one it would replace.[13]

One way to sustain an unironic reading of the epithet is to compare the sage's mass deception to the 'noble lie' of Plato's *Republic* by which a philosopher disseminates a myth (μυθολογοῦντες, 415a3) among the populace to subdue them to the useful and the good (414b–415d). So O'Sullivan: 'The lesson, however false, can be understood as ἥδιστον, since it puts an end to the age of brutality ... and led to a benign, more civilized era.'[14] There is indeed some affinity between these two political uses of lying, though I would be happier if Sisyphus used an adjective that specifically stressed the lie's utility (for example, Pl.'s χρησμοῦ, 415c5). An alternative that is closer to the interpretation I will offer is a dazzling metapoetic reading of the passage by Tim Whitmarsh, who sees in the deceiving sage a reflection of the tragedian's power to 'introduce "sweet" lies about the gods for the sake of maintaining social order'.[15] In this reading, ἥδιστον has the sense 'beguiling' and recalls the 'honeyed words' (ἔπεα ... μείλιχα, *Theog.* 84) by which Hesiod's Muse-inspired king quells social unrest; so too the sage's false tale (ψευδεῖ λόγῳ, 26) is a prototype of fiction, like the Muses' 'lies (ψεύδεα) like the truth' (*Theog.* 27–8). Whitmarsh is right, I think, to

---

11 O'Sullivan and Collard (2013, 445, with n. 8).
12 Davies (1989, 22).
13 Cf. Collard and Cropp (2008, 674 n. 6); Diggle (1996, 103). Nauck's κέρδιστον, 'craftiest' or 'most devoted to profit', would introduce the note of manipulativeness without being ironic (cf. Σίσυφος ... ὃ κέρδιστος γένετ' ἀνδρῶν, *Il.* 6.153) but this brings in a stray, distracting point to justify assuming that greed was the inventor's motive. Guthrie (1969, 244 n. 4) supported κέρδιστος by comparing Eur. *El.* 743–4: φοβεροὶ δὲ βροτοῖσι μῦθοι | κέρδος πρὸς θεῶν θεραπείας; but his cynical reading of these lines (that is, frightening tales bring profit to priests) is disputable: Stinton (1976, 82–3).
14 O'Sullivan (2012, 178); see also O'Sullivan and Collard (2013, 445 n. 8). Hesk (2000, 179–88) also develops the parallel.
15 Whitmarsh (2014, 118).

argue that ἥδιστον is unironic and comes out of Greek reflections on the pleasures of fiction: but rather than taking Hesiod as the prime intertext here, I will adduce some passages from fifth- and fourth-century rhetoric and poetics to show that ἥδιστον colors the sage not as a cynical manipulator but as an artful narrator and successful persuader. Appealing to the pleasure that audiences take in the marvelous will explain the complete acceptance of his lie.

There is no need to establish that ἡδονή is a central value in Greek poetics, but two technical terms in Sisyphus's introductory lines support exploring the meta-discursive function of ἥδιστον. The first is the meaning of πρέποντι in 39. Why are the heavens a 'fitting' or 'appropriate' place for the gods to dwell? The reason has nothing to do with the nature of the gods or the heavens but is because the sage would most astonish (ἐξέπληξεν) men if he put the gods there.[16] This use of πρέπον to describe what is appropriate to the purposes of the storyteller rather than what is socially or morally 'fitting' appears to have been an innovation of sophists like Gorgias and Hippias.[17] An example of this new, aesthetic sense is Herodotus's use of the root to say that, although the truth of the matter is that Helen ran off with Paris to Egypt, Homer decided to have her go to Troy, 'because (the Egyptian version) was less well suited to his epic than the one he used' (οὐ γὰρ ὁμοίως ἐς τὴν ἐποποιίην εὐπρεπὴς ἦν τῷ ἑτέρῳ τῷ περ ἐχρήσατο, 2.116).

The astonishment the sage was aiming to arouse is the second and key critical concept here, ἔκπληξις. This word described an overpowering but intensely pleasurable feeling of amazement, an effect that the critical tradition held to be characteristic of great poetry and rhetoric.[18] Aristotle associates ἔκπληξις with the marvelous (τὸ θαυμαστόν) and the incredible (ἀδύνατα, *Poet.* 1460a13, b23–9), and recommends it to epic poets, tragedians and storytellers generally because 'the marvelous is sweet, as is indicated by the fact that everyone adds it in when telling stories because they want to gratify their listeners' (τὸ δὲ θαυμαστὸν ἡδύ· σημεῖον δέ, πάντες γὰρ προστιθέντες ἀπαγγέλλουσιν ὡς χαριζόμενοι, *Poet.* 1460a17–18). Traces of the term in Gorgias and Aristophanes show that the concept was already at work in fifth-century critical discourse,[19] but an unnoticed and particularly rich comparandum can be found in a passage of Pindar where

---

16 With τοὺς θεούς (not mortals) as its object, ἄγων in 38 makes perfect sense (as his creations, he can lead them wherever he wishes); the emendation λέγων is banal and otiose after λέγων in 24.
17 As Pohlenz (1933, 54–5) argued. Cf. Russell (1981, 88).
18 Arist. *Poet.* 1454a4, 1455a17; Pl. *Ion* 535b–c; [Demetr.] *Eloc.* 101; Plut. *De aud. poet.* 25d; [Longinus] 15.2.
19 For Gorgias see *Helen* § 16 and cf. § 13 on τοὺς τῶν μετεωρολόγων λόγους; Walsh (1984, 89–92); for Aristophanes, *Frogs* 144, 962 and Russell (1981: 132–4).

he ventriloquizes how an enlightened mythographer would analyze the story of how Pelops got his ivory shoulder.

In *Olympian* 1 Pindar rejects the cult myth that the ivory shoulder was fashioned by the gods to replace the part of Pelops that a distracted Demeter had nibbled on at Tantalus's feast.[20] As an alternative he offers a demythologized and naturalized explanation: the 'ivory' shoulder was merely an extraordinarily beautiful birthmark (*Ol.* 1.26-7). He then digresses to explain how such false tales about the gods win credence (28-34):

ἦ θαύματα πολλά, καί πού τι καὶ βροτῶν
φάτις ὑπὲρ τὸν ἀλαθῆ λόγον
δεδαιδαλμένοι ψεύδεσι ποικίλοις
   ἐξαπατῶντι μῦθοι.

Χάρις δ', ἅπερ ἅπαντα τεύχει τὰ μείλιχα θνατοῖς,
ἐπιφέροισα τιμὰν καὶ ἄπιστον ἐμήσατο πιστόν
ἔμμεναι τὸ πολλάκις

> Surely marvels are many, but when mortals talk of them they doubtless go beyond the true account, their stories, embroidered with intricate lies, deceive: for *Kharis* (Charm), who makes all that is appealing for mortals, has many a time rendered even the incredible credible by bestowing her favor.

Because many things in the world surpass the limited understanding of mortals, in talking of them they often go beyond the true account (τὸν ἀλαθῆ λόγον, 28b) and embellish it with artful lies (ψεύδεσι ποικίλοις, 29). The reason they do so is to invest their stories with 'charm' (χάρις), the power that makes all things agreeable (μείλιχα) and welcomed. If Charm bestows her favor, she can make even a tale of divine cannibalism, provided it is cunningly wrought, be taken as truth – at least until a wise exegete, like Pindar, comes along.

If we recognize a fundamental continuity between this passage and Aristotle's observation some century and a half later that people add an element of the marvelous (τὸ θαυμαστόν) to their stories because it is sweet

---

20 On this text see further Ford (2019, 13–21). Many of the same ideas congregate in the famous *Nem.* 7.19–24 in which Pindar says that using deceptive stories to trick people is its own form of wisdom or expertise (σοφία δὲ κλέπτει παράγοισα μύθοις). His example is 'Homer of the sweet verses' (τὸν ἀδυεπῆ … Ὅμηρον) who has exaggerated the story (λόγον) of Odysseus's travails (πάθαν) beyond the facts; but because something awe-inspiring inheres in his lies and devices (ψεύδεσί οἱ ποταναῖ τε μαχανᾷ σεμνὸν ἔπεστί τι), his false account has been accepted by the mass of people, whose minds are blind to the truth (τυφλὸν δ' ἔχει ἦτορ ὅμιλος ἀνδρῶν ὁ πλεῖστος).

(ἡδύ) and will gratify their listeners (χαριζόμενοι, *Poet.* 1460a18), we can see that the sage's 'sweetest teaching' about gods stands in this continuum. He sought to raise people's fear of the skies to the level of astonishment, 'an overpowering feeling of wonder or surprise' as Aristotle defines ἔκπληξις (θαυμασιότης ... ὑπερβάλλουσα, *Top.* 4.126b17). By situating his gods in the skies he cleverly turned the terror people felt at celestial phenomena into awe at the power of these purposeful, superhuman beings. Astonishment made the tale sweet, and that sweetness charmed people into embracing the story and ceasing from lawlessness.

In this light διδαγμάτων ἥδιστον remains a paradox, but not an ironic one aimed at criticizing the inventor or scorning belief in gods. The sage is indeed, like Sisyphus himself, cunning, deceptive and manipulative, but as a narrator, as one skilled at using stories to play on his audience's emotions. I hope that this interpretation gives a clear and pertinent sense to these words, but it also suggests a path through the rest of the fragment, where the figurative language becomes dense and the precise sequence of thought is often not clear. Accordingly, I would like to conclude by considering some problems of text and interpretation in the rest of the cosmological argument (29–40) that can be clarified by keeping in mind that the primary function of this 'sweetest' teaching was to produce fear of the gods.

The first and most important textual point to address is to reject Musgrave's unnecessary, nearly universally accepted emendation in 30 of ὀνήσεις ('benefactions') for πονήσεις.[21] This introduces a positive aspect of the gods in the skies that would accord with the account of Prodicus, who said that the ancients considered everything that was nourishing and beneficial to life to be gods, so that bread, for example, was worshipped as Demeter, fire as Hephaestus and so on.[22] Praise for the gifts from 'the god who put our bestial life in order' was put onstage by Euripides (*Supp.* 201–13), where among these gifts is 'the rain from heaven that nourishes what grows in the earth and quenches our bellies' thirst'. Mentioning the benefits as well as the dangers that come from the skies might be thought to increase the motivation for law-abidingness by adding gratitude and hopes of reward to fear of celestial punishment. But this obscures the inventor's tactical brilliance by muddling the text's consistent focus on fear (see δέος, 13; φόβους, 29; δεινὰ 32; φόβους, 37). The picture drawn by the sage is much closer to one given by Democritus, who held that when the ancients beheld the disturbances of the heavens (τὰ ἐν τοῖς μετεώροις παθήματα),

---

21 It is printed by Snell (1971), Davies (1989), Pechstein (1998), Collard and Cropp (2008), O'Sullivan and Collard (2013), and accepted by so learned a scholar as Henrichs (1975, 98); it is rejected by Krumeich *et al.* (1999, 559 n. 17).

22 See Henrichs (1975).

such as thunder, lightning, conjunctions of stars and eclipses, they were frightened and thought they were caused by gods.²³

With the transmitted πονήσεις, a coherent sequence of ideas emerges. It begins with the sage's knowledge (ἔγνω, 29) that what he thinks of as 'heavenly bodies circling overhead' (τῆς ὕπερθε περιφορᾶς, 31) were a source of terror and toil for mortals in their primitive way of life (ταλαιπώρῳ βίῳ, 30). For they observed²⁴ that in that place was lightning, the terrifying crash of thunder and the 'flashing of the star-eyed sky'.²⁵ The latter lyrical image might be thought to evoke some attractive, positive aspect of the heavens (marking the seasons? a guide to navigation?) in line with Prodicus and Euripides; but no such example is given, and the phrase can easily refer to the Democritean ἐν τοῖς μετεώροις παθήματα.²⁶ At this point, the focalization shifts back from what mortals see to what the sage knows (I have signaled the shift in perspective with a dash). In 34–5 the lyricism intensifies²⁷ as 'the beautiful embroidery of Time, that wise craftsman' describes how the sky appears to the sage: like Euripides' 'blessed' man, who 'gazes upon the unageing order of immortal nature' (ἀθανάτου καθορῶν φύσεως | κόσμον ἀγήρων, fr. 910.5–6 TrGF), the sage beholds not disorder and danger in the heavens but a tapestry, a work of artful design whose maker was not any divine demiurge but Time itself. He knows that the heavens are not the abode of gods but an intricate arrangement that has arisen in the course of time as the elements found their natural places, taking their proper motions through the cosmos. What mortals fear coming down from these skies is only the approach of a fiery lump of metal (for example, a comet or meteor)²⁸ or water setting out on its way to earth. This is the 'truth' (26) of the matter which he hides from his hearers.

23 A 75 DK (= ATOM D207 Laks-Most); cf. B 30 DK (= ATOM D210 Laks-Most).
24 Snell's κατεῖδον persuasively distinguishes between the wise man's knowledge (ἔγνω) that the sky was a source of fear for mortals from their observation (κατεῖδον, LSJ A II) of frightening celestial phenomena.
25 With Dihle (1977, 42), I prefer σέλας, transmitted by Aetius, to Sextus's δέμας ('frame, structure'); the focalization now shifts to mortals, and what they see is flashes of light not a structure.
26 As in Pl. *Hp. mai.* 285c1, τὰ περὶ τὰ ἄστρα τε καὶ τὰ οὐράνια πάθη. Cf. *Ion* 531c7 and *Phd.* 96b9. In the background are the destructive storms sent by a just Zeus in Homer that destroy the crops of mortals: *Il.* 5.87–92, 16.384–92 etc.
27 Notable, along with the compound, transferred epithet ἀστερωπόν, are the personification and metaphor in Χρόνου ποίκιλμα (cf. ψεύδεσι ποικίλοις in *Ol.*1. 29), the kenning λαμπρὸς ἀστέρος μύδρος and the ornamental epithet ὑγρὸς ὄμβρος.
28 The phrase is usually taken to refer to the sun moving across the sky; for example, Pechstein (1998, 339), citing schol. on Eur. *Or.* 982: Εὐριπίδης μύδρον λέγει τὸν ἥλιον, whence Nauck's ἡλίου. But ὅθεν governs the storms as well, and so the poet must be thinking of some moving celestial body approaching earth (LSJ στείχω I b) from the sky, as rain does: so Guthrie (1969, 244 n. 1); Davies (1989: 23).

Sisyphus sums up his account of the cosmological teaching with a difficult set of lines (37–40):

τοίους πέριξ ἔστησεν ἀνθρώποις φόβους,
δι' οὓς καλῶς τε τῷ λόγῳ κατῴκισεν
τὸν δαίμον' οὗτος ἐν πρέποντι χωρίῳ,
τὴν ἀνομίαν τε τοῖς νόμοις κατέσβεσεν

37–40 del Pechstein 37 τοίους πέριξ ἔστησεν Meineke: τοιούτους περιέστησεν Sextus: τοιούσδε περιέστ. Grotius 37–8 φόβους / δι' οὓς Sextus: φόβου / στοιχούς Musgrave 38–9 τῷ λόγῳ … οὐκ Sextus: τῶν λόγων … οὕνεχ' Diggle 39 δαίμον' οὗτος Diels: δαίμονα οὐκ Sextus: δαίμον' οἰκεῖν Hermann 40 del. Luppe

Such were the fears with which that man hedged in human beings, through which he very finely both located the god in an appropriate place for his story and quelled lawlessness with laws.[29]

However the opening of 40 is reconstructed, Sisyphus highlights the fears of heaven-sent ills aroused by the cosmological argument. Among the other issues, the position and meaning of καλῶς is relevant to this study since, as noted, it picks up ἥδιστον at 25. I take the adverb in common with both verbs linked by τε … τε (my translation signals this by adding 'very'): with κατῴκισεν, Sisyphus commends the sage's artfulness as a liar in finding an appropriate spot[30] to place the gods; with κατέσβεσεν, καλῶς broadens out into its usual senses and judges the results of this imposition to be a fine thing. With this judgment the speech concludes, but, as has already been said, the calm, rational speculations enunciated here may well have been assailed in the rest of the play.

I have argued that διδαγμάτων ἥδιστον, if read in the context of fifth-century reflections on lying and persuasion, is an apt and precise paradox and should not be changed. It refers to the pleasure that the discourse about the heavens, false as it was, gave audiences and that won the sage's story

---

29 Diggle (1996) emends more extensively, but his translation is compatible with the views here: 'Such were the fears with which he hedged mankind around. By way of these fears he both neatly, for the sake of his fiction, located god in a suitable place and quelled lawlessness with laws.' Pechstein (1998, 342) deleted these lines as a confused and interpolated summary of 1–36, whereas I have argued they recapitulate only the cosmological doctrine of 24b–36.
30 So O'Sullivan and Collard (2013, 447 n. 12) translate the diminutive χωρίῳ and argue against the contention of Dihle (1977, 39) that, because tragic diction avoids diminutives, the word strongly points to the fragment coming from a satyr-play. Nonetheless, that remains a real possibility, and there may be some lightness in this final summary.

universal assent (at least until Sisyphus came along). I have also suggested that the fragment as a whole offers a well-structured and neatly expressed imitation of contemporary 'sophistical' discourse whose predominant tone is not ironic or cynical contempt, but a sophisticated pleasure in fabulation, an enjoyment of the elegant and ingenious combination of false theology with materialist physics to produce a declamation that is, if not wholly serious or true, undoubtedly charming.

Works Cited

Bett, Richard. 2002. 'Is there a Sophistic Ethics?' *Ancient Philosophy* 22: 235–62.
Billings, Joshua. 2016. 'Dramatic Appendix'. In *Early Greek Philosophy*, vol. 9: *The Sophists Part 2*, edited by A. Laks and Glenn Most, 256–365. Cambridge, MA: Harvard University Press.
———. 2021. *The Philosophical Stage: Drama and Dialectic in Classical Athens*. Princeton: Princeton University Press.
Collard, Christopher, and M. J. Cropp. 2008. *Euripides*, vol. 8: *Fragments: Oedipus–Chrysippus. Other Fragments*. Cambridge, MA: Harvard University Press.
Collard, Christopher, M. J. Cropp, and K. H. Lee, eds. 1995. *Euripides: Selected Fragmentary Plays I*. Warminster: Aris and Phillips.
Davies, Malcolm. 1989. 'Sisyphus and the Invention of Religion ("Critias" TrGF 1 (43) F 19 = B 25 DK)'. *BICS* 36: 16–32.
Diggle, James. 1996. 'Critias, Siyphus (fr. 19 Snell, 1 Nauck)'. *Prometheus* 22: 103–4.
Dihle, Albrecht. 1977. 'Das Satyrspiel *Sisyphos*'. *Hermes* 105: 28–42.
Ford, Andrew. 2019. 'Mythographic Discourse Among Non-mythographers: Pindar, Plato and Callimachus'. In *Host or Parasite? Mythographers and Their Contemporaries in the Late Classical and Hellenistic Periods*, edited by J. Marincola and Allen Romano, 5–27. Berlin: De Gruyter.
Guthrie, W. K. C. 1969. *A History of Greek Philosophy*, vol. 3. Cambridge: Cambridge University Press.
Henrichs, Albert. 1975. 'Two Doxographical Notes: Democritus and Prodicus on Religion'. *HSCP* 79: 93–123.
Hesk, Jon. 2000. *Deception and Democracy in Classical Athens*. Cambridge: Cambridge University Press.
Kahn, Charles. 1997. 'Greek Religion and Philosophy in the Sisyphus Fragment'. *Phronesis* 42: 247–62.
Kleingünther, Adolf. 1933. 'ΠΡΩΤΟΣ ΕΥΡΕΤΗΣ'. *Untersuchung zur Geschichte einer Fragestellung*. Leipzig: Dieterich.
Krumeich, R., N. Pechstein and B. Seidensticker. 1999. *Das griechische Satyrspiel*. Darmstadt: Wissenschaftliche Buchgesellschaft.
Laks, André, and G. W. Most. 2016. *Early Greek Philosophy*, 9 vols. Cambridge, MA: Harvard University Press.
O'Sullivan, Patrick. 2012. 'Sophistic Ethics, Old Atheism, and "Critias" on Religion'. *CW* 105: 167–85.

O'Sullivan, Patrick, and Christopher Collard, eds. 2013. *Euripides: Cyclops and Major Fragments of Greek Satyric Drama*. Oxford: Oxford University Press.

Pechstein, Nicholas. 1998. *Euripides Satyrographos: ein Kommentar zu den Euripideischen Satyrspielfragmenten*. Stuttgart: Teubner.

Pohlenz, M. 1933. 'τὸ πρεπόν: Ein Beitrag zur Geschichte des griechischen Geistes'. *GGG* 16: 53–92.

Russell, Donald. 1981. *Criticism in Antiquity*. Berkeley: University of California Press.

Snell, Bruno. 1971. *Tragicorum Graecorum Fragmenta*, vol. 1. Göttingen: Vandenhoeck & Ruprecht.

Stinton, T. C. W. 1976. '*Si credere dignum est*: Some Expressions of Disbelief in Euripides and Others'. *Proceedings of the Cambridge Philological Society* 22: 60–89.

Sutton, Dana. 1981. 'Critias and Atheism'. *CQ* 31: 33–8.

Walsh, George. 1984. *The Varieties of Enchantment: Early Greek Views on the Nature and Function of Poetry*. Chapel Hill: University of North Carolina Press.

Whitmarsh, Tim. 2014. 'Atheistic Aesthetics'. *CCJ* 60: 109–26.

CHAPTER 8

The Whetstone of Love: Helen's Blemished Beauty

Dustin W. Dixon

John Lyly's *Euphues* (1578 CE) fabricates a detail of Helen's appearance: a scar on her chin, which, according to Lyly, Paris called a *cos amoris*.[1] Helen's so-called 'whetstone of love' appears in a list of historical and mythological exempla (Greek, Roman, Judeo-Christian) of physical imperfections and vices of character. 'In all perfect shapes', Lyly says, 'a blemish brings rather a liking every way to the eyes, than a loathing any way to the mind' (sig. B1r).[2] In Helen's case, this counterfactual loathing evokes the oldest traditions of her as an object of scorn and shame that do not need to be rehearsed here. Though Lyly seems to have invented this particular blemish that rids Helen of the perfect beauty that canonically defines her, he is not the first to imagine a Helen with physical imperfections.[3] This chapter explores this unorthodox tradition of Helen's appearance in classical antiquity.

Though it is a minor mythological variant, we find several instances of Helen depicted as a figure whose appearance, in some cases, is imperfect and, in others, could elicit disgust. Within this tradition, she is depicted with a small facial scar, or with a more prominent wound, or as wrinkled

---

1 This chapter has been informed by my work with Jeff and engagement with his scholarship, which began even before I was his student. In an undergraduate seminar on Aristophanes, I read his essay, 'Older Women in Attic Comedy', which led me to apply to the PhD program at Boston University. While I was studying drama with Jeff, he encouraged me to work on the fragments of tragedy and of comedy, and our conversations inspired my dissertation on mythological comedy. This chapter picks up some of those threads and returns to the final seminar I took with him, which explored the idea of fiction through a study of Euripides' *Helen* and Aristophanes' *Women at the Thesmophoria*.
2 Maguire (2009, 59–65) surveys the fascination with Helen's moles, dimples and eyebrows in post-classical literature. On Helen in Greek and Roman antiquity and beyond, see also Blondell (2013) and Edmunds (2016).
3 Nor is Lyly the last to imagine Helen's imperfections, which reappear, for instance, in C. S. Lewis's incomplete 'After Ten Years' and in Margaret Atwood's *The Penelopiad*.

in old age, or even as what the ancients would categorize as grotesque. As we will see, the ancient sources treat her blemished appearance differently from Lyly. Even in the unorthodox depictions of Helen in ancient literature and art, her blemishes do not, as Lyly would have it, sharpen her beauty but rather reinforce the canonical tradition that her beauty manifests a truly dangerous allure. And so those who are keen to upend traditional mythology by subverting Helen's most well-known feature nevertheless reinforce the upended myths in other ways. Even in the most extreme cases of a grotesque Helen, her ugliness does not subvert the canonical association of her appearance with danger.[4] The treatments of Helen's physical imperfections are more nuanced than such a straightforward subversion.[5] Through my exploration of this minor tradition, I will argue that Helen's blemished beauty invites audiences to recall – and to recoil from – the horrors of the Trojan War.

To begin from a pat articulation of ancient Greek views on how one's appearance reflects one's character, we can turn to Aristophanes' *Women at the Thesmophoria*.[6] The tragedian Agathon adapts a commonplace that male beauty signals positive characteristics (such as virility, virtue or intelligence), and he applies the idea to the production of poetry. Euripides' Kinsman proposes that the inverse must be true, too, so that ugliness suggests a defect of character (164–9):

ΑΓΑΘΩΝ	καὶ Φρύνιχος – τοῦτον γὰρ οὖν ἀκήκοας – αὐτός τε καλὸς ἦν καὶ καλῶς ἠμπίσχετο· διὰ τοῦτ' ἄρ' αὐτοῦ καὶ καλ' ἦν τὰ δράματα. ὅμοια γὰρ ποιεῖν ἀνάγκη τῇ φύσει.
ΚΗΔΕΣΤΗΣ	ταῦτ' ἄρ' ὁ Φιλοκλέης αἰσχρὸς ὢν αἰσχρῶς ποιεῖ, ὁ δὲ Ξενοκλέης ὢν κακὸς κακῶς ποιεῖ.
Agathon	And Phrynichus – you must have heard of him – was both beautiful and beautifully dressed. And that's why his plays were also beautiful. For as we are made, so must we compose.
Kinsman	That must be why the revolting Philocles writes so revoltingly, and the base Xenocles so basely …![7]

---

4 On treatments of Helen's canonical beauty, see Worman (1997).
5 On ugliness, and whether it is the opposite of beauty, see Rosenkranz (2015) and Eco (2007).
6 On beauty in the Greek imagination, see Konstan (2014).
7 Except where noted, translations of Aristophanes are from Henderson's Loebs; all others are my own. The text of the comic fragments follows *PCG*.

Though they are discussing qualities of poetry, the joke whimsically extends the notion that a beautiful man (καλός) is noble (καλός) and an ugly man (αἰσχρός, κακός) is base (αἰσχρός, κακός).[8]

The significance of the beauty of women, however, is more fraught, even paradoxical. While female beauty can signify qualities deemed valuable attributes of women, as Ruby Blondell notes, there was a 'pervasive fear that where character is concerned the most beautiful women will be not merely not the best, but the very worst'.[9] Pandora, a mythological predecessor of Helen, is made beautiful to trick the god Epimetheus in Zeus's initial step toward punishing mankind, and Hesiod succinctly captures the intrinsic paradox of women's beauty when he calls Pandora a καλὸν κακόν ('a beautiful bad', *Theogony* 585). Female beauty, desirability and danger are often mutually constitutive in the Greek imagination, and it is this very paradox that makes the minor tradition of Helen's imperfect beauty a compelling one to unpack. I do so by tracing this tradition of the blemished Helen backwards in the literary tradition. Analyzing the tradition in such a way happens to allow us to trace Helen's life backwards from death to birth: Helen in the underworld (Lucian's *Dialogues of the Dead* of the second century CE), aged Helen (Ovid's *Metamorphoses* of c. 8 CE), Helen's prime (Euripides' *Helen* of 412 BCE and Cratinus's *Dionysalexandros* of 430 or 429 BCE) and, in the end, Helen's birth (Cratinus's *Nemesis* of 431 BCE).[10] This reverse-chronological approach, both to the tradition and to Helen's life, brings to the surface an important aspect of my argument in this chapter: Helen's canonical beauty is teased more forcefully in comedy than by subsequent adaptors.

The Deceased and the Aged Helen

Imagining a Helen that scarcely appears in the classical Greek tradition that preferred to apotheosize the daughter of Zeus, Ovid's *Metamorphoses* (15.225–36) and Lucian's *Dialogues of the Dead* (5, featuring Menippus and Hermes) depict a Helen who ages, revealing how time mars the flesh of all mortals, even the most beautiful.

In Lucian's dialogue, Menippus, led on a tour of the underworld by Hermes, is keen to see beautiful men and women of the mythological past,

---

8 There are well-known exceptions to the idea that one's physical appearance corresponds to one's character. In the *Iliad*, for example, Nireus is very beautiful (κάλλιστος, *Il.* 2.673), second only to Achilles, but feeble (ἀλαπαδνός, *Il.* 2.675), and Hector chides his brother Paris for his lack of courage despite his exceptional beauty (*Il.* 3.39–45).

9 Blondell (2013, 3); see also Konstan (2014, 72–80).

10 On these dates for the *Dionysalexandros* and for the *Nemesis*, see Bianchi (2016, 207–10) and Godolphin (1931), respectively. Storey (2006, 114–16) argues that the *Dionysalexandros* was produced in 437 or 436.

but now these are nothing but skulls and bones. At the end of their brief exchange that centers on the deceased Helen, Hermes compares her beauty to that of a flower (*Dial. mort.* 5.2):

> ἐπεὶ καὶ τὰ ἄνθη ξηρὰ ὄντα εἴ τις βλέποι ἀποβεβληκότα τὴν βαφήν, ἄμορφα δῆλον ὅτι αὐτῷ δόξει, ὅτε μέντοι ἀνθεῖ καὶ ἔχει τὴν χρόαν, κάλλιστά ἐστιν.

> Since, if one sees even flowers that are withered and have cast off their color, they obviously will seem to him to be disfigured (ἄμορφα); when, however, they bloom and have their hue, they are most beautiful (κάλλιστα).

The analogy confronts the reader with the impossibility of describing what Helen really looked like. Defying description, her indeterminate, incomparable beauty can only be gestured toward, paradoxically, through comparisons such as this one, and Helen's mythological beauty is brought into reality through analogy to a familiar, common object.[11] While the exceeding beauty (κάλλιστα) is surely the strongest point of comparison between Helen and the flower, by evoking the flower's disfigured (ἄμορφα) state, Lucian invites his audience to consider Helen's current condition as a pile of bones in similar terms.

The transience of Helen's beauty is unusual but suits the moralizing tone of the dialogue. Earlier in the conversation, when Hermes identifies the beautiful men and women of the mythological past, Menippus protests: 'I see only bones and skulls that are bare of flesh, all of them the same' (ὀστᾶ μόνα ὁρῶ καὶ κρανία τῶν σαρκῶν γυμνά, ὅμοια τὰ πολλά, 5.1). With the macabre pun on γυμνά, both 'bare' and 'nude', Menippus unwittingly sees Helen naked, but death and time have rendered her nudity unappealing and equal to that of everyone else (ὅμοια τὰ πολλά). Menippus, therefore, cannot identify Helen's bones, and Hermes picks up a skull and asserts, 'This very skull is Helen' (τουτὶ τὸ κρανίον ἡ Ἑλένη ἐστίν, 5.1). Hermes' confidence is unfounded but, at the same time, succinctly recapitulates Menippus's frustration at his inability to tell Helen apart from the others. It does not matter which skull Hermes picks up and claims to be Helen, because they are all, in their current ugly (ἄμορφα) state, the same. By showing that the beauty for which Helen continues to be known is merely fleeting and, in the end, equal to that of all mortals, the dialogue moralizes about the vanity of the living.

Hermes' identification of Helen's skull prompts Menippus to ponder the great loss of life for the sake of bones. He asks, 'And therefore on

---

11 See Maguire (2009, 35–82) on the challenges of depicting and describing Helen's beauty.

account of this [Helen's skull] were the thousand ships filled from all of Greece and so many fell, Greeks as well as foreigners, and so many cities were overturned?' (εἶτα διὰ τοῦτο αἱ χίλιαι νῆες ἐπληρώθησαν ἐξ ἁπάσης τῆς Ἑλλάδος καὶ τοσοῦτοι ἔπεσον Ἕλληνές τε καὶ βάρβαροι καὶ τοσαῦται πόλεις ἀνάστατοι γεγόνασιν; 5.2). Menippus contemplates the devastation of the Trojan War fought, in his formulation, not for a woman but for a thing (τοῦτο). Menippus's use of this neuter demonstrative to refer to the skull, rather than a feminine demonstrative to refer to Helen, almost projects her current disfigurement onto the past and overlooks her reputed beauty. The setting of the underworld, where he is surrounded by the bones of Helen and those who died at Troy (Achilles and Nireus are singled out), makes Menippus's disbelief even more poignant. The bones attest to the devastation wrought for the sake of Helen's beauty that, as he can see with his own eyes, is ephemeral.

It is a question that scrutinizes the traditional values of the mythological past, but I read in Menippus's scrutiny a confirmation of those very values. Menippus certainly upholds the notion that female beauty presents a dangerous allure to men. More provocatively, by referring to Helen's skull, his question implies that the disfigured do not merit such loss of life while he makes no such protest about dying for the beautiful. Therefore, his question serves to tie a war's worth to the appearance of the women for which it is fought. Beauty signifies that the danger a man undergoes merits the risk. By the unspoken logic of Menippus's questions, Helen's perfect beauty would be worth marshaling the massive forces of Greece against those of Troy. Hermes' rebuttal, which includes the floral analogy quoted above, confirms this reading: 'But you did not see the woman living, Menippus, for even you would say that there is no culpability "in suffering a long time for this woman"' (5.2). Hermes' selective quotation of the Trojan elders in the *Iliad* (3.157), who then presently change their minds (3.159–60), leaves unresolved whether only an immortal god should so esteem something ephemeral.

Ovid's depiction of Helen in her old age contemplating her own diminished beauty strikes a similar note. The scene comes in the final book of Ovid's *Metamorphoses* in the account of Pythagoras's teachings about the nature of the cosmos and its intrinsic mutability. Arguing that cosmic flux ensnares the bodies of human beings, he cites the aging of Helen as an example (15.232–6):

'flet quoque, ut in speculo rugas adspexit aniles,
Tyndaris et secum, cur sit bis rapta, requirit.
tempus edax rerum, tuque, invidiosa vetustas,
omnia destruitis vitiataque dentibus aevi
paulatim lenta consumitis omnia morte!'

'Helen weeps, too, when she observes the wrinkles of an old woman in the mirror, and she asks herself why she was abducted twice. Time, the devourer of things, and you, jealous age, weaken everything and you consume everything, mutilated by the teeth of time, in tenacious death.'

Ovid's *Metamorphoses*, uniquely of the accounts discussed in this chapter, offers us Helen's own perspective on her changed appearance, and this melancholy tableau could be read within the long tradition of storytelling more sympathetic to Helen.[12] And yet she finds common ground with Lucian's Menippus. She sees in her wrinkled flesh not the wisdom of time, but loss, and the expression of loss invites consideration of the worth of her beauty and the danger it poses. Her wrinkled appearance recalls, for her, her two abductions, at the hands of Theseus and, more famously, of Paris. This elision of her beauty's disappearance and Paris's seizing her subtly evokes the Trojan War, already looming in the background after it was recounted earlier in the epic. With the war evoked, the apostrophe of time and age, whose all-encompassing obliteration is reinforced by the repetition *omnia … omnia*, suggests not only Helen's surely impending death but also all destruction of the past. Thus Ovid's retrospective look at Helen's vanished beauty gestures toward the ineffable loss of so many Greeks and Trojans for the sake of her appearance.

The Defaced Helen

Turning now to our texts from fifth-century Attic drama (Cratinus's *Nemesis* and *Dionysalexandros*, Euripides' *Helen*), we do not find canonical version of myths about Helen, but we do enter the canonical temporality of her story: her birth, her abduction by Paris and the aftermath of the war. What I find audacious about these dramas is that they do not treat Helen's beauty retrospectively, as Lucian and Ovid do; instead, they depict Helen as having physical imperfections in the time of her life when her beauty is canonically idealized.

We continue our study backwards through Helen's life with Euripides' *Helen*, a play that engages traditional representations of her by reimagining a Helen who spent the war in Egypt while a copy of her went to Troy.[13] *Helen* depicts the titular heroine in Egypt after the war, her husband Menelaus unwittingly discovering her there and their plotting to flee the Egyptian king Theoclymenus. The first line of the prologue, 'These beautiful-maiden streams of the Nile' (Νείλου μὲν αἴδε καλλιπάρθενοι ῥοαί, *Hel*. 1), establishes

---

12 See Austin (1994).
13 On the tradition of Helen's copy, see Wright (2005, 56–157) and Allan (2008, 18–28).

both the setting and the theme of beauty (κάλλος) and serves, in the words of Eric Downing, as 'the engine to the traditional story about Helen'.[14] On Charles Segal's influential reading of the play, Helen's beauty 'mediates between the epistemological and the ethical themes, illusion and war. It signifies ... a promise of happiness in a strange and violent world'.[15]

I draw attention to the double of Helen's beauty, her potentially dangerous monstrosity, as a theme that subtends the play's exploration of her beauty and its consequences.[16] Helen herself introduces the idea of her monstrosity when she recounts the details of her birth (256–9):

ἆρ' ἡ τεκοῦσά μ' ἔτεκεν ἀνθρώποις τέρας;
γυνὴ γὰρ οὔθ' Ἑλληνὶς οὔτε βάρβαρος
τεῦχος νεοσσῶν λευκὸν ἐκλοχεύεται,
ἐν ᾧ με Λήδαν φασὶν ἐκ Διὸς τεκεῖν.

Did the woman who bore me bear a monstrosity for men? For neither Greek nor foreign women produce a white vessel for chicks, in which they say Leda bore me from Zeus.[17]

The opening rhetorical question has a grammatical ambiguity, so that τέρας ('monstrosity') could serve as a predicate accusative (thus, 'Did the woman who bore me bear me as a monstrosity for men?') or, as I have rendered it here, the direct object of the main verb. Though the next sentence suggests the latter reading, the momentary ambiguity begins to associate Helen herself with monstrosity. The noun τέρας, with its subtle association with an image or spectacle, and the evocation of color (λευκόν, white) invite the audience to visualize the egg.[18] While Cratinus's comedy *Nemesis* brings the egg onstage as an outrageously large (and surely funny) prop, in Euripides' tragedy Helen's description of her birth projects her own disgust and horror onto the egg, a monstrous object that reifies the danger of her beauty.[19] Her ominous description of the impossibility of her birth from an egg, in fact, serves to forbode the danger that she knows she has posed to both Greeks (Ἑλληνίς) and foreigners (βάρβαρος). The noun τεῦχος reinforces

14 Downing (1990, 2).
15 Segal (1971, 569).
16 Jendza (2020, 140–6) discusses Menelaus's ugliness and Helen's beauty in *Helen*.
17 Diggle's OCT suggests deleting 257–9, but Allan (2008, *ad* 257–9), to my mind rightly, defends their retention. Here, I follow Diggle's ordering of the lines, which Kovacs's Loeb rearranges so that line 256 comes after 259.
18 Gorgias (*Hel.* 16) and Aristotle (*Poet.* 1453b) associate τέρας and its cognates with sight.
19 Henderson (2013, 246) notes the parallel between Cratinus's *Nemesis* and Euripides' *Helen* and suggests that Euripides uses the story of Helen's birth from an egg as an antitype to explore the fictiveness of myth.

the point, as it can refer to a hollow container but also to the machinery of war, as it does frequently in epic and in tragedy.[20] The following line, 'For my life and affairs are a monstrosity (τέρας)' (260), completes Helen's projection, and she goes on to wish that an uglier appearance (αἴσχιον εἶδος) were exchanged for her beauty (ἀντὶ τοῦ καλοῦ, 263).

While Helen's anxiety about the war has been transferred anachronistically to the egg from which she was born, its monstrosity manifests in Helen herself later in the play when she fulfils her wish to take on a different appearance. When Helen plots with her husband Menelaus to escape Egypt, she plans to change her dress and mar her face in the guise of mourning (1087–9):

ἐγὼ δ' ἐς οἴκους βᾶσα βοστρύχους τεμῶ
πέπλων τε λευκῶν μέλανας ἀνταλλάξομαι
παρῇδί τ' ὄνυχα φόνιον ἐμβαλῶ †χροός†.

After I go into the house, I will cut my hair, exchange my white peplos for a black one and launch bloody nails in my cheek.

Though it would be too strong to claim that Helen symbolically becomes the egg here, she dons its monstrous danger. The white (λευκῶν) peplos that she wears evokes the color of the egg (τεῦχος νεοσσῶν λευκὸν, 258). Though it is perhaps, admittedly, a tenuous connection after more than 800 lines, this passage confirms that the peplos she wears is white, and so a visual link between Helen and the egg is forged when she mentions its color. She also echoes the martial language (τεῦχος or 'vessel') used in the circumlocution for the egg by couching her plan to scratch her face in starkly violent terms (φόνιον means 'bloody' and 'murderous'; ἐμβαλῶ carries connotations of a military assault).[21] Her costuming is a blitz.

Upon her return to the stage in this new costume, we see the full transfer of the monstrosity of the egg onto the otherwise innocent, real Helen. In her plan to flee, Helen (re)appropriates her mythological persona that had been assumed by the phantom, as she now poses a danger to another male foreigner, this time Theoclymenus. Her disfigurement here is not simply part of a disguise that will allow her to deceive her warden and suitor but also symbolizes the consequences of men's attempts to safeguard and to control her sexuality, which Helen now controls herself. We see here an example of Henderson's distinction between women in tragedy and in comedy: 'In tragedy, as in myth generally, the female world is typically portrayed as a

---

20 For example, Hom. *Il.* 4.222, *Od.* 24.498; Soph. *Aj.* 572; Eur. *Andr.* 617.
21 Extending the image, the next choral ode (1107–64) recounts the destruction of the Trojan War.

threat to the men's: women are essentially wild (the Amazons are paradigmatic) and must be tamed in the interest of civilization (defined as male).'²² In the destruction of her own beauty, we find, surely, liberation for Helen and, at the same time, the imagined wildness of women so threatening to male social order. This is the paradox of Helen's beauty, her καλὸν κακόν, as Euripides depicts a Helen whose evil bubbles to the surface through her manipulation and reappropriation of her beauty.²³

The Ugly Helen

Comedy weds the canonical myths of Helen and this alternative tradition of a blemished heroine, though the comic poets offer a more radical and unadulterated version of this trope than those we have seen thus far. I suggest that they are more radical insofar as the Helen of traditional myths appears in the comic costume (a grotesque masque and padded suit). The beauty of comedy's Helen has not been lost to time, as in Ovid and Lucian, nor has it been sacrificed for an elaborate plot, as in Euripides. Rather, her beauty never existed.²⁴

As the hypothesis to the *Dionysalexandros* attests, Cratinus has repurposed a myth about the origins of the Trojan War to criticize Periclean belligerence as the principal cause of the Peloponnesian War (test. i.44–8).²⁵ The hypothesis suggests that this topical content was subsumed under the

---

22 Henderson (2010, 28).
23 Aristophanes' *Women at the Thesmophoria* seems to gesture toward Helen's reappropriation of her beauty when the Kinsman, now playing the role of Helen from Euripides' *Helen*, expresses shame about his appearance: αἰσχύνομαί σε τὰς γνάθους ὑβρισμένη ('I feel shame – for the violation of my jowls', 903). Here, the Kinsman cleverly mocks both his own chin, which he had shaved as part of his disguise, and, likely, Helen's defacement in Euripides' play.
24 It may be objected that the costumes of comedy are conventional and so no special significance should be deduced. On this debate, see the essays by Winkler (1990) and Foley (2000) as well as Revermann (2006, 146–59) on comic ugliness. I note also that the mimetic dynamics of the mythological plays under consideration here differ from the parodies of tragedy in, for example, Aristophanes' *Women at the Thesmophoria*. In Euripides' attempted rescues of his Kinsman that parody Euripidean tragedy, the rescue *qua* metatheatrical *mise en scène* fails, in part, because it is a *mise en scène*. The Kinsman fails to become Helen. As Zeitlin (1981, 314) has argued, '[I]n the parody, the theatrical confusion lies in the refusal to allow the same character/actor to bear more than one name …'. In Cratinus's mythological comedies, however, the actors adopt the mythological characters as their primary identity, and so the theatrical illusion casts an actor as Helen. On the issues of actors, characters and identities in antiquity, see Easterling (2002) and Duncan (2006), and on Helen and theatrical illusion specifically, see Bassi (2000) and Dixon and Garrison (2021, 47–66).
25 'In the drama, Pericles is mocked (κωμῳδεῖται) very persuasively through innuendo (δι' ἐμφάσεως) for bringing the war upon the Athenians' (test. i.44–8). On the

mythological plot. The title *Dionysalexandros* gives away the major innovation: Dionysus plays the part of Paris both in judging the beauty contest of the three goddesses and in abducting Helen (test. i.20–3). After the abduction, Dionysus takes Helen back to Ida, and when the Greeks come looking for her, he hides Helen in a basket and disguises himself as a ram (test. i.25–33). The god causes so much trouble that the Prince of Troy intervenes in the play's denouement.

Though the fragments provide frustratingly little supplement to the hypothesis's precis, it attests to the play's interest in difference, identity and appearance. Whether the goddesses are aware that Dionysus, not Paris, judges the contest, the disparity between the canonically beautiful Paris and the comically grotesque Dionysus is underscored by Aphrodite's unusual bribe. He is so hideous that she bribes him not with Helen, the usual bribe, but promises to make him 'very beautiful and desirable' (κάλλιστόν τε καὶ ἐπέραστον, 17–18).[26] For their part, the goddesses of the beauty pageant likely appeared in grotesque form as well. The characters in the play exemplify ancient comedy's tendency toward what Michael Silk has called the 'recreative' nature of Aristophanic characters, who tend to 'enjoy some relationship with "reality", but a less straightforward one than the mimetic relationship implied by "reality"'.[27] Cratinus treats characters who are all, save the chorus of Satyrs, canonically beautiful in mythological 'reality', but the play recreates them as ugly not in a fictional plot but rather in the context of a canonical myth, the Judgment of Paris.

So the play's interest in beauty makes the final scene described in the hypothesis particularly interesting. After Paris tracks down Dionysus and Helen, he intends to surrender the pair to the Greeks. Instead (test. i.37–9):

ὀκνούσης δ(ὲ) τῆς Ἑλένη(ς) ταύτην μ(ὲν) οἰκτείρας ὡς γυναῖχ' ἕξων ἐπικατέχ(ει)

When Helen hesitates, he pities her and takes her as his wife.

Our comic lovers depart from the motivations of their epic counterparts. Part of the humor surely lies in the inversion of their canonical beauty and in the couple's willingness, despite appearances, to marry.[28] The comic

Dionysalexandros generally, see recently Bakola (2010, *passim*), Storey (2011, 284–7) and Bianchi (2016, 198–301).

26 See recently Sells (2019, 99–102) on how erotic beauty drives the plot of the *Dionysalexandros*.
27 Silk (2000, 221). See also Taaffe (2014, 54): 'plot, character, and text all indicate that "woman" is primarily a mimetic construct'.
28 Compton-Engle (2015, 28–45) offers an excellent survey of the evidence for staging men's and women's bodies onstage, and she notes that not all comic characters wear

costume humorously upends the trope of the bride's beauty, traditional even in Greek antiquity. Less humorous, it seems, but more puzzling is the stated motivation of Paris: he is not enraptured by Helen's beauty but moved by pity (ταύτην ... οἰκτείρας, 38).[29] Perhaps it is precisely because Helen appears in grotesque costume, cleaved from her canonical beauty, that Paris's motivations differ.

The audience may or may not have shared Paris's pity, but, as we have seen, Euripides and Ovid portray a sympathetic Helen who, nevertheless, is indivisible from the destruction of Troy. Cratinus, too, was capable of such nuance, and his selection of myth is particularly evocative in light of this tradition of a blemished Helen. We can detect in the play's ending a Lucianic matrix of humor and the grotesque, joy and death that, as Mario Telò shows, is not foreign to the dynamics of fifth-century comedy.[30] There is humor in the reversals of canonical beauty. Joy in the imminent wedding. Grotesque in the comic costume. Death in the war, both the Trojan War that is also now imminent and the Peloponnesian War that Cratinus satirized. Indeed, as the allegorical readings of the *Dionysalexandros* remind us, the comedians assimilated the Trojan War to the Peloponnesian War, whose outbreaks share, in the comic treatment, a *casus belli*: the abduction of women.[31] In Matthew Wright's assessment, the comic poets played a part in developing the myths of the Trojan War as 'a symbol of the concept of problematic causation' of war in the fifth century.[32] We can also propose, in light of the tradition of Helen's blemished beauty, a new significance to Cratinus's selection of Helen's abduction as subject of his play. This myth is particularly concerned with control of Helen's beauty, but the audience of the *Dionysalexandros* see an ugly version of Helen. When Dionysus abducts her, her reputation for beauty is upended by her grotesque mask. Her padded costume would invite the audience to question the worthiness of an assault when the Greeks invade to take her back. And just as the monstrous egg of Euripides' *Helen* serves as a warning, so the bride's grotesque mask and padded costume embody the danger of the union to Paris and

---

grotesque costumes onstage. Vase-paintings, however, do depict a Helen in the traditional padded suit of the comic stage (Apulian bell-krater, 375–350 BCE, Bari, Mus. Arch. 8014; Apulian bell-krater, 370–350 BCE, Matera, Mus. Naz. 9579).

29 Finglass (2016) notes that Paris's pity in the *Dionysalexandros* has been largely overlooked in scholarly criticism.
30 Telò (2020).
31 Compare Aristophanes' *Acharnians* (515–39), evoking Herodotus's rationalizing account of the abduction of women as the cause of the Trojan War (1.1–5). On my reading of the evidence, many of these interpretations push the allegorical nature of Cratinus's play too far. I am more convinced by the limited allegorical reading of Bakola (2010, 181–208) than by the reading of Schwarze (1971, 6–24), who sees allegory everywhere.
32 Wright (2007, 413).

are a harbinger of the carnage that invariably stalks the joy of this day. It is the difference between the beautiful Helen familiar to the audience and the comic, grotesque Helen that would give spectators pause. That Paris has already seen the great lengths to which the Greeks would go to take Helen back from Dionysus reinforces the ephemerality of whatever joy comes from his decision to marry her. Though Helen has lost her beauty, war will come.

Cratinus's intervention in the traditional depictions of Helen is thrown into relief by the poet's own *Nemesis*. Like the *Dionysalexandros*, this comedy seems to have lampooned Periclean warmongering within the ostensibly mythological plot of Helen's conception and birth.[33] It also seems to have treated Helen as a κακὸν καλόν. In the play, Zeus transforms into a swan to trick the goddess Nemesis into having sexual intercourse, Nemesis bears an egg that is given to Leda to incubate and hatch, and Helen is born from it. Cratinus thus follows the tradition of the *Cypria* that makes Nemesis, rather than Leda, Helen's mother.[34] Making the goddess of retribution her mother cements Helen as a potential evil. Making her the child of an avian Zeus and a female goddess engenders her monstrous hybridity.

My reading focuses on one of the several fragments of the *Nemesis* that allow a glimpse at this comedy in ways that the fragments of the *Dionysalexandros* do not. Cratinus's play, even as it foreshadows Helen's future danger, expresses great joy for her birth. Hermes advises Leda on the incubation (fr. 115):[35]

Λήδα, σὸν ἔργον· δεῖ σ' ὅπως εὐσχήμονως
ἀλεκτρυόνος μηδὲν διοίσεις τοὺς τρόπους,
ἐπὶ τῷδ' ἐπῴζουσ', ὡς ἂν ἐκλέψῃς καλὸν
ἡμῖν τι καὶ θαυμαστὸν ἐκ τοῦδ' ὄρνεον.

Leda, your task: you must not differ from the practices of a graceful hen, clucking over this, so that you might hatch for us a beautiful and marvelous chick from it.

The gruff σὸν ἔργον ('your task'), which Bakola identifies as paratragic,[36] conveys the weight of the assignment, though it is surely worth the promise of a καλόν ('beautiful') and θαυμαστόν ('marvelous') offspring. Here, Cratinus offers his audience yet another metamorphosis and deception in a

---

33 The pursuit of topical references is encouraged by the setting of the play in Sparta and an assimilation of Zeus to Pericles in fr. 118.
34 See Henderson (2012, 2–7) on the mythological background and Cratinus's treatment of the myth.
35 I follow Henderson (2012, 7) on attributing this fragment to Hermes.
36 Bakola (2010, 170).

comedy devoted to these themes. The incubation requires a transformation of Leda's temperament as she must perform the role of a bird to incubate the egg. The deception comes in Hermes' claim that the egg will bear something 'beautiful'; because the adjective's noun, 'bird' (ὄρνεον), is delayed to the last word of the next line, the hyperbaton winks ironically at those in the audience who know their myths of Helen. A beautiful hatchling, yes, but not a bird. This divine deception is reminiscent of the gifting of Pandora to mortals.

The egg evocatively exemplifies myth's ability to move between the tragic and the comic modes. While Euripides introduces the egg as a monstrous object of shame for Helen, Cratinus brings it onstage as an absurd prop.[37] The demonstrative pronouns (τῷδ', τοῦδ') indicate that the egg appears onstage, and a vase-painting, whose visual cues align with the known details of Cratinus's play, captures the absurdity of staging Helen's hatching.[38] No gods are present, and we can see Helen emerging from an egg and looking at a man and a woman, very likely her mortal adoptive parents Leda and Tyndareus. A blanket around the egg suggests a human, rather than avian, mode of incubation. The low platform is the stage. Admittedly, the actor playing Helen – was it a child actor or an adult actor? – does not appear to be wearing the traditional comic garb, and so she may not, truly, be an example of a blemished Helen.[39]

Regardless, like the other accounts discussed in this chapter, this play blends beauty and grotesqueness, and the scene on the vase expresses a subtle pessimism about futures born from ephemeral delight. The rollicking scene of Helen's birth afforded an opportunity for physical humor that would rival anything we find in Aristophanes' preserved comedies. Tyndareus whacks an egg with an axe. A nervous Leda looks on. A slave gestures to stop. Helen emerges. The scene must have been hilarious, enthralling, frenetic, joyous. There is danger, however, as well, but it looms for Helen. As Tyndareus wields the axe and is poised to strike the egg once more, the figure on the right holds his hand up in warning. I interpret this to mean that Tyndareus is recoiling from his last, successful attempt to crack the egg, and when it hatches unexpectedly, the slave alerts him not to let the axe fall again. The vase-painting, however, also depicts a kind of suppressed desire in its threat to Helen: one more fall of the axe would forestall much suffering for so many Greeks and foreigners. Might someone in

---

37 On Cratinus's large props, including the egg, see Bakola (2010, 239–42).
38 Apulian bell-krater, 380–370 BCE, Bari, Mus. Naz. 3899. On the vase, see Walsh (2009, 135–7). Sells (2019, 53–88) discusses the iconography of humorous vases such as this one.
39 We can compare the depiction of an unmasked, young figure, who is probably Achilles, in a comic scene depicting the centaur Chiron on an Apulian bell-krater (c. 380–370 BCE, London, British Museum 1849,0620.13).

the audience not have been tempted to stand up and yell, 'One more time, Tyndareus!'? Would that have been said in jest?

Cratinus's *Nemesis* thus domesticates Helen's threat that the *Dionysalexandros* makes Panhellenic. The King and Queen of Sparta incubate an egg about whose contents the gods have lied. The Prince of Troy, out of pity, chooses a marriage that will engage his city in a war with the Greeks. In both plays, there are ominous warnings about the danger she poses, both in the plot but also in encoding that danger within the visual signs of the unusual and the grotesque.

I do not want to convey, however, that the comedies of Helen were so overtly dour. There is no reason to suspect that the tone of the *Dionysalexandros* and the *Nemesis* were similar to that of the melancholy aged Helen in Ovid's *Metamorphoses*, though we may suspect affinities with Lucian's dialogue of Hermes and Menippus. Instead, I find the patterns of associating even a blemished Helen with danger – whether in comedy, epic or satire – suggestive. In particular, while Cratinus's treatment of Helen seems to have reinforced the tradition that views her as another Pandora, the costuming conventions of comedy almost demand engagement with and reimagining the Hesiodic paradox of female beauty and the complicated Greek views of physiognomy. Cratinus does not simply invert the standard by treating her as a κακὸν κακόν ('ugly evil'), nor do, for that matter, Euripides, Ovid or Lucian. Rather, Cratinus crafts a Helen who could embody καλὸν κακόν in various ways. Does she embody 'a beautiful bad', 'a noble abomination', 'an evil beauty' or 'an ugly nobility'? Cratinus reimagines καλὸν κακόν in his recreation of Helen into an ugly body, one that, nevertheless, reinscribes, even as it may tease, the ideologies of misogyny reflected in her canonical, perfect, gendered beauty. The mythological tradition with its panoply of variants holds more tenaciously to Helen as an avatar of danger and as a symbol of the Trojan War's ruin than it does her beauty.[40] Though her charms are thought to be temporary, no matter how ugly or monstrous or time-worn Helen is, she still beguiles menacingly.

Works Cited

Allan, William. 2008. *Euripides: Helen*. Cambridge: Cambridge University Press.
Austin, Norman. 1994. *Helen of Troy and Her Shameless Phantom*. Ithaca, NY: Cornell University Press.
Bakola, E. 2010. *Cratinus and the Art of Comedy*. Oxford: Oxford University Press.

---

40 Cf. Edmunds (2016, 193): '[T]he power of Helen, if she has any, does not come from her beauty.'

Bassi, Karen. 2000. 'The Somatics of the Past: Helen and the Body of Tragedy'. In *Acting on the Past: Historical Performance Across the Disciplines*, edited by Mark Franko and Annette Richards, 13–34. Hanover: Wesleyan University Press.
Bianchi, Francesco Paolo. 2016. *Kratinos*, vol. 2. Heidelberg: Verlag Antike.
Blondell, Ruby. 2013. *Helen of Troy: Beauty, Myth, Devastation*. Oxford: Oxford University Press.
Casolari, Federica. 2003. *Die Mythentravestie in der griechischen Komödie*. Münster: Aschendorff.
Compton-Engle, Gwendolyn. 2015. *Costume in the Comedies of Aristophanes*. Cambridge: Cambridge University Press.
Diggle, James. 1981–94. *Euripidis Fabulae*, 3 vols. Oxford: Oxford University Press.
Dixon, Dustin W., and John S. Garrison. 2021. *Performing Gods in Classical Antiquity and the Age of Shakespeare*. London: Bloomsbury Academic.
Downing, Eric. 1990. 'Apatê, Agôn, and Literary Self-Reflexivity in Euripides' *Helen*'. In *Cabinet of the Muses: Essays on Classical and Comparative Literature in Honor of Thomas G. Rosenmeyer*, edited by Mark Griffith and Donald J. Mastronarde, 1–16. Atlanta: Scholars Press.
Duncan, Anne. 2006. *Performance and Identity in the Classical World*. Cambridge: Cambridge University Press.
Easterling, Patricia. 2002. 'Actor as Icon'. In *Greek and Roman Actors: Aspects of an Ancient Profession*, edited by Pat Easterling and Edith Hall, 327–41. Cambridge: Cambridge University Press.
Eco, Umberto. 2007. *On Ugliness*, translated by A. McEwen. New York: Rizzoli.
Edmunds, Lowell. 2016. *Stealing Helen: The Myth of the Abducted Wife in Comparative Perspective*. Princeton: Princeton University Press.
Finglass, Patrick. 2016. 'The Pity of Paris: Cratinus' *Dionysalexandros*'. *Eikasmos* 27: 93–9.
Foley, Helene P. 2000. 'The Comic Body in Greek Art and Drama'. In *Not the Classical Ideal: Athens and the Construction of the Other in Greek Art*, edited by Beth Cohen, 275–311. Leiden and Boston: Brill.
Godolphin, F. R. B. 1931. 'The *Nemesis* of Cratinus'. *CP* 26: 423–6.
Henderson, Jeffrey. 1998–2002. *Aristophanes*, 4 vols. Cambridge, MA: Harvard University Press.
———. 2010. *Three Plays by Aristophanes: Staging Women*, 3rd edn. New York and London: Routledge.
———. 2012. 'Pursuing Nemesis: Cratinus and Mythological Comedy'. In *No Laughing Matter: New Studies in Old Comedy*, edited by C. W. Marshall and George Kovacs, 1–12. London: Bloomsbury.
———. 2013. 'Comic Scenes in Greek Tragedy'. In *The Encyclopedia of Greek Tragedy*, vol. 1, edited by Hanna M. Roisman, 245–8. Malden, MA: Wiley-Blackwell.
Jendza, Craig. 2020. *Paracomedy: Appropriations of Comedy in Greek Tragedy*. Oxford: Oxford University Press.
Kassel, Rudolf, and Colin Austin. 1983–. *Poetae Comici Graeci*, 8 vols. Berlin: De Gruyter.

Konstan, David. 2014. *Beauty: The Fortunes of an Ancient Greek Idea*. Oxford: Oxford University Press.

Maguire, Laurie. 2009. *Helen of Troy: From Homer to Hollywood*. Malden, MA: Wiley-Blackwell.

Nesselrath, Heinz-Günther. 1990. *Die attische mittlere Komödie: ihre Stellung in der antiken Literaturkritik und Literaturgeschichte*. Berlin: De Gruyter.

Revermann, Martin. 2006. *Comic Business: Theatricality, Dramatic Technique, and Performance Contexts of Aristophanic Comedy*. Oxford: Oxford University Press.

Rosenkranz, Karl. 2015. *Aesthetics of Ugliness: A Critical Edition*, edited and translated by A. Pop and M. Widrich. London: Bloomsbury.

Schwarze, Joachim. 1971. *Die Beurteilung des Perikles durch die attische Komödie und ihre historische und historiographische Bedeutung*. Munich: C. H. Beck'sche.

Segal, Charles. 1971. 'The Two Worlds of Euripides' *Helen*'. *TAPA* 102: 553–614.

Sells, Donald. 2019. *Parody, Politics and the Populace in Greek Old Comedy*. London: Bloomsbury Academic.

Silk, Michael S. 2000. *Aristophanes and the Definition of Comedy*. Oxford: Oxford University Press.

Solmsen, Friedrich, R. Merkelbach and Martin West. 1990. *Hesiodi Theogonia, Opera et Dies, Scutum, Fragmenta Selecta*. Oxford: Clarendon Press.

Storey, Ian. 2006. 'On First Looking into Kratinos' *Dionysalexaandros*'. In *Playing Around Aristophanes*, edited by Lynn Kozak and John Rich, 105–25. Oxford: Aris and Phillips.

———. 2011. *Fragments of Old Comedy*, 3 vols. Cambridge, MA: Harvard University Press.

Taaffe, Lauren K. 2014. *Aristophanes and Women*. New York: Routledge.

Tarrant, Richard J. 2004. *Ovid: Metamorphoses*. Oxford: Oxford University Press.

Telò, Mario. 2020. 'Laughter, or Aristophanes' Joy in the Face of Death'. In *Aristophanic Humour: Theory and Practice*, edited by Peter Swallow and Edith Hall, 53–68. London: Bloomsbury Academic, 2020.

Walsh, David. 2009. *Distorted Ideals in Greek Vase-Painting: The World of Mythological Burlesque*. Cambridge: Cambridge University Press.

Wilson, Nigel G. 2007. *Aristophanis Fabulae*, 2 vols. Oxford: Oxford University Press.

Winkler, John J. 1990. 'Phallos Politikos: Representing the Body Politic in Athens'. *Differences* 2: 29–45.

Worman, Nancy. 1997. 'The Body as Argument: Helen in Four Greek Texts'. *CA* 16: 151–203.

Wright, Matthew. 2005. *Euripides' Escape-Tragedies: A Study of Helen, Andromeda and Iphigenia Among the Taurians*. Oxford: Oxford University Press.

———. 2007. 'Comedy and the Trojan War'. *CQ* 57: 412–31.

Zeitlin, Froma. 1981. 'Travesties of Gender and Genre in Aristophanes' *Thesmophoriazousae*'. *Critical Inquiry* 8: 301–27.

CHAPTER 9

Virginity and the Post-mortem State of the Body: Reading Mary and Hippolytus in Dialogue
Chris Synodinos

The purpose of this study is primarily to revisit the textual tradition of the *Transitus Mariae* with a view to reflecting upon aspects of changes of Mary's body in its state of perpetual virginity upon completion of her earthly life.[1] Mary's bodily changes reflected in the tradition of her dormition and assumption pertain to the mystical transformation of her body (1 Cor. 15:51). Her virginity is briefly discussed as a token of exemption from retribution in a Scriptural context and therefore as an agent of post-mortem incorruption. This essay then puts the figure of Mary in dialogue with representations of the Greek mythical hero Hippolytus, especially as he is represented in Euripides' play. Through the lens of the *Transitus Mariae*, Hippolytus's refusal to honor Aphrodite is discussed as hubristic behavior producing an adverse effect: the arousal of Nemesis exacting retribution by way of deformity in death.

It has been claimed that, seen from the perspective of the canonical gospels, the various apocrypha may show limited affinity to the way the myths of Greek drama relate to Greek philosophy – a case in point being the *Transitus Mariae* apocryphal prose. Mary's dormition is an event upon which there is unanimous agreement in the entire *Transitus* apocryphal literature. Mary's bodily changes in the tradition of her dormition and assumption relate now to a quasi-resurrectional state, now to a genuine resurrectional state of her post-mortem body. The assumption of Mary's body occurs in the *Transitus Mariae* as a concomitant event in favor of which only partial consensus has been reached in the pertinent apocryphal literature.

---

1 In the course of preparing my dissertation, which is a Latin patristic text, I received assistance of inestimable value from Professor Henderson, who displayed deep and extensive knowledge of patristic literature. I can never adequately express my gratitude to him for the generosity with which he shared his knowledge of patristics with me, a knowledge also reflected in his work as an editor of the Loeb's *The Apostolic Fathers*. Accordingly, my chapter reflects Professor Henderson's knowledge of patristics and has been inspired by it.

It has been contended that belief in the Virgin's bodily assumption arose as a corollary of her divine maternity, which is itself inextricably linked to her perpetual virginity – a fundamental conviction of the Early Church and central to major branches of today's mainstream Christianity. It is notable that human virginity, as an indelible mark of human nature before the Fall, is commonly shared by Christ, Mary and John the Evangelist, the only central figures in early Christian spirituality whose bodies in Scripture, tradition and legend respectively merited assumption and incorruptibility before the Judgment. It has been posited that John's virginity and purity of soul may have added credence to the legend of his assumption to await Christ's Judgment in heaven.[2] Mechthild of Magdeburg, the visionary and mystic of the thirteenth century, beholds John the Evangelist, the prince of virgins, in one of her revelations and testifies to the incorruptibility of his body, being 'spiritually buried in sleep but glowing like a fiery crystal' (Magdeburg 2.3.48). As regards Mary's chastity, on the other hand, she was a consecrated virgin at the Temple, which she entered in her infancy, being devoted by her mother to the service of the Lord. The fact that she was vowed to a life of perpetual virginity can be gleaned from the *Protoevangelium Jacobi*,[3] an apocryphon whose goal was, according to Quasten,[4] 'to prove the perpetual and inviolate virginity of Mary before, in, and after the birth of Christ'. This fact is likewise attested to, even if indirectly, by the canonical gospels (Luke 1:26-38). Mary's divine maternity carries the presupposition of her virginity as an implied necessity just as the economy of the redemption in Christ necessitates the presupposition of Mary's divine maternity. Accordingly, Mary's assumption as manifestation of her privileged sharing in the resurrection of Christ through her unique involvement in the economy of salvation is inextricably linked to her virginity, by which this salvific involvement is primarily qualified.

The dogma of the assumption of Mary was promulgated by the apostolic constitution *Munificentissimus Deus* on 1 November 1950 by Pius XII.[5] As regards theological research in support of this apostolic constitution, four investigators stand out: Frs M. Jugie, A. Wilmart, Dom B. Capelle and A. Wenger. Jugie's contribution in particular consisted in the publication of the two forms of John of Thessalonica's homily on the dormition of Mary, one establishing the short, or authentic, text of John's narrative (T), the other the longer, or interpolated version (T1).[6] The import of Jugie's publication

---

2 For the origin and textual sources of this legend, see Lefèvre (1954, 178 n. 4). All translations are mine unless otherwise stated.
3 Smid (1965, 8-9, 15).
4 Quasten (1983: 120-1).
5 O'Carroll (1983, 55).
6 Jugie (1926, 349-57, 375, 405). For the superiority of the interpolated version, see Wenger (1955, 20 n. 2) and *Capelle* (1940, 225-8).

rested, among other things,[7] on the fact that it offered the first critical edition of the second of the two witnesses that the Greek Church possesses on either the dormition or the dormition and the assumption of Mary, the first being that of ps.-John the Evangelist.[8] At the time of Jugie's publication, ps.-John the Evangelist and John of Thessalonica's homilies were thought to be connected.[9] This connection eventually proved incorrect due to Dom Wilmart's publication of a Latin *Transitus*,[10] the oldest Latin *Transitus* apocryphon known at that time.[11] Wilmart's apocryphon showed an obvious affinity with John of Thessalonica's T and T1 texts. Jean Rivière was the first to take note of this connection, albeit his view of the connection proved erroneous in that he made John of Thessalonica dependent on Wilmart's Latin apocryphon.[12] The dependence was eventually challenged by Dom Capelle. Capelle observed that MS *M*, one of the Latin *Transitus* witnesses entered in Wilmart's apparatus criticus, offered a text common to a number of other *Transitus* narratives and that it moreover featured additional elements of unknown provenance. A comparison of twenty characteristic variants entered in MS *M* of Wilmart's apparatus with recensions T and T1 of John of Thessalonica's text convinced Capelle that, although independent of one another, John's text, MS *M* and Wilmart's Latin *Transitus* were all derived from a common ancestor. This ancestor, which was Greek, not Latin, Capelle designated as Π (Π = πηγή, 'the source'), adding that it was eminently desirable for this text to be found.[13] Such a text – if not Π, at all events one answering closely Dom Capelle's description of the archetype – was at length located thanks to the assiduous labor of Fr. Wenger, who dubbed his newfound witness *R* and was additionally fortunate to discover an early Latin version of it, 'subsequent no doubt to *R*, yet antecedent of all the Latin witnesses of the text' hitherto known.[14] If *R* is not in fact Capelle's Π, it is at least, according to Wenger, a descendent of Π predating all the Latin versions and John of Thessalonica as well.[15]

The most diversified formal feature of the *R* texts, as well as of the other *Transitus* textual families collectively considered, is the epilogue, because of a steadily repeated structural element contained therein: as the account enters its final phase in the various apocryphal and homiletic

---

7 Wenger (1955, 22).
8 Wenger (1955, 17).
9 O'Carroll (1983, 59).
10 This is Transitus C in Clayton's stemma, which is an adapted version of Wenger's stemma; see Clayton (1990, 9–10).
11 Rivière (1936, 323–62).
12 Wenger (1955, 20).
13 Wenger (1955, 20–2).
14 Wenger (1955, 10, 22).
15 Wenger (1955, 22).

versions of the *Transitus* narratives, a number of recurrent motifs are variously interwoven around the theme of the separation of body and soul at life's end. These recurrent motifs, which are both theological and literary, form the dominant cluster of primary motifs, around which the *Transitus* narratives evolve. The primary motifs come in two varieties: leading primary and accessory primary motifs. Subordinate clusters of secondary motifs within these narratives gravitate to the dominant cluster. The variety of the primary motifs and the diverse ways in which they coalesce, augmented by the impact of subordinate clusters with secondary motifs, appear to account for the abundance of the *Transitus* narratives in the daunting proliferation of witnesses both of the same textual family and of the same recension of the source in which they occur. The leading primary motifs interwoven around the central theme of the soul's removal may be divided into two classes: I. (a) the soul is assumed to fly off by itself or (b) said to be taken to heaven; II. (a) the body is carried off to heaven before or after burial, or (b) interred and never spoken of again. If II(a), the body is translated to blessed realms, namely, heaven or paradise, and a number of accessory primary motifs occur, relating to the following tabulated headings:

1. agency whereby the transference is effected;
2. manner in which the transference is effected;
3. state of the body during transference;
4. time at which the transference is effected;
5. end for which the transference is effected;
6. place toward which the transference is directed.

The accessory primary motifs, which may be further designated as the adverbial relations of the body, combine variously in the narratives that contain them to reflect the dogmatic presuppositions of the monastic community or social milieu in which these narratives arise.

Specialists in biblical apocryphal literature have long postulated Egypt to be the country of provenance of the archetypal *Transitus* narrative.[16] As a rule, this contention is not elaborated further. Notwithstanding, in an erudite dissertation bearing on the soul's separation from the body in apocryphal literature and on the Egyptian motifs occurring therein, Louise Dudley has amply evinced the Egyptian provenance of a number of standard motifs commonly shared by her sources, including the narratives of the *Transitus Mariae*.[17] One highly likely point of contact between an archetypal *Transitus* narrative and Egyptian cultural elements (antecedent to the

---

16 James (1983, 194).
17 Dudley (1911, 18–24, 115–18, 135–9, 151).

conversion of Egypt, particularly in the Coptic recensions) is, for instance, the enshrouding of Mary's soul – a motif highly suggestive of the mummification process, as Dudley insightfully notes.[18] Additional motifs, shown by Dudley to be of Egyptian provenance, are the motifs of the 'refusal to die', of the 'angels by whom the soul is removed', the 'body-and-soul-speech' motif and the like.[19] Such common theological inheritance shared by pre-Christian and post-conversion Egypt, albeit observed predominantly in Marian studies, is not limited to Mary but likewise applies to the cases of Christ and the saints and to symbols as well. Wallis Budge commented upon the likelihood of dogmatic debates being fueled in early Christian Egypt by proselyte attempts to accommodate old native beliefs within the framework of the new confession.[20] The fact is that late antique Egypt had truly turned into a hotbed of amalgamation in religious thought – at least with regard to parts of Lower Egypt – as is evinced to some extent by the so-called epistle of Hadrian in the *Historia Augusta*. Some of the terms proposed for the syncretic processes afforded by the fluidity of the religious situation in Egypt in the first three centuries CE were 'function borrowing', 'cult adoption' and 'religious transference'.[21] Such designations appear to be valid for charting the paths of shared common ground between an old and a new set of religious beliefs in late antique Egypt. The Early Church itself would likely acquiesce to the use of such terms, construing them in reference to the principles of the *praeparatio evangelica*; to wit, the contention that the supreme being 'left not himself without witness' among mankind but by way of natural theology revealed to the early humans some salvific truths (Acts 14:17), the ultimate explication of which he deferred to future generations.[22] The notion of *praeparatio evangelica* would thus seem to encode a design universal in scope, transcending localities and implying that '[w]here ever it is accepted that Grace perfects nature but does not destroy it, we find Christianity sweeping up into its own orbit the rhythms of nature'.[23] Accordingly, function borrowing and religious transference would be construed within the scope of 'the fundamental relations between the archetypal myth and its ectypes'.[24] Ectypes (or variants on a pattern) of virginity that are parallel to Mary's virginity, for instance, could encompass intergender instances such as that of Hippolytus[25] – virginity being

---

18 Dudley (1911, 133 n. 16).
19 Dudley (1911, 18–24, 30–47, 104-10, 139–41).
20 Wallis Budge (1904, 2:220).
21 Higgins (2012, 71-2).
22 Cooper (1877, 3).
23 Sayers (1981, 84).
24 Sayers (1981, 84).
25 I am using Euripides' *Hippolytus* as the oldest extant full version of the legend of Hippolytus on record.

one archetypal way of striving to approximate the divine by endorsement of *hagneia* (ἁγνεία), a state reflected in chastity and in causing the arousal of divine awe.

In *hagneia*, and cognate words stemming from the same root, Greek shows the idea of holiness, grasped in a very broad sense.[26] The reference is to the notion of 'taboo' and its primary meaning, namely, that which arouses religious awe. Likewise, the root underlying *hagneia* and kindred words originally conveyed the idea of something striking religious awe into the mind and of the actual feeling aroused. Moreover, the same root denotes both something positive, inspiring awe, reverence and worship as well as something foul that excites abhorrence – and accordingly someone or something sullied with it.[27] Thus the adjective *hagnos* (ἁγνός) refers initially to one that inspires religious awe, that is taboo. In tragedy, the word is employed additionally in the sense of ritual purity achieved, for instance, through lack of defilement by bloodshed or sexual pollution. The latter instance gives rise to the notion of 'chastity' in *hagneia*, while on the other hand purity internalized and moralized leads to the idea of the 'morally immaculate' entity.[28] In their respective realities, Mary and Hippolytus share chastity as an attribute of nearly sacramental character in a unique way: the inner journey of each, culminating ultimately in personal intimacy with the divine, seems in their case to cause the term *hagneia* to decontract progressively from the notion of 'chastity', with which it initially applies to each of the two, and revert to the earlier meaning of taboo – as awe-striking in Mary's or awful in Hippolytus's case. Intimacy with the divine ensues implicitly from chastity as a rule and manifests in various wonderworks.[29] Still, what singles out Mary's and Hippolytus's virginities is in each case the explicit impact of this physical condition in establishing a conscious-driven rapport with the godhead that leads to theosis.[30] Mary is fully aware of how her chastity is inextricably linked to her divine maternity (see Mary's song in Luke 1:46-55). Hippolytus's 'theosis', on the other hand, subtly implied by Aphrodite (παρθένῳ ξυνὼν ἀεί | ... | μείζω βροτείας προσπεσὼν ὁμιλίας, 'constantly haunts the maiden goddess, having attained to more than mortal companionship', Eur. *Hipp.* 17-19), is consistently attempted in the main by way of chastity.[31] Mary's virginity is meant to carry universal significance, and Mary extols God's intimacy. But the intimacy is generated on the initiative of the divine. Mary does not earn

---

26   Roloff (1952-3, 114).
27   Roloff (1952-3, 114); cf. εὔδαιμον and κακόδαιμον respectively in their original sense.
28   Roloff (1952-3, 115).
29   Fehrle (1908, 53-6).
30   I understand *theosis* both in the broader sense of assimilation to the divine as well as in its stricter theological application in Mary's case.
31   Bremer (1975, 275-7).

it, neither does she solicit it; she merely assigns it to the initiative of God (Luke 1:48). Still, Mary's world is transcendent; not so Hippolytus's own: in his striving for divine assimilation,[32] he has surpassed the natural limitations imposed by the human condition and has thus laid himself open to an attack by opposing forces.[33]

Hippolytus's firmness of purpose in his chastity fails to win him the sympathy of his audience, much less Aphrodite's goodwill. His conduct is strange and incomprehensible and therefore wrong; Euripides makes it clear from the outset that in his pursuit of the impossible Hippolytus is out of touch with popular feeling.[34] The meadow imagery, with which his *rhēsis* opens and also functions as a trope of virginity in implying Hippolytus's inviolability (cf. 73–8), alienates his Athenian audience by being advisedly devoid of sensuality and the erotic overtones with which meadows and gardens would tend to be routinely associated in the Greek mind.[35] At the very outset of his characterization in the *rhēsis* (73–86), Hippolytus's *hagneia* (πρόσωθεν αὐτὴν ἁγνὸς ὢν ἀσπάζομαι, 'I salute her [sc. Aphrodite] from a respectful distance since I am undefiled', Eur. *Hipp.* 102), echoed in the trope of the 'undefiled meadow' (ἀκήρατος λειμών), is close to coming full circle by reverting via a semantic shift back to the original notion of awe-inspiring taboo. By this time, his inner journey has reached a point at which his intimacy with the divine is starting to strike religious awe tinged with dread into the minds of his audience,[36] notably in the wake of his awful fixation on rejecting sexuality. The dynamics of retribution has been set in motion by extravagance. Hubris has invited Nemesis,[37] and punishment is meted out to Hippolytus owing to a disposition that reflects in the same physical condition for which reward is offered to Mary. Still, virginity does not apply to Mary as it does to Hippolytus. To speak in Aristotelian terms, by being spared the original fall through *praeredemptio*, or anticipated redemption, and accordingly the ensuing actualization of sexuality as well, Mary reverts to the state of unrealized sexuality before the Fall of Man.[38] This is true, even if it is posited that

---

32 Bremer (1975, 275-7).
33 Bremer (1975, 277).
34 Bremer (1975, 277).
35 See Motte (1973, 150–3, 214-16 and *passim*) and Bremer (1975, 276-7).
36 Bremer (1975, 277): 'In complete sincerity he [Hippolytus] puts himself aloof from humanity ... His sense of being superior to the πολλοί, expressed scenically in 73–78, is expressed philosophically in 79–81, the passage about "innate virtue," and mystically in 84–86: "of all mortals I am the only one to converse with you"'.
37 I am using this term in the sense of deified abstraction, not as the deified force personified in Greek drama and later Greek theology; see Henderson (2012, 2-7).
38 I understand 'reverts' in the sense that albeit spared the fall through divine economy in her immaculate conception, Mary would still have been subject to it in being human.

grace impacts Mary's sexuality and everything that comes with it *post veniendo*, not *praeveniendo*.[39] Consequently, Mary's sexuality is not actualized. Nevertheless, Mary's chastity is critical to the attainment of her theosis,[40] a presupposition which contributes to her deification construed as sanctification.[41] Conversely, seen from the perspective of Mary's world, Hippolytus's sexuality is actualized, even if not activized.[42] It is dormant, yet possessed, not potential, sexuality.[43] Strictly on the premise of actualized sexuality, Hippolytus is therefore, presumably, on more solid ground in allowing for tentative gender identity scrutiny from a modern perspective,[44] even if gender identity in his case is not entirely free of speculation, not entirely self-bestowed, and with the stipulations that would appear to apply.[45]

Asexuality is not infrequently referenced in the context of Hippolytus's virginity, without it always being clear whether it is employed strictly as *terminus technicus* or in a broader sense,[46] including anaphrodisia. The first of the two readings of asexuality referenced, namely, as *terminus technicus*, seems inapplicable because it fails to conform fully to the definition of

---

39 Eastern theology maintains that, although sharing in the original sin, Mary is entirely cleansed from it by grace *post veniendo*.
40 Mary's *virginitas mentis*, *sensus* and *corporis* ensue from the postulate of *praeredemptio*.
41 Mosser (2021, 136).
42 Cole (2017, 96) observes that 'Hippolytus inadvertently sexualizes the natural environment that he describes', and Lambert (2019, 136) notes that Hippolytus likewise 'sexualizes the meadow'.
43 For instance, due to celibacy, asexuality and so forth. Aristotle discriminates between actuality and potentiality and further between two forms of actuality, citing the example of the relation between knowledge possessed (ἐπιστήμη) and knowledge exercised (θεωρεῖν). Hicks (1907, 307), elaborating on Arist. *De anima* 412a10, observes that '[t]he former, the possession of knowledge real but latent, is an inchoate, provisional actualization'.
44 Mowat (2018) questions the legitimacy of ascribing modern gender identity to ancient sexualities but concludes that – presumably by referring to them – Classics can nonetheless afford us an opportunity for self-probing and assessing others through the prism of modern identity categories. It may also be telling that he goes on to discuss contemporary asexuality issues by referencing, yet not directly connecting with, the myth of Hippolytus.
45 Mowat (2018) grants that no [gender] identity can be assigned to Hippolytus but contends that his virginity 'says a lot ... about expectations of masculinity and sexuality'.
46 By 'terminus technicus', I understand the use of the term as defined by AVEN (the Asexual Visibility and Education Network) with the proviso that asexuality, strictly considered, covers a wide spectrum of diversity and attitudes in sexual orientation; see Chu (2014, 88, 89–91). For AVEN, see https://www.asexuality.org/?q=overview.html. By 'broader sense', on the other hand, I understand, as Chu (2014, 89) suggests, the invalidity of 'the assumption that all asexuals are completely opposed to both engaging in sex of any kind and being in a romantic relationship'.

an asexual person as 'one who does not experience sexual attraction'.[47] We know of Hippolytus's specified dismissive anaphrodisia: that he does not experience sexual attraction toward women, but it is unclear how inclusive his anaphrodisia is. If it is true that his diction and conduct admit of homoerotic interpretation at the subtextual level,[48] Hippolytus would automatically disqualify as an asexual person. This means that he would disqualify if, for instance, the meadow imagery, with which his *rhēsis* opens, were to be read as 'a masterful portrayal of intense puritanism, beneath the surface of which sexual passion is bubbling'.[49] Accordingly, Hippolytus seems to be an unlikely asexual on at least two counts: first, for lack of adequate evidence supporting a comprehensively unerotic disposition,[50] not *praxis*,[51] in light of his specifically selective anaphrodisia; second, on account of his putative repressed eroticism, detected in the subtext of the *Hippolytus*.[52] On explicit evidence gleaned from the text, the nature of Hippolytus's anaphrodisia points to a celibate,[53] not asexual virginity. Moreover, the association of his sexually abstemious disposition with femininity, an axiomatic assumption in his social setting, contributes to his being viewed as a 'freak'[54] who easily crosses over to 'queerness' by reason of his committed virginity in the eyes of his of original audience.[55]

Construing male virginity, even if not at Hippolytus's level of commitment, as a gender-specific status peculiar to femaleness appears to occur as a motif in the Menoeceus episode of Euripides' *Phoenician Women* as

---

47 The lack of comprehensive sexual attraction is presumably meant to be inclusive as the outstanding feature lying at the heart of any definition of asexuality here referenced.
48 See Craik (1998, 43) and Lucas (1946, 68).
49 Lambert (2019, 135): 'Euripides' layered intertextual references here to the meadow topos in Greek lyric poetry, redolent of sexual danger, temptation, "deflowering" and rape, as well as the bee, associated with sexual chastity, and with both Artemis and Aphrodite, make Hippolytus's opening speech a masterful portrayal of intense puritanism, beneath the surface of which sexual passion is bubbling.' For other instances of Hippolytus's imputed repressed sexuality, see Lambert (2019, 135-6). Lambert (2019, 133) apparently construes Hippolytus's shunning of women in terms of celibacy, not asexuality.
50 Craik (1998, 43) and Lucas (1946, 68).
51 See n. 46.
52 See n. 49.
53 Lambert (2019, 133-4).
54 Lucas (1946, 67-8).
55 Ingram (2003, 451): '[F]irst ... at least until the late Middle Ages, "Roman Catholic discourse" celebrated virginity as a holy state; second ... "Protestant discourse" demystified and even devalued virginity; third ... women who retained their virginity in Protestant cultures boldly resisted imperatives to marry; fourth ... committed virginity presented a threateningly aberrant sexual orientation in those contexts and might therefore be profitably studied as "queer".

well – presumably a novelty of Euripides' own crafting.[56] Accordingly, terms like 'freak' and 'queer' make sense to be used of Hippolytus as likely perceived by his original audience. They do so from the audience's perspective because they help diffuse the tension caused by negative awe and the modes of aversion that Hippolytus's chastity activates and because they help maintain binary-gendered masculinity by coding the aberrant conduct of a male as female. He is classified as 'a maiden trapped in a man's body',[57] yet his identity remains a mystery like that of his namesake 'transvestite' statue.[58] There is even more on identity here: the uncanny coincidence of Mary's church being erected over and superimposed onto the Hippolytus Hall in Madaba, Jordan.[59] What we seem to have in this fused monument is a representation of an axis, unifying two types of *hagneia* semantically narrowed down to 'virginity', with taboo overtones of haunting awe resurfacing in the structures that celebrate the two figures. Artemis's statement that Hippolytus will lie 'in the darkness beneath the earth' (Eur. *Hipp.* 1416) relegates him to the department of sprites and ghosts – to the cultus of heroes. Theirs are the rituals of aversion, the 'ceremonies of riddance'.[60] Hippolytus's virginity fails. He claims *virginitas corporis* (1003) but admits to defiling his *virginitas sensus* (1004–5, 653–5);[61] we know nothing about his *virginitas mentis*, although Phaedra is aware that hers is sullied (317). Dwelling in the realm of aversion, Hippolytus conjures up the taboo awe of aversion.[62] In that sense, he misses the *Creaturvergötterung* which Mary attains. Still,

---

56 Swift (2009, 70-1) draws attention to the unnecessary emphasis laid on Menoeceus's virginity in *Phoenician Women* and contends that 'by insisting on Menoeceus's virginity as the reason for his sacrifice, the play assimilates him to the (female) virgins of the other sacrifice-myths'. Swift likewise cites Craik's remark that Tiresias's imagery, portraying Menoeceus as a πῶλος (Eur. *Phoen.* 947), is a trope 'more commonly used of *parthenoi* [young females]'.
57 According to Lambert (2019, 136), this would be the modern equivalent of Hippolytus's statement that 'he has a maiden's soul' (παρθένον ψυχὴν ἔχων, 1006). For an effeminized reading of Hippolytus in Euripides' tragedy, see Goff (1990, 65-7).
58 The statue of Hippolytus, purported to be of Hippolytus of Rome, features the seated, 'rainbow-clad' figure of a bearded man, possibly a philosopher, dressed in man's apparel from the waist up but draped as a woman from the waist down, apparently as a result of an earlier and a more recent reassembly of the original statue's fragments, unearthed in Rome, allegedly in the burial grounds of the Via Tiburtina; see Brent (1995, 3-50).
59 The latter, a Roman structure of the early sixth century, depicts scenes from Euripides' play, while the former dates to the end of the same century.
60 Harrison (1908, 8).
61 For Phaedra's *impuritas mentis*, see n. 29; cf. n. 41.
62 Harrison (1908, 59): 'It did not escape that acute observer of man and his language, Archbishop Eustathius, that this word [ἄγος] and its cognate ἅγιος, holy, had in ancient days a double significance, that holy was not only pure but also polluted … The word lies deep down in the ritual of ancient sacrifice and of ancient religious thought … [I]t is tinged with, though not quite the equivalent of, expiation'.

in his own province, lying under Mary's church in Madaba, he achieves *Gottvereinigung* of a chthonic sort,[63] short of entering Artemis's domain. As Lucas puts it: '[T]here is poetry in the relation between man and goddess which seems so close, yet fails at last to transcend the limitations imposed on human natures and divine'.[64]

Works Cited

Bremer, J. M. 1975. 'The Meadow of Love and Two Passages in Euripides' *Hippolytus*'. *Mnemosyne* 28: 268-80.

Brent, Allen. 1995. *Hippolytus and the Roman Church in the Third Century: Communities in Tension Before the Emergence of a Monarch-Bishop*. Leiden: Brill.

Capelle, Bernard. 1940. 'Les anciens récits de l'Assomption et Jean de Thessalonique'. *Recherches de théologie ancienne et médiéval* 12: 209-35.

Chu, Erica. 2014. 'Radical Identity Politics: Asexuality and Contemporary Articulations of Identity'. In *Asexualities: Feminist and Queer Perspectives*, edited by K. J. Cerankowski and Megan Milks, 79-99. New York: Routledge.

Clayton, Mary. 1990. *The Cult of the Virgin Mary in Anglo-Saxon England*. Cambridge: Cambridge University Press.

Cole, Emma. 2017. 'Paralinguistic Translation in Sarah Kane's *Phaedra's Love*'. In *Adapting Translation for the Stage*, edited by Geraldine Brodie and Emma Cole, 90-103. New York: Routledge.

Cooper, W. R. 1877. *The Horus Myth in Its Relation to Christianity*. London: Hardwick and Bogue.

Craik, Elizabeth M. 1998. 'Language of Sexuality and Sexual Inversion in Euripides' *Hippolytos*'. *Acta Classica* 41: 29-44.

Dudley, Louise. 1911. 'The Egyptian Elements in the Legend of the Body and Soul'. PhD diss., Bryn Mawr College.

Fehrle, Karl-Heinz Eugen. 1908. *Die kultische Keuschheit im Altertum*. Naumburg: Lippert & Co.

Goff, Barbara E. 1990. *The Noose of Words: Readings of Desire, Violence and Language in Euripides' Hippolytos*. Cambridge: Cambridge University Press.

Harrison, Jane Ellen. 1908. *Prolegomena to the Study of Greek Religion*, 2nd edn. Cambridge: Cambridge University Press.

Henderson, Jeffrey. 2012. 'Pursuing Nemesis: Cratinus and Mythological Comedy'. In *No Laughing Matter: New Studies in Old Comedy*, edited by C. W. Marshall and G. A. Kovacs, 1-12. London: Bloomsbury.

Hicks, R. D. 1907. *Aristotle: De Anima*. Cambridge: Cambridge University Press.

Higgins, Sabrina. 2012. 'Divine Mothers: The Influence of Isis on the Virgin Mary in Egyptian *Lactans*-Iconography'. *Journal of the Canadian Society for Coptic Studies* 3-4: 71-9.

---

63 For *Gottvereinigung* by way of chastity, see n. 29.
64 Lucas (1946, 69).

Ingram, Randall. 2003. Review of *Pure Resistance: Queer Virginity in Early Modern English Drama* by T. A. Jankowski. *Journal of the American Academy of Religion* 71: 451-3.
James, Montague Rhodes. 1983. *The Apocryphal New Testament*. Oxford: Clarendon Press.
Jugie, Martin. 1926. *Homélies mariales byzantines*, vol. 2. Paris: Firmin-Didot.
Lambert, M. 2019. 'Decolonizing the Classics Curriculum in South African Universities with Euripides' *Hippolytus*'. *Akroterion* 64: 127-44.
Lefèvre, Yves. 1954. *L' Elucidarium et les Lucidaires*. Paris: E. de Boccard.
Lucas, D. W. 1946. 'Hippolytus'. *CQ* 40: 65-9.
Mosser, Carl. 2021. 'Orthodox–Reformed Dialogue and the Ecumenical Recovery of *Theosis*'. *Ecumenical Review* 73: 131-51.
Motte, A. 1973. *Prairies et jardins de la Grèce antique: de la religion à la philosophie*. Brussels: Palais des Académies.
Mowat, Chris. 2018. 'Queering Hippolytus: Asexuality and Ancient Greece'. *Notches*. https://notchesblog.com/2018/05/17/queering-hippolytus-asexuality-and-ancient-greece/.
Neumann, Hans, ed. 1990. *Mechthild von Magdeburg: Das fließende Licht der Gottheit: nach der Einsiedler Handschrift in kritischem Vergleich mit der gesamten Überlieferung*, vol. 1. Munich: Artemis.
O'Carroll, Michael. 1983. *Theotokos: A Theological Encyclopaedia of the Blessed Virgin Mary*. Wilmington, DE: Michael Glazier, Inc.
Quasten, Johannes. 1983. *Patrology*, vol. 1. Allen, TX: Christian Classics.
Rivière, J. 1936. 'Le plus vieux transitus latin et son dérivé grec'. *Revue de théologie ancienne et médiévale* 8: 5-23.
Roloff, Karl-Heinz. 1952-3. 'Caerimonia'. *Glotta* 32: 101-38.
Sayers, Dorothy L. 1981. 'Types of Christian Drama: With Some Notes on Production'. *VII: Journal of the Marion E. Wade Center* 2: 84-99.
Smid, Harm Reinder. n.d., c. 1965. *Protoevangelium Jacobi: A Commentary*, translated by G. E. van Baaren-Pape. Assen: Van Gorcum.
Swift, L. A. 2009. 'Sexual and Familial Distortion in Euripides' *Phoenissae*'. *TAPA* 139: 53-87.
Wallis Budge, Ernest A. 1904. *The Gods of the Egyptians; or, Studies in Egyptian Mythology*. Chicago: The Open Court Publishing Company.
Wenger, Antoine. 1955. *L'Assomption de la T.S. Vierge dans la tradition byzantine du VIe au Xe siècle: études et documents*. Paris: Institut français d'études byzantines.

CHAPTER 10

Literal Truth, Mythic Truth and Narrative in Longus's Daphnis and Chloe

William Owens

The novel was a new genre in antiquity.[1] A consensus dates the earliest surviving example, Chariton's *Callirhoe*, to the middle decades of the first century CE.[2] Authors who mentioned the form tended to disparage it: because it was fiction; because it dealt with erotic themes; perhaps just because it was new.[3] Ancient moralists, philosophers and rhetoricians thought and wrote about fiction and narration, but not about the fictional prose narratives that we call novels. When commentators sought examples to illustrate their thinking about fictional narratives, they seldom illustrated this thinking with examples drawn from the ancient novels. As John Morgan observes, 'in antiquity the novel was drastically undertheorized'.[4]

This is the context in which the present essay discusses evidence in *Daphnis and Chloe* for Longus's own thinking about his genre. I argue that the author used two conceptual frameworks for thinking about genre. Longus reflects on the truth value of his fiction through allusion to Hesiod's encounter with the Heliconian Muses in the *Theogony* and through engagement with a dichotomy between *logos* and *mythos* that emerged in the classical period. He also triangulates his narrative through comparison and contrast with three forms of narration identified in rhetorical treatises:

---

1 In the preface to the Longus/Xenophon of Ephesus Loeb, Jeffrey Henderson dedicated the *Daphnis and Chloe* translation to William McCulloh, his acclaimed Greek professor at Kenyon College. After reading *Daphnis and Chloe* with Professor McCulloh, Jeff (2009, vi–vii) notes, he was so captivated that, like Goethe, he resolved to return to the novel every year and learn something new of its beauty. The present essay is another such return, a return, in this case, in honor of Jeff.
2 See the discussion of Tilg (2010, 36–82).
3 Cf. the discussion of Reardon (1991, 46–53). Owens (2020) suggests that an early association of the new genre with formerly enslaved authors and readers also contributed to its disparagement.
4 Morgan (1993, 176). Reardon (1991, chh. 3 and 4) is helpful.

history (*historia*, ἱστορία), myth (*fabula*, μῦθος) and fiction (*argumentum*, πλάσμα). While this essay does not reveal an ancient definition of the novel, it may show us a practitioner of the novel genre thinking about its nature.

Longus and Hesiod, *Mythos* and *Logos*

Daphnis and Chloe are in love by the end of book 1. In their naïveté, each thinks that they have been struck by some sort of physical illness.[5] Neither even knows the name of Eros, that is, of Love. Early in book 2, Philetas, an elderly cowherd, comes upon the protagonists with their flocks. He tells them of a noontime encounter in his garden with a beautiful, naked boy, who will turn out to be Eros. After mocking Philetas's futile attempts to grab hold of him, the boy speaks: Despite his appearance, he is older even than Cronus and time itself. He tells Philetas that long ago he had united him with Amaryllis, the mother of his children. Each morning now he 'herds together' (ποιμαίνω, 2.5.4) Daphnis and Chloe, after which he visits Philetas's garden, delights in the flowers and plants and bathes in the springs. The waters in which he has bathed, the boy tells Philetas, give the garden its beauty. He then clambers away up the myrtle bushes, revealing the wings on his back and a quiver before disappearing. Philetas tells the protagonists that they 'have been consecrated' (κατέσπεισθε, 2.6.2) to Eros, that Eros is looking after them.

Daphnis and Chloe take pleasure in the account 'as if they had been listening to a *mythos* and not a *logos*' (ὥσπερ μῦθον οὐ λόγον ἀκούοντες, 2.7.1) and ask Philetas what Eros is and what he can do. Philetas replies that Eros is a god 'young, beautiful and winged' (νέος καὶ καλὸς καὶ πετόμενος), who 'rules the elements, rules the stars, rules his fellow gods' (κρατεῖ μὲν στοιχείων, κρατεῖ δὲ ἄστρων, κρατεῖ δὲ τῶν ὁμοίων θεῶν), and, in fact, is more powerful than even Zeus (2.7.1–2). The power of Eros is felt through all nature. Philetas has seen his power in bulls, in billy goats and in himself; when lovesick for Amaryllis, he 'forgot about food, took nothing to drink, and got no sleep' (καὶ οὔτε τροφῆς ἐμεμνήμην οὔτε ποτὸν προσεφερόμην οὔτε ὕπνον ᾑρούμην, 2.7.4). The old herdsman concludes that 'There is no remedy for Eros, none to drink, to eat or chant in songs, except kissing, embracing and lying down together with naked bodies' (Ἔρωτος γὰρ οὐδὲν φάρμακον, οὐ πινόμενον, οὐκ ἐσθιόμενον, οὐκ ἐν ᾠδαῖς λαλούμενον, ὅτι μὴ φίλημα καὶ περιβολὴ καὶ συγκατακλιθῆναι γυμνοῖς σώμασι, 2.7.7).[6]

Longus combines two traditions involving the god. In erotic poetry and art, Eros is a beautiful but naughty boy, the son of Aphrodite. But in an earlier tradition, present, for example, in Hesiod's *Theogony*, he is

---

5 Chloe describes her symptoms at 1.14; Daphnis at 1.17.
6 Henderson (2009, 69 n. 24) observes a correction of Theocritus 11.1–3.

the oldest deity after Chaos itself, an elemental force driving creation (*Theog.* 116–22).[7] Longus emphasizes the Hesiodic associations of his Eros in parallels between the epiphany to Philetas in the garden and the epiphany of the Muses to Hesiod on Helicon. Hesiod and Philetas are both musical herdsmen. Hesiod receives his poetic gift from the Muses while he is herding his lambs. Philetas boasts to Daphnis and Chloe that he used to herd his cows by music alone (μόνῃ μουσικῇ, 2.3.2). Both epiphanies occur, apparently at noon, in secluded places: the slopes of Helicon and Philetas's garden.[8] The Muses bathe in the three streams that flow down Mount Helicon, Permessos, Hippocrene and Olmeios; Eros bathes in the three springs that water Philetas's garden (πηγαῖς τρισὶ κατάρρυτος, 3.3.5).[9]

In each epiphany, divinity chides the poet-herdsman. The Muses reproach Hesiod, and perhaps all herdsmen, as lowly rustics, 'mere bellies' (ποιμένες ἄγραυλοι, κάκ' ἐλέγχεα, γαστέρες οἶον, *Theog.* 26). In Longus, divine abuse takes a gentle turn when Eros pelts Philetas with myrtle berries (2.4.4). The divinities then pronounce their powers and confer distinction on the poet-herdsmen. The Muses tell Hesiod that they know how to say false things that seem like things that are true and, when they wish, to speak the truth (*Theog.* 27–8). They give him a laurel staff, the symbol of the divine song that they breathe into him (αὐδὴν | θέσπιν, *Theog.* 31–2).[10] In *Daphnis and Chloe*, Eros asserts his powers to Philetas and notes the distinction he had conferred on the herdsman: after he became old, Philetas, alone of men, had a vision of the boy-god (μόνος ἀνθρώπων ἐν γήρᾳ θεασάμενος τοῦτο τὸ παιδίον, 2.5.5). Finally, as the Muses are the source of Hesiod's divine song, Eros causes the beauty in Philetas's garden, which is watered by the springs in which the god bathes.

Some elements here could be common to the literary epiphany: a poet encountering a divinity alone in a remote location at midday.[11] Other details suggest that Longus had the epiphany of the Heliconian Muses in mind: both Philetas and Hesiod are herdsmen; both are chided by the divinity they encounter; three sources of water flow through each setting.[12] The carefully

---

7 Cf. Bowie (2019, 176).
8 Noon was a traditional time for divine epiphanies; see Petridou (2015, 210–14). Longus has specified noon as the time for Eros's epiphany (ἀμφὶ μέσην ἡμέραν, 2.4.1), while a later tradition sets the epiphany on Helicon at noon (cf. *Anth. Pal.* 9.64, μεσημβρινά).
9 Cf. Athanassakis (2004, 37); also, West (1988, 63).
10 Longus does not note a staff in his initial description of Philetas, who, it turns out, walks with the aid of one (ἐπερεισάμενος τῇ βακτηρίᾳ, 2.4.3).
11 Cf. Petridou (2015, 196–201, 210–25).
12 Oblique evidence that Longus was thinking about Hesiod in this episode may also be indicated in Philetas's name, which associates the character with the Hellenistic scholar and poet Philetas of Cos. Bowie (1985, 68–77) argues that Philetas of Cos created Lycidas, a herdsman poet in *Idyll* 7, who, in a noon-time epiphany evocative of Hesiod, confers on the narrator his staff, a symbol of his poetic authority.

constructed allusion is relevant to how the protagonists react to Philetas's story: they are delighted as if they were hearing a *mythos* and not a *logos* (ἐτέρφθησαν ὥσπερ μῦθον οὐ λόγον ἀκούοντες, 2.7.1). Longus reflects here a distinction between *mythos* and *logos* that emerged in the classical period, which distinguished philosophic thinking from traditional ways of understanding the world.[13] *Logos* indicated the reasoning, empiricism and application of evidence of the philosopher. A construct emerged, as R. L. Fowler puts it, 'in which poetry, imaginative myth, gods and unknowable prehistory are on one side of a cognitive and chronological line; on the other side are prose, reasoning (*logos*), humans, empirical investigation and the verifiable facts of recent history'.[14] Henderson's Loeb translation, 'as if they were listening to a story and not fact', aligns with the dichotomy.

Longus's editorial comment, 'as if they were hearing a *mythos* and not a *logos*', contrasts the perspective of his innocent protagonists and that of his sophisticated readers. Daphnis and Chloe take what Philetas said as if it really happened, as *logos*. They are naïve readers in contrast to Longus's actual readers, who for the most part would have taken in Philetas's tale not as truth, but as a part of a fictive narrative that is itself not true. Such readers would suspend their disbelief when reading the Philetas episode, indeed the whole novel, and enjoy *mythos* as *mythos*, not *logos* as if it were *mythos*.[15] However, the issue is more complicated than this contrast between *mythos* and *logos* and two types of readers. What the Muses tell Hesiod is itself a *mythos* (τόνδε δέ με πρώτιστα θεαὶ πρὸς μῦθον ἔειπον, *Theog.* 24). In this instance, we are looking at the older notion of *mythos*, which was, in Bruce Lincoln's formulation, 'an assertive discourse of power and authority that represents itself as something to be believed and obeyed'.[16]

The Muses' *mythos* is their assertion that they know how to say many lies that are like true things and know also, should they wish it, to sing the truth (ἴδμεν ψεύδεα πολλὰ λέγειν ἐτύμοισιν ὁμοῖα, | ἴδμεν δ' εὖτ' ἐθέλωμεν ἀληθέα γηρύσασθαι, *Theog.* 27–8). Longus could have seen here an archaic precedent for his own writing: he, too, knew how to tell lies that seem like the truth. In addition, it seems that the author of *Daphnis and Chloe* is playing with two understandings of *mythos* and truth. The first involves truth considered as an accurate account of events: truth as *logos* as is implied in the conceit that Philetas's story was a factual account. The second understanding involves symbolic truth implied in the notion of

13 On this point, see Morgan (2000, ch. 1); Lincoln (1999, 37–43).
14 Fowler (2011, 47).
15 Gill (1979, 65) describes reading fiction as a game in which both authors and readers 'share in a willed pretense, treating what is unreal as real, and what is invented as actual'.
16 Lincoln (1999, 17–18). Cf. Morgan (2000, 16): 'before the Presocratics the world of myth was characterized by indemonstrable truth and poetic authority; the word *mythos* similarly connoted authoritative, efficacious and performative speech'. Also, Fowler (2011).

mythos as authoritative speech.[17] Ewen Bowie's comment on the passage picks up on this archaic valuation: 'the sense of μῦθος here is that of "myth", a story whose value lies in its deeper meaning rather than its literal truth'.[18] We may see here an additional dimension in which the Hesiodic epiphany is relevant to Longus's own writing. He implies not only that he knows how to tell lies that seem like the truth but also how through these lies to express deeper truths that carry the venerable if unverifiable authority of *mythos*.

Myth, History and the Novel

Longus found in rhetorical treatises that discuss non-forensic narration a second conceptual framework for his narrative. The treatises vary in detail, but Longus seems to engage with a tradition that recognized three varieties of non-forensic narration: *mythos* (*fabula* in the Latin treatises); *historia* (*historia*); *plasma* (*argumentum*).[19] Longus acknowledges all three forms in his narrative, suggesting at different times that he is writing either *mythos*, *historia* or *plasma*. At the same time, Longus suggests that each of these genres is limited in its application to his own narrative. We may see here the author triangulating his own narrative in relation to the genres of non-forensic narration.

The tripartite division of narration is reflected in Cicero's *De Inventione* and in Sextus Empiricus's critique, *Against the Grammarians* (*Adv. gr.*). Classification of the three types depends on their relationship to actual events. Cicero defines *fabula* as narration 'composed of things that were neither true nor similar to the truth' (*in qua nec verae nec veri similes res continentur*, *De inv.* 1.27; cf. *Adv. gr.* 264, μῦθος δὲ πραγμάτων ἀγενήτων καὶ ψευδῶν ἔκθεσις). In illustration, he quotes a line from Pacuvius's lost tragedy *Medea* referring to the winged snakes that pulled Medea's chariot. In this system of classification, *fabula* represents the supernatural element of tragedy or myth. *Historia* is an account of an actual deed, remote from our times (*gesta res, ab aetatis nostrae memoria remota*, *De inv.* 1.27; cf. *Adv. gr.* 263, ἡ μὲν ἱστορία ἀληθῶν τινῶν ἐστι καὶ γεγονότων ἔκθεσις). The third type of non-forensic narration is the one with possible application to the novel. *Argumentum* is the narration of something that has been made up but which could, nonetheless, have happened (*est ficta res, quae tamen fieri*

---

17 This is the sense in which Hesiod declares that he will tell his brother Perses some 'authoritative truths', at *WD* 10: ἐγὼ δέ κε Πέρσῃ ἐτήτυμα μυθησαίμην. See Lincoln (1999, 218 n. 5) on the text of *Theog.* 24, where ἀληθέα γηρύσασθαι represents the *lectio difficilior* in place of ἀληθέα μυθήσασθαι, which, if an error, could have been motivated by the notion of *mythos* as an authoritative declaration.
18 Bowie (2019, 179).
19 See discussions of Barwick (1928), Greco (1998), Calboli Montefusco (2006), Feddern (2017).

potuit, De inv. 1.27; cf. *Adv. gr.* 263, πλάσμα δὲ πραγμάτων μὴ γενομένων μὲν ὁμοίως δὲ τοῖς γενομένοις λεγομένων). In contrast to the miraculous events, creatures and transformations of *fabula, argumentum* conforms with the laws of the natural world. Cicero's illustration of *argumentum*, a passage from Terence's *Andria*, implies that this form also conforms to the norms of the social world, for the plots of New Comedy were socially realistic despite their fiction.[20] The example anticipates a discussion of the need for verisimilitude in forensic narration that follows (*De inv.* 1.29), in which Cicero expresses the rhetorician's concern for verisimilitude not only in terms of the laws of the physical world but also in terms of narrative coherence, motivation, and social relations and expectations.

Mythos *and Not* Mythos

There is a suggestion that Longus is writing a form of *mythos* in book 2, after Chloe has been taken by a raiding party from the city of Methymna. Pan appears in a dream to the Methymnaean commander Bryaxis, threatens him for seizing a girl 'out of whom Eros wants to make a myth' (ἐξ ἧς Ἔρως μῦθον ποιῆσαι θέλει, 2.27.2) and commands him to release her (2.26–7). Bowie here sees a 'self-referential' remark that 'is hard not to refer' to Longus's novel itself.[21] This understanding of the mythic character of *Daphnis and Chloe* can align with a Hesiodic understanding of *mythos*; though fiction, Longus's narrative contains deeper truths about human love in the context of nature and society. Longus, too, may have thought of his narrative as this sort of *mythos*. However, the text reveals significant engagement with the understanding of *mythos* that emerged in opposition to *logos*, in which *mythoi* indicated the myths of mythology, traditional stories concerning the gods and heroes and supernatural events, that is, the conception of *mythos* in the rhetorical treatises.

Myths of this sort abound in *Daphnis and Chloe*. Three myths of transformation have been inserted in the main narrative: Daphnis tells Chloe a myth about the transformation of Phatta, a female cowherder, into a woodpigeon (1.27); Lamon tells the story of Pan's pursuit of the nymph Syrinx and her transformation into the panpipes (2.34); Daphnis tells Chloe the myth of Pan's attempt to rape Echo and the nymph's physical dismemberment and transformation into the natural phenomenon of echo (2.23). Eros, Pan and the Nymphs enter the main narrative when different characters dream about them. The protagonists' stepfathers, Lamon and Dryas, have

---

20 Sextus Empiricus refers to comedy (and mimes) in illustration of the type.
21 Bowie (2019, 204). Cf. Reardon (1994, 146): *Daphnis and Chloe* is 'something less than a novel, perhaps; Eros has made a μῦθος of Chloe, a fable – as Longus predicts, in 2.27'. Also, MacQueen (1985).

the same dream on the same night, in which the Nymphs give Daphnis and Chloe over to a winged boy who touches the two with an arrow and commands the stepfathers to make them tend flocks (1.7). Later, the Nymphs reassure Daphnis in a dream that Chloe will come to no harm after being taken prisoner by the Methymnaeans; as noted above, Pan orders the Methymnaean commander in a dream to release Chloe (2.26–7). Daphnis sees the Nymphs in a dream a second time: they instruct him where he can find the fortune that enables him to marry Chloe (3.27). Daphnis's real father Dionysophanes dreams that Eros, at the Nymphs' request, assents to the protagonists' marriage and instructs him how to find Chloe's father (4.34). These are not, strictly speaking, myths, but mythic elements. The gods who appear in these dreams are real to the characters, who act in accord with what they see.

This type of *mythos*, *mythos* as understood in the rhetorical treatises, is associated with the pleasure that is central to Longus's novel. In the Proem, the unnamed narrator, a stand-in for the author, boasts that his story will be 'a pleasurable possession for all mankind' (κτῆμα δὲ τερπνὸν πᾶσιν ἀνθρώποις, Pr. 3), an allusion to Thucydides' claim that his history would be 'a possession for all time' (κτῆμά ... ἐς αἰεί, Thuc. 1.22.4). Thucydides' history is a lasting possession because it is something of value, that is, a text that offers the diligent reader understanding about how states conduct themselves and go to war. However, Thucydides concedes that, despite its utility, some of his audience will find his history rather unpleasing because he has omitted a mythological element (καὶ ἐς μὲν ἀκρόασιν ἴσως τὸ μὴ μυθῶδες αὐτῶν ἀτερπέστερον φανεῖται, 1.22.4). For Thucydides, this mythological element, *to mythōdes*, appears to be close to the *mythos* of the rhetorical treatises. In an earlier passage, he attributes the quality of *mythōdes* to the *logographoi* who please their audiences with accounts that are both unverifiable and unbelievable (τὰ πολλὰ ὑπὸ χρόνου αὐτῶν ἀπίστως ἐπὶ τὸ μυθῶδες ἐκνενικηκότα, 1.21.1).[22]

Longus's novel is a pleasurable possession not only because it is about something pleasant, love, but also because the author has embedded fabulous *mythoi* in the main narrative. These *mythoi* are associated with pleasure. Accordingly, Daphnis and Chloe heard Philetas's account of Eros, notionally a *logos* in the ironic context of the main narrative, with pleasure, as if they were hearing a *mythos*. This is also the case with the inserted *mythoi* dealing with transformation. Daphnis's narration to Chloe of the Phatta story is one of the pleasures of their first summer together (τοιάσδε τέρψεις αὐτοῖς τὸ θέρος παρεῖχε, 1.28.1). At the rustic party celebrating

---

22 Flory (1990), who is followed by Hornblower (1991, 59), argues that *to mythōdes* refers to exaggerated patriotic stories. Morgan (2011, 559–60) argues that in excluding *to mythōdes* Thucydides is trying to draw the line between history and fiction.

Chloe's deliverance from the Methymnaeans, Philetas declares that Lamon's telling of the Syrinx story was sweeter than song (μῦθον ᾠδῆς γλυκύτερον, 2.35.1). Chloe's pleasure at Daphnis's account of the dismemberment of Echo was such that she gave him many more kisses than promised (ταῦτα μυθολογήσαντα τὸν Δάφνιν οὐ δέκα μόνον φιλήματα ἀλλὰ πάνυ πολλὰ καταφίλησεν ἡ Χλόη, 3.23.5).

However, Longus does not appear to think of *Daphnis and Chloe* itself as this kind of *mythos*. He distinguishes each of the tales of transformation from the main narrative through the device of an internal narrator. Philetas's waking vision and the dreams that introduce the other mythic elements also mark them out from the main narrative, where events conform with what is possible in the real world.[23] Longus may also distance the ideology of his main narrative from that of inserted *mythoi*. Each inserted tale narrates how the destruction of a young woman results in something associated with beauty and pleasure: in the song of the woodpigeon, in the panpipes, in the phenomenon of echo. Chloe's pleasure in the tale of Echo's gruesome fate may seem especially incongruous. The pleasure that these *mythoi* offer seems to derive from the aestheticization of disturbing violence, and Jack Winkler has asked a reasonable question: 'Could Longus be inviting or at least allowing his readers to wonder at the arbitrariness, the unnaturalness, of a sexual order that inexorably transforms females into victims?'[24] Pan declared in Bryaxis's dream vision that Eros wanted to make a *mythos* out of Chloe. This may not have been the sort of story that Longus had in mind for his heroine.

Historia *and Not* Historia

In the Proem, Longus claims that he is writing *historia*. The narrator describes that, while hunting on Lesbos, he came upon a painting dedicated to the Nymphs. The painting depicted events in the life of Daphnis and Chloe: how they fell in love and how, after many vicissitudes, they were able to marry. The narrator calls this picture a 'history of love' (ἱστορίαν ἔρωτος, Pr. 1). After consulting with a guide (Pr. 3), the narrator writes the story that follows. Such framing represents Longus's narrative not as a fiction that he invented, but a transcription of a painting that recorded things that really happened: a history, 'an exposition of things that are true and things that have happened' (cf. *Adv. gr.* 263, ἡ μὲν ἱστορία ἀληθῶν τινῶν ἐστὶ καὶ

---

23 Philetas's story is distinguished from the main narrative through the device of an internal narrator. The epiphany itself might be thought of as a waking dream. Cf. Petridou (2015, 5): 'the borderline between dream visions and waking visions is not to be drawn easily'.
24 Winkler (1990, 104).

γεγονότων ἔκθεσις). Longus's engagement with Thucydides and the nature of historical writing is in earnest.[25] However, the claim that he is writing about an actual love affair is a pose aimed at facilitating the 'game of fiction', the pretense shared between author and reader that events narrated in the fictional text are real.[26]

Longus returns to his engagement with *historia* in his account of the mini war between Methymna and Mytilene (2.19-20; 3.1-2).[27] The author narrates the events that lead to war: a peasant steals the rope that moored a boat used by young Methymnaean aristocrats on vacation; the vacationers relocate to another part of the coast, near the protagonists' district; they secure their boat with a cable woven from grass; while they are hunting, their barking dogs scare Daphnis's goats onto the shore, where there is nothing to eat but the grass cable; the boat and all their possessions drift out to sea; the young men blame Daphnis and try to drag him off; Daphnis's fellow peasants come to his rescue; there is a trial and a fight, in which the Methymnaean aristocrats are bested; they return home, tails between their legs, and give a false account of what happened to the Methymnaean assembly, which declares war. Rather than a 'history of love', Longus seems to be writing real, if trivial, history with a concatenation of cause and effect grounded in logic, nature and human motivation. However, this deep dive into the causes of the Mytilene-Methymna mini war seems less an emulation of Thucydidean exactness (cf. Thuc. 1.22.2, ὅσον δυνατὸν ἀκριβείᾳ) than a parody, one that cries out: 'Too much information!'[28]

Parody may distinguish Longus's story from real historical *logos* in terms of style. An event that happens when Chloe is taken prisoner during the war distinguishes the story from *historia* in terms of plot. Ancient readers knew that in the real world prisoners of war were routinely enslaved and that slaves were subject to sexual exploitation.[29] Events such as these are the subject of history. However, Chloe is not meant to be the subject of history. The Nymphs reassure Daphnis in a dream that Chloe will not be taken to Methymna and be a slave (μήτε εἰς τὴν Μήθυμναν κομισθεῖσα δουλεύοι, 2.23.3), and Pan intervenes and rescues her, because, the god declares, she is a girl of whom Eros wants to make a myth (2.27.1-2).

---

25 The allusion to Thucydides is well known: Cueva (1999), Luginbill (2002), Trzaskoma (2005).
26 Morgan (1993) discusses the means and implications of the ancient fiction writer's adoption of a historiographical pose in the case of Heliodorus.
27 On the Thucydidean aspects of this part of the narration, cf. Trzaskoma (2005).
28 The account of events resulting in the Mytilene-Methymna mini war may allude to Thucydides' lengthy account of the many and complex disputes between Athens and Corinth leading up to the Peloponnesian War (Thuc. 1.23-57).
29 Gaca (2010).

Plasma *and More than* Plasma

Chloe's story appears on the verge of being hijacked by *historia* when *mythos* comes to rescue it. However, as we have seen, young women in *mythoi* fare no better than women in real life who are taken captive in war. This is the context in which we should consider Longus's allusion to the third variety of non-forensic narration, *plasma*. Cicero's discussion of this form focused on the conformity of *argumentum* to the laws and conventions of the natural and social worlds: an *argumentum* was a fictive account of something that could happen (*est ficta res, quae tamen fieri potuit*, *De inv.* 1.27). Sextus Empiricus suggests the affinity of *plasma* to *historia*: an account of things which, if they have not happened, are recounted in a manner similar to things that have (πλάσμα δὲ πραγμάτων μὴ γενομένων μὲν ὁμοίως δὲ τοῖς γενομένοις λεγομένων, *Adv. gr.* 264).

Longus alludes to *plasma* in book 4, when Lamon reveals to his master Dionysophanes that the protagonist is not his natural son but a foundling he found exposed in the fields (4.19). Dionysophanes is shocked at this information and orders his slave 'to tell the truth and not to make up things that seem like lies about how he came to have a son' (τἀληθῆ λέγειν μηδὲ ὅμοια πλάττειν μύθοις ἐπὶ τῷ κατέχειν τὸν υἱόν, 4.20.1). In his comment on the passage, Ewen Bowie observes, 'The tale that Lamon claims to be true is, after all, L.'s own narrative.'[30] Dionysophanes' order to his slave 'not to make things up' (μηδὲ … πλάττειν) serves as a reminder of the made-up events of the novel itself, the πλάσμα that is *Daphnis and Chloe*.[31]

While the authors of the treatises were not thinking of the ancient novels in their discussions of narration, evidence suggests that Longus drew on the rhetoricians in associating his narrative with the rhetoricians' *plasma*.[32] The treatises cite comedy in illustration of this type of narration; Cicero, for example, refers to Terence's *Andria*. The final book of *Daphnis and Chloe* is rich in allusion to stereotypical characters and situations drawn from New Comedy: a slave suspected of lying; an irate master; a recognition and recognition tokens; a marriage. There is also a parasite, Gnathon, who has the same name as the parasite in Terence's *Eunuchus*. Longus was undoubtedly familiar with rhetorical treatises dealing with narration. It seems possible

---

30 Bowie (2019, 287).
31 Dionysophanes' suspicion that Lamon was lying reflects the stereotype of the dishonest slave. There may also be an allusion here to the association between the novel genre and slaves as tellers of tales argued by Owens (2020).
32 Morgan (1993, 190) remarks on the absence of intentionality in the rhetorical discussions of *argumentum* or *plasma*: this type of narration could be represented both by a plausible lie intended to deceive and by a realistic fiction intended to entertain.

that he saw in the discussions in those texts on *plasma* and *argumentum* a framework for thinking about his own narrative.[33]

However, Longus distinguishes *Daphnis and Chloe* from the *plasma* of New Comedy. Dionysophanes' command 'to tell the truth and not to make up things that seem like lies' playfully re-engages with the *mythos* of the Heliconian Muses, who knew how to say many lies that are like true things but also how to sing the truth (*Theog.* 27–8). Thus, the author draws into association his two conceptual frameworks: Hesiod and the rhetorical treatises. Dionysophanes' command contrasts true *logos* with lying *mythos*. Lamon's story is true in the delimited terms of Longus's fiction, but the reminder of the Heliconian Muses suggests that *Daphnis and Chloe* contains a deeper truth, the unverifiable but authoritative truth of archaic *mythos*. In that respect Longus may have sought to distinguish his narrative from *plasma* as it was understood by the rhetoricians and represented in New Comedy.

Conclusion

Through allusion to the Heliconian Muses, Longus finds venerable authority for his fiction. Like the Muses, he is able to say 'many lies that are like true things'. By attaching the Hesiodic concept of *mythos* to philosophy's *logos–mythos* dichotomy, Longus plays with the concepts of literal and mythic truth. Thus, like the Muses, he also knows how to say true things in the archaic sense in which *mythos* was true. Through reference to the forms of narration (myth, history and fiction) discussed in rhetorical treatises, Longus triangulates his own narrative, which both is like and not like each of these forms. Bryan Reardon read *Daphnis and Chloe* as a text suspended between idealized *mythos* and a novel proper, whose *logos* aims more at realistic representation. This essay suggests that the author himself may have thought of his narrative along similar lines.

Works Cited

Athanassakis, Apostolos N. 2004. *Hesiod: Theogony, Works and Days, Shield*. Baltimore: Johns Hopkins University Press.

Barwick, K. 1928. 'Die Gliederung der *Narratio* in der rhetorischen Theorie und ihre Bedeutung für die Geschichte des antiken Romans'. *Hermes: Zeitschrift für klassische Philologie* 124: 261–88.

Berti, Marisa. 1967. 'Sulla interpretazione mistica del romanzo di Longo'. *Studi Classici e Orientali* 16: 343–58.

---

33 On Longus and New Comedy, see Berti (1967), Pandiri (1985), Zeitlin (1994).

Bowie, Ewen L. 1985. 'Theocritus' Seventh *Idyll*, Philetas and Longus'. *CQ* 35: 67–91.
———. 2019. *Longus: Daphnis and Chloe*. Cambridge: Cambridge University Press.
Calboli Montefusco, Lucia. 2006. 'Cic. *Inv.* 1.27 and *Rhet. Her.* 1.12 F.: The Question of the *Tertium Genus Narrationis*'. In *Papers on Rhetoric 7*, edited by Lucia Calboli Montefusco, 17–29. Rome: Herder.
Cueva, Edmund Paul. 1999. 'Longus and Thucydides: A New Interpretation'. *GRBS* 39: 429–40.
Feddern, Stefan. 2017. 'Zur Erzähltheorie in *de Inventione* (*Inv.* 1,27), in Der *Herennius-Rhetorik* (*Rhet. Her.* 1,12f.) und beim *Anonymus Seguerianus* (53–55)'. *Gymnasium* 124: 247–75.
Flory, Stewart. 1990. 'The Meaning of τὸ μὴ μυθῶδες (1.22.4) and the Usefulness of Thucydides' History'. *CJ* 85: 193–208.
Fowler, Robert Louis. 2011. '*Mythos* and *Logos*'. *JHS* 131: 45–66.
Gaca, Kathy L. 2010. 'Telling the Girls from the Boys and Children: Interpreting Παῖδες in the Sexual Violence of Populace-Ravaging Ancient Warfare'. *ICS* 35-6: 85–109.
Gill, Christopher. 1979. 'Plato's Atlantis Story and the Birth of Fiction'. *Philosophy and Literature* 3: 64–78.
Greco, Maria. 1998. *De Inventione: M. T. Cicerone*, vol. 3. Galatina: Congedo.
Henderson, Jeffrey. 2009. *Longus: Daphnis and Chloe. Xenophon of Ephesus: Anthia and Habrocomes*. Cambridge, MA: Harvard University Press.
Hornblower, Simon. 1991. *A Commentary on Thucydides*, vol. 1: *Books I–III*. Oxford: Clarendon Press.
Lincoln, Bruce. 1999. *Theorizing Myth: Narrative, Ideology, and Scholarship*. Chicago: University of Chicago Press.
Luginbill, Robert Dean. 2002. 'A Delightful Possession: Longus' Prologue and Thucydides'. *CJ* 97: 233–47.
MacQueen, Bruce D. 1985. 'Longus and the Myth of Chloe'. *ICS* 10: 119–34.
Morgan, John R. 1993. 'Make-Believe and Make Believe: The Fictionality of the Greek Novels'. In *Lies and Fiction in the Ancient World*, edited by Christopher Gill and T. P. Wiseman, 175–229. Austin: University of Texas Press.
———. 2011. 'Fiction and History: Historiography and the Novel'. In *A Companion to Greek and Roman Historiography*, edited by John Marincola, 553–64. Malden, MA: Blackwell.
Morgan, Kathryn. 2000. *Myth and Philosophy from the Presocratics to Plato*. Cambridge: Cambridge University Press.
Owens, William M. 2020. *The Representation of Slavery in the Greek Novel: Resistance and Appropriation*. London: Routledge.
Pandiri, T. A. 1985. '*Daphnis and Chloe*: The Art of Pastoral Play'. *Ramus* 14: 116–41.
Petridou, Georgia. 2015. *Divine Epiphany in Greek Literature and Culture*. Oxford: Oxford University Press.
Reardon, Bryan P. 1991. *The Form of Greek Romance*. Princeton: Princeton University Press.

———. 1994. '*Muthos ou Logos*: Longus's Lesbian Pastorals'. In *The Search for the Ancient Novel*, edited by James Tatum, 135–47. Baltimore: Johns Hopkins University Press.

Tilg, Stefan. 2010. *Chariton of Aphrodisias and the Invention of the Greek Love Novel*. Oxford: Oxford University Press.

Trzaskoma, Stephen. 2005. 'A Novelist Writing "History": Longus' Thucydides Again'. *GRBS* 45: 75–90.

West, M. L. 1988. *Theogony and Works and Days*. Oxford: Oxford University Press.

Winkler, John J. 1990. *The Constraints of Desire: The Anthropology of Sex and Gender in Ancient Greece*. London: Routledge.

Zeitlin, Froma I. 1994. 'Gardens of Desire in Longus's *Daphnis and Chloe*: Nature, Art, and Imitation'. In *The Search for the Ancient Novel*, edited by James Tatum, 148–70. Baltimore: Johns Hopkins University Press.

CHAPTER 11

The Body's Borders: Violation and the Visual in the Carmina Priapea

Tyler T. Travillian

There are remarkably few readings of the *Carmina Priapea* (*CP*), even though it has been known to the modern world since about 1340. Only since the turn of the millennium have scholars moved beyond using the *Carmina Priapea* indirectly, as, for example, Richlin did in *The Garden of Priapus*, where she mined the text for documentary evidence about Roman attitudes toward women and male homosexuals. In that text, she saw Priapus as representing a type of aggressive and violent male sexuality, saying that Priapus 'remains a *symbol* of mastery'.[1] The scholarship that treats the poems directly has focused mainly on categorizing, for example, the qualities and sources of individual poems, the types of poems, the metrical arrangements.[2] This has started to change.[3] The first dedicated reading of the *Carmina Priapea*, by Niklas Holzberg, reads through the poems linearly, as if (he says) an erotic novel in which the Protagonist, Priapus, transforms from potent to impotent.[4] At the end of this novel, the poet identifies himself with Priapus and converts the storyline into a metapoetic statement that small, seemingly impotent verse carries a big wallop. This is a valid reading, but it is important to remember that the *Carmina Priapea* make up not a linear novel but a book of epigrams.

1 Richlin (1992, 125).
2 Kloss (2003) and Höschele (2008) have documented the metrical arrangement of the poems; Bianchini (2001) the sources of individual passages and quotations; Buchheit (1962) the 'types' of poems; Clairmont (1983) and Travillian (2011) the MSS. The two best works on the *CP* to date are the introduction by W. H. Parker (1988) and the introduction and commentary by Callebat (2012), which mainly updates W. H. Parker's introduction, expands Bianchini's sources and adds linguistic commentary.
3 Vallat (2008) and Vallat (2012); Plantade (2008); Prioux (2008); Höschele (2008); Travillian (2017). Young (2015a) has noteworthy work on sensation, sensualism and touch, while Young (2015b) reads the *CP* as a metacommentary on the relationship between obscenity and Latin as a literary language. O'Connor (2019) is a throwback to the old, cataloguing type.
4 Holzberg (2005).

Epigrams come with their own expectations: they are polyvalent by nature, they demand to be read non-sequentially,[5] and they make social commentary. This is not to discount Holzberg's reading, which remains a way to read the text. Young offers another way, touching on the juxtaposition of the physical threats of 'bodily regulation' within the poems and the elegant – if not effete – 'sensory experiences available through its poetic form', that is, the figured touch of Priapus, and the all-too-real sonic caresses of the *Priapea*-as-poetry.[6] I suggest that another of the senses, the gaze, shows the reader a way to combine and expand on Holzberg and Young's readings, revealing two other simultaneous readings that are necessarily in tension, that necessarily comment on each other: a Priapic Reading, which uses sexual humor and invective to enforce social norms on those lower in the social hierarchy, and a Subversive Reading that destabilizes and re-evaluates the elite masculinity that the poems at first appear to reinforce.

The Priapic Reading: Visual Pleasure and Priapic Poetry

I call the first of these the Priapic reading after the so-called 'Priapic pose' of elite Roman male sexuality: the elite male uses sexual humor and invective to enforce social norms on those lower in the social hierarchy. Sexual threat (that is, violating the body's borders) is a metaphor for assertion of questioned dominance.[7] This reading is active in the *Carmina Priapea*: in fact, it is the dominant reading. But what is absent from the dominant reading is an acknowledgment that these poems are a written text, and so the threat is active only through the gaze. Indeed, the first poem in the collection explicitly states the importance of the gaze, inviting us to 'read these

---

5   See Martial 13.3.8, *Addita per titulos sua nomina rebus habebis: | praetereas, si quid non facit ad stomachum* ('You'll have the proper names added to the items via titles: | so pass over anything if it doesn't suit your fancy'); 14.2.4, *Lemmata si quaeris cur sint adscripta, docebo: | Ut, si malueris, lemmata sola legas* ('If you ask why titles have been added, I'll tell you: | so that, if you prefer, you may read just the titles'); 10.1, *fac tibi me quam cupis ipse brevem* ('Make me [the book] as short as you want').

6   Young (2015a, 185), though she perhaps overstates the relationship between the sensualism some find in poetry-*qua*-poetry and 'unmanly' pleasure.

7   Richlin (1992, 140–1). A fuller version of the quotation: 'The main victims of sexual invective – women, old women, and pathic homosexuals – represent by their sexual behavior the social behavior that the narrator wishes to dissociate from himself … The phallus is the source of both interpersonal dominance and sexual mastery, as at Horace I.2.44 [*Sermones*], where the servants punish the adulterer by urinating upon him; the penis contains and ejects both urine and semen, stain and seed. Conversely, Priapus threatens rape, a sexual punishment, against thieves, committers of a non-sexual crime that yet infringes on Priapus' property. Sexual threat is thus a metaphor for assertion of a questioned dominance over personal property.'

poems with the same eyes with which you look at this [Priapus's phallus]' (1.8). It is worth noting, too, that the poem genders the reader as masculine from the beginning (*lecture*, 'you about to read', 1.1) investing us, as it were, in the male gaze, much as cinema did in Mulvey's original formulation of Gaze Theory.[8]

Women in the *Carmina Priapea* are always portrayed as lustful, falling into three basic categories: the prostitute on display, the matron who only pretends to be chaste and the sexually voracious old woman. All three are linked by sexual appetite. If we look at poem 4:

> Obscenas rigido deo tabellas,
> Ducens ex Elephantidos libellis,
> Dat donum Lalage rogatque, temptes,
> Si pictas opus edat ad figuras.

> As she brings the stiff god obscene
> sketches from Elephantis's manual,
> Lalage gives them as a gift and asks you to find out
> if she can reproduce the poses painted there.

The poem invites the reader first to visualize the obscene pictures from Elephantis's sex manual (juxtaposed on Priapus's stiffness), then to picture Lalage, whom we remember as a love interest from Horace, *Odes* 1.22, and finally to put himself vicariously in the position of judge, and perhaps collaborator, as she tries out the positions. One could hardly imagine a better candidate for what Mulvey calls the phallocentric scopophilic gaze: a male viewer is taking pleasure from watching a woman as sexual object and is using that view to reinforce her place in society as object to the male subject. One could hardly imagine a better candidate, but the collection improves upon itself with poem 19, in which the poet describes an erotic dancer. Instead of inviting us to imagine the image as before, the poet gives us six rather detailed lines:

> Hic quando Telethusa circulatrix,
> Quae clunem tunica tegente nulla
> Extis latius altiusque motat,[9]
> Crisabit tibi fluctuante lumbo:
> Haec sic non modo te, Priape, posset
> Privignum quoque sed movere Phaedrae.

---

8 Mulvey (1975).
9 The Latin of this line is terribly corrupt, but the sense is clear.

If ever Telethusa, the streetwalker,
who, without a shred of clothing covering her ass,
shakes ever longer and deeper than her guts,
will twerk for you with rolling loins:
she, doing this would make not only you
twitch, Priapus, but even Phaedra's stepson.

The dancer, Telethusa (both 'the one who initiates' and 'the one who brings to a finish'), is so erotic, the poet tells us, she could arouse even mythology's archetypal asexual, Hippolytus. And poem 27 continues in this fashion, with another four lines describing another erotic dancer.[10]

The second type of woman is the matron who only pretends to be chaste. We see this in *CP* 8:

Matronae procul hinc abite castae:
Turpe est vos legere impudica verba
Non assis faciunt euntque recta:
Nimirum sapiunt videntque magnam
Matronae quoque mentulam libenter.

Matrons, go far from here, if you're respectable:
It's shameful for you to read shameless words.
They don't care a bit and go right on:
no wonder! Matrons too are wise/have taste[11] and
gladly look at a big *mentula*.

Here, the matron is the one looking, but the reader is watching her do it, one might say, as if through a keyhole. The warning comes too late: any matron who has made it this far has already compromised her matronly status, and the reader knows it, so he gets to imagine her as not so chaste, as liking the same objectifying sexuality he likes – inscribing the male fantasy

---

10 *Deliciae populi, magno notissima circo, | Quintia, vibratas docta movere nates, | Cymbala cum crotalis, pruriginis arma, Priapo | Ponit et adducta tympana pulsa manu: | Pro quibus, ut semper placeat spectantibus, orat, | Tentaque ad exemplum sit sua turba dei* ('The darling of the people, so well known in the great circus, Quintia, skilled at shimmying and shaking her buttocks, dedicates her cymbals and castanets, lust's weapons, to Priapus and her drums, too, beaten with her hand held close; in exchange for which, she asks that she always delight her spectators and that her crowd always be taut, just like the god').

11 For 'taste' as another important sense in the *CP*, see also *CP* 71. Young (2018, 143) mistakes the register by reading *sapiunt* as 'they taste' = 'they suck on a huge cock'. *Sapere* never means 'to taste' in the active sense – that is reserved for *gustare*. The innuendo lurking beneath 'they have good taste' is more muted and indirect: at most, 'matrons, too, have got the taste'.

onto the inner life of the female figure with her gaze. This theme is reprised more explicitly in poem 66,[12] and we see there a voyeuristic gaze that enjoys watching the secret, sexual side of women – or rather, inscribing on women a sexual side as imagined by the Priapic gaze of the male readers.

The third type is the old woman, figured always as unattractive and sexually voracious. For example, poem 12:

> Quaedam iunior Hectoris parente,
> Cumaeae soror, ut puto, Sibyllae,
> Aequalis tibi, quam domum revertens
> Theseus repperit in rogo iacentem,
> Infirmo solet huc gradu venire
> Rugosasque manus ad astra tollens,
> Ne desit sibi mentula rogare.
> Hesterna quoque nocte dum precatur,
> Dentem de tribus excreavit unum.
> 'Tolle, inquam, procul et iube latere
> Scissa sub tunica stolaque russa,
> Ut semper solet, et timere lucem,
> Qui tanto patet indecens hiatu,
> Barbato macer eminente naso,
> Ut credas Epicuron oscitari!'

A certain woman rather young (compared to Hector's mother!), a sister, I think, to the Cumaean Sibyl, the same age as you, whom Theseus, when he came home, found lying on a funeral pyre, she, with her faltering step, tends to come here, and lifting her wrinkled hands to the stars, she asks that there be a *mentula* for her, too. And last night, while she was praying, she spat out one of her three teeth. 'Pick it up', I say, 'and make it hide far away under your torn shirt and red dress, like it usually does, and make it shy from the light, that "tooth" that's right out in the open – indecent! – in such a gaping maw, tiny with a hairy nose sticking out above it so that you'd think it was Epicuros yawning!'

This is incredibly vivid and visual: the woman is the form of old age, hobbling and wrinkled, and she opens her dress to Priapus, only to be brutally rejected. We might categorize this as a Narcissistic gaze – the other type of

---

12 *Tu quae, ne videas notam virilem,* | *Hinc averteris, ut decet pudicam:* | *Nimirum, nisi quod times videre,* | *Intra viscera habere concupiscis* ('You who – lest you see the mark of a man – turn away from here (as befits a proper woman); doubtless you will, unless ... the thing you're afraid to look at, you long to have inside your guts').

pleasurable gaze Mulvey identified in cinema. The audience, our elite male reader here, gets pleasure by identifying with the 'alpha male' of the scene (Priapus) as he uses his masculinity to assert control over the environment, in this case rejecting the old woman for transgressing proper female behavior, which she does by seeking sex actively and thinking to act on a male rather than being a passive participant. The same theme reappears, just as brutally, at poems 32, 46 and 57.[13]

Men also appear in the *Carmina Priapea*, but only two types. The first is the thief, who is threatened with bodily violation (rape), and the second is the *cinaedus*, who willingly seeks out bodily violation. The elite Roman male is supposed only to be the active partner in any sexual activity.[14] Taking the passive role removes him from status as *vir* ('real man') and reduces him to the status of mere *homo*, a male of any of the socially subordinate classes. So for a thief to be raped is a social as well as physical violation, a theme taken up by poem 15.

> Commisso mihi non satis modestas
> Quicumque attulerit manus agello,
> Is me sentiet esse non spadonem.
> Dicat forsitan haec sibi ipse: 'nemo
> Hic, inter frutices, loco remoto
> Percisum sciet esse me.' sed errat:
> Magnis testibus ista res agetur.

> Whoever should bring hands that don't quite keep to themselves to the plot entrusted to me, that man will feel that I am no eunuch. He might perhaps say these things to himself: 'No one here among the shrubs in this remote place will know that I have been raped'; but he's wrong: the case will be argued by these great witnesses/testicles.

---

13 *CP* 32: *Uvis aridior puella passis, | buxo pallidior novaque cera, | collatas sibi quae suisque membris | formicas facit altiles videri, | cuius viscera non aperta Tuscus | per pellem poterit videre haruspex, | quae suco caret usque pura pumex, | nemo viderit hanc ut expuentem, | quam pro sanguine pulverem scobemque | in venis medici putant habere, | ad me nocte solet venire et affert | pallorem maciemque larualem. | Ductor ferreus, insularis aeque | lanternae videor fricare cornu* ('A "girl" more dried out than grapes, and sallower than boxwood or new wax, who makes ants, compared to her and her arms, look well fed, whose entrails a Tuscan haruspex could inspect through her skin without even opening her up, who is so bone dry and pure pumice that no one has seen her spit, whom doctors think has dust for blood and sawdust in her veins, *she* is accustomed to come to me at night and *she* brings her pallor and ghastly thinness. I seem to be an iron lampholder rubbing the horn of a corner lamp').

14 H. Parker (1997, 47–65).

And here Priapus threatens not just the physical rape but also social rape, bringing in the societal normative gaze of shame culture. We might note that Priapus also forces the reader's (mental) eyes onto his abnormally large (and therefore virile?) testicles. This is the Narcissistic gaze again, as the reader aligns with Priapus punishing the theft. There is, however, also an undercurrent of shock and surprise, the beginning of the notion that the reader might not be entirely in on the joke, but rather the butt of it. There are quite a few more of these thief poems.[15]

The second type of male figure is the pathic male: the male who is not only debased by taking the passive role in sex acts, but is figured as preferring it: the *cinaedus*.[16] This figure is lambasted for taking the female role, as we can see at poem 45:

> Cum quendam rigidus deus videret
> Ferventi caput ustulare ferro,
> Ut Maurae similis foret puellae,
> 'Heus, inquit, tibi dicimus, cinaede,
> Uras te licet usque torqueasque,
> Num tandem prior es puella, quaeso,
> Quam sunt, mentula quos habet, capilli.'

> When the stiff god saw a certain man singeing his hair with a hot iron so that he would be like a Moorish girl, he said, 'Hey, I'm talking to you, *cinaedus*. Even if you burn yourself and twist yourself all the way up, surely, I ask, you still aren't any more a girl than the hairs of your head are a *mentula*'s short-and-curlies.'

The *cinaedus* is visually determined, a state imposed upon an individual from the outside, just as objectifying sexuality was imposed upon the matron earlier. The figure appears again explicitly at poems 25 and 46. Most interestingly, the thief and *cinaedus* types merge at the end of poem 51.[17] Here, Priapus asks why all the thieves come to his little yard when

---

15 CP 17, 22, 23, 24, 28, 30, 31, 35, 38, 44, 51, 52, 55, 56, 58, 59, 64, 69, 71, 72, 77 – for a total of twenty-three poems.

16 The question remains open whether the *cinaedus* as such was a true social category with which individuals identified, or if it was only a category used to censure, malign and socially injure.

17 *Quid hoc negoti est quave suspicer causa | Venire in hortum plurimos meum fures, | Cum, quisquis in nos incidit, luat poenas | Et usque curuos excavetur ad lumbos? | ... | Quae cuncta quamvis nostro habemus in saepto, | Non pauciora proximi ferunt horti. | Quibus relictis in mihi laboratum | Locum venitis, improbissimi fures: | Nimirum apertam convolatis ad poenam, | hoc vos et ipsum, quod minamur, invitat* ('What business is there here, or why should I see so many thieves come into my garden, when whoever falls upon me

the neighboring plots are at least as fruitful. He concludes that the thieves must like the punishment he doles out, equating them with *cinaedi* and appearing to make good on the threat of poem 15 to expose the thieves publicly. The author controls how the reader sees (literally) the thief by drawing attention to physical violation.[18] Although explicit visual imagery is less prevalent in these poems, it seems to me that we might still link the poems to the audience's Narcissistic gaze that takes pleasure in watching (or imagining that they see) Priapus dole out appropriate punishments to those who transgress proper masculine behavior. In favor of this reading, *viri* (real men) are almost wholly absent from the *Carmina Priapea*. Only men who violate the norms appear. So instead of acting in the poems, *viri* have as their surrogate Priapus, who takes on the role of norm-enforcer. This permits the reader to imagine himself as the *vir*, filling out the last role in the Roman gender schema. But having Priapus as their surrogate introduces real problems for how the reader sees *viri*.

The Subversive Reading: Visual Ambiguities

The Priapic Reading relies on the gaze, but the gaze runs both ways. It invites us to look for a subversive reading. The first indication of this reading comes early, at poem 10:

> Insulsissima quid puella rides?
> Non me Praxiteles Scopasve fecit,
> Non sum Phidiaca manu politus;
> Sed lignum rude villicus dolavit,
> Et dixit mihi: 'tu Priapus esto!'
> Spectas me tamen et subinde rides:
> Nimirum tibi salsa res videtur
> Adstans inguinibus columna nostris.

> You utterly witless girl, why are you laughing? Praxiteles didn't make me, nor did Scopas, nor was I polished by Phidias's hand, but the bailiff hacked me out of raw wood and said to me, 'You shall be Priapus.' Yet you keep looking at me and then laughing. It's no

---

pays the penalty and is hollowed out all the way to the curve of his loins? [*Lines 5–22: a list of the vegetables that do not grow well in this garden.*] And although we have all these things in our plot, the neighboring gardens bear just as many. But with these abandoned, all you shameless thieves come into my spot to work. No doubt you flock to a penalty that's right out in the open and what we threaten is the very thing that attracts you!').

18 Young (2015a, 197) goes further and argues that the reader is also merged with the thief and *cinaedus* by assimilating *poema legere* ('to read the poem') to *poenam/pomam legere* ('to pluck the penalty/fruit').

wonder you see the situation as a joke: there's a column standing at attention on my loins!

Here we see Priapus subject to the female gaze. It is the female gaze that is determining the body of Priapus.[19] Priapus is usually thought of as exhibitionistic – since seeing his phallus equates to being visually penetrated by it – but he does not hold up well here, and it is the reaction that makes it so: the girl laughs at him, which turns him from a figure of threat to a figure of fun (*salsa*). She emasculates him, turns him back into wood, and suddenly it is her gaze that is doing the penetrating.

Poem 10 brings with it a realization that may surprise the casual reader: nowhere in the *Carmina Priapea* does Priapus act. He threatens and blusters, but he never acts.[20] 'Sexual threat', Richlin says, 'is a metaphor for the assertion of questioned dominance',[21] but what happens when the threat-maker is incapable of carrying out those threats? Are they disarmed? Unmanned? Even Priapus's speech acts, such as they are, are not public – they are only made in front of the person threatened and so carry no true consequence. That is quite significant for the representative of the active male opposed to the acted upon – namely, women and non-normative males. Looking at it this way, we can return to the poems depicting old women. In poem 12, Priapus tells the woman to scram, but we do not know if she did. We are not told what happens next. This stands in contrast to Horace, *Serm.* 1.8, where the Priapus statue frightens away witches that have come in the night. There we are told explicitly that 'they ran to the city' (*illae currere in urbem*, 1.8.47). If we read this in context, the following poem, 13, seems like a re-assertion of deflated masculinity: *Percidere, puer, moneo! futuere, puella! | Barbatum furem tertia poena manet!* As if he says, 'I'll rape boys, girls and men.' But what about the old woman? She is noticeably absent, as if he wants to forget. It grows more meaningful when we compare poem 32, where the woman does in fact use Priapus sexually. Here he is the passive

---

19 Priapus is visualized as a rough hack. Among other motives, this may be a pre-emptive aesthetic comment by the poet defending the poems against the polished, Callimachean aesthetic.
20 How do you enact a threat through words or poems? You have to make the reader complicit in carrying out the threat by the very act of reading the words. The *CP* attempt this in the riddle poems: 7, 54, 55 and 67. In 7, sounding out the lisp (*te pe dico*) enunciates the threat: *te pedico*. In 54, drawing out the riddle (*CD si scribas temonemque*) inscribes the *phallus* directly. In 55, the final pun, *Gallus* as ethnonym and *gallus* as eunuch, reinscribes the *falx* as phallus. In 67, the reader spelling out the first syllables (*pe-di-ca-re*), is once again caught, as in 7, in the act of pedication. These all end up being notional violations, and they do not discriminate among readers, affecting the *vir* as well as the *cinaedus* and the *femina*. This non-discrimination undercuts their efficacy as true threats and enforcers of social norms.
21 Richlin (1992, 140–1).

partner, inasmuch as he had sex against his will. He is riding close to the definition of the pathic *cinaedus*. In poems 51–6 the thieves get back their own, too. On the surface 51 blasts the thieves for being *cinaedi* – pathics – but to score the point, Priapus must belittle the size of his own 'garden' and inadvertently points out his own impotence: the thieves are the ones acting, not Priapus. As we might by now expect, poem 52 is a programmatic 'steal and you'll be raped' poem that comes after Priapus has had to lower his gaze, so to speak, but 53 reminds the god that he is minor and should be content with just a little: he is just not big enough.[22] And to cap it off, in poem 55, the thieves steal Priapus's sickle so that he is not only impotent and passive, but now he is a eunuch who has to ask his master in 56 to orally rape thieves for him.[23] Here we see a return to the laughter from poem 10 and a direct invocation of the gaze. This is really the depth of Priapus's degradation, a depth we see more fully explored in poem 73.

> Obliquis quid me, pathicae, spectatis ocellis?
> Non stat in inguinibus mentula tenta meis.
> Quae tamen exanimis nunc est et inutile lignum,
> Utilis haec, aram si dederitis, erit.

> Why are you looking at me with sidelong eyes, you tarts? It's not a *mentula* standing taut on my loins, this thing which, lifeless now and useless wood, will nevertheless be useful, if you will dedicate your altar to it.

Priapus openly acknowledges the female gaze here as he did earlier, and he admits that he is just lifeless and useless wood. Where in poem 10 he was still masculine enough to be embarrassed by his ineffectiveness, here he offers to serve a male role only if the women will take the active part by

---

22 *Contentus modico Bacchus solet esse racemo, | Cum capiant alti vix cita musta lacus, | Magnaque fecundis cum messibus area desit, | In Cereris crines una corona datur. | Tu quoque, dive minor, maiorum exempla secutus, | Quamvis pauca damus, consule poma boni*
   ('Bacchus is used to being happy with a modest bunch of grapes, even when the deep vats can hardly hold the quickened must, and when a large threshing floor isn't enough for the fertile harvests, only one crown is given to Ceres' hair. You, too, lesser god, following the examples of the greater ones: though I give but little, consider them a good man's fruit').
23 *Derides quoque, fur, et impudicum | Ostendis digitum mihi minanti? | Heu! Heu! me miserum! quid ista lignum est, | Quae me terribilem facit videri? | Mandabo domino tamen salaci, | Ut pro me velit irrumare fures* ('You're laughing, too, thief, and showing me the dirty finger when I threaten you? Woe is me! Why is that thing wood that makes me seem frightful? Still, I will entrust to my lusty master that he be willing to rape [orally] thieves on my behalf').

'dedicating their altar'. The juxtaposition of *pathicae* with *non stat mentula tenta* vividly brings out the contrast: 'I'm no good for passive women. I can only play the male role if you take the lead.' This casts Priapus clearly as a *cinaedus*, the very opposite of the *vir*.

Seeing Double: A Generic Question

Moving beyond Priapus's rhetoric, we see a multiplicity of gazes operating with and against each other: (1) the subaltern gaze of women and thieves, (2) the 'reader's gaze', simultaneously penetrating and penetrated, and (3) an inscrutable 'author's gaze', setting the poems in the context of their cycles and adjoining pieces. Each of these gazes reinforces and undermines Priapus – and thus the elite Roman male reader, the *vir*, who identifies with him. So how are we to read the *Carmina Priapea*? The ambiguity of the multiple gazes comes clear through the lens of genre. The topic has largely been avoided because the poems seem so unique.[24]

The *Carmina Priapea* are satire and, as such, fundamentally political. Susanna Morton Braund identifies four key features of satire: the presence of playfulness and criticism, the familiar, its distortion and urban, polyglot audience. Each of these clearly applies to the *Carmina Priapea*: the poems form a playful critique of Priapus, the worship of Priapus and Roman aggressive sexuality in general. On the axis of the familiar and its distortions, at the micro level, the poems make jokes, which are by definition a distortion of the familiar,[25] and on a macro level the poems distort the god himself, turning him from a protector of fertility and travelers into a symbol of ludicrously impotent aggression. The setting, too, is often urban[26] and presupposes fluency in Greek.[27] The cleverness

---

24 The scholars who come closest to discussing genre are W. H. Parker (1988), who assumes a Priapic genre without discussion, Bianchini (2001, 49), who assumes the same, saying that it 'is independent and autonomous, yet valorizing certain salacious, biting, and explicitly erotic ideas already present in comic and satiric authors'. Callebat (2012, xxxiii–xxxvi) considers the poems too diverse to classify but decides they are definitely not satire but rather 'ethnographie burlesque', which he defines as material taken from the social sphere that is mocked and poked fun at (that is, satire). Goldberg (1992) does not address the question.

25 Jokes, by their very nature, work by setting up an expectation (that is, engaging the familiar) and then exaggerating or reversing the expected conclusion (that is, distortion). It is the cleavage between the expectation and the distorted conclusion that we experience as humor.

26 Note especially the temple (*templi parietibus tui notavi*, CP 2.10), the shrine (*sacellum*, CP 14.2), the urban prostitute (*circulatrix*, CP 19.1), the Via Sacra (CP 21.4) and the mention of the Suburan neighborhood (CP 40.1).

27 CP 68 reinterprets the *Iliad* and the *Odyssey* in terms of sexual conflicts – over Helen and Penelope – and includes several words in Greek that were not naturalized into

and high degree of literary allusion in the poems suggest that the audience is in fact metropolitan and only pretending to take on a rural mask as part of the book's conceit. Finally, the tone of apparent anger and aggression (usually undercut by the impotence of the speaker or by some other factor) is the same tone Roman satire strikes. Nor is satire's close association with play (*ludus*) absent. As Thomas Habinek notes, 'Roman satire describes itself as play more often than it describes itself as satire. Its playfulness consists in part of its relationship to other, ostensibly more serious, literary genres (for example, epic, oratory, history).'[28] So too the explicit self-description of the *Carmina Priapea* in the two introductory poems: *CP* 1 names the poems themselves *lusus ... procaces* ('bold play'), while *CP* 2 begins by calling the poet *ludens* (playing). The collection rounds out the association with play at *CP* 70, where Priapus complains that a dirty pauper has 'played a trick' on him (*illusit*). Thus the *Carmina Priapea* follow satire closely in content and attitude, and in fact seem to be establishing from the very first poems an explicit relationship with that genre.

The form of the *Carmina Priapea*, however, does not fit traditional Roman satire: the poems are hendecasyllables, elegiac couplets and choliambs, not dactylic hexameter; and they are short: from two to thirty lines each. Instead, they closely resemble epigrams of the Neronian and Flavian eras, particularly Lucillius and Nicharcus, whom the *Carmina Priapea* occasionally quote from and allude to.[29] Gideon Nisbet describes the epigrams of these authors as short, witty poems that build to a 'point' and are in some way satirical, incorporating 'a range of anti-realist strategies: paradox, hyperbole, parody,' and as conveying a particularly rough kind of misogyny[30] – and this is just what we see in the *Carmina Priapea*. But as close as the *Carmina Priapea* come to Nicharcus's and Lucillius's kinds of epigram in strategies and form, epigrammatic books were rarely themed, and we know of none with extended focus on a single character, the way we see in the longer poems of satire. So we have a genre form here that takes its content and attitude from satire but many of its strategies and structure from Neronian-era epigram, situating it precisely at the focal point of genre in the Derridean sense: the edge between two spaces where an author creates something new.

_{Latin. Note also the Greek proper names throughout, the particular wordplay on Sirius and Erigone at *CP* 62 and the use of Greek at *CP* 72.4, if the reading *bracchia macra* is correct.}

28 Habinek (2005, 177).
29 I omit Martial here due to the uncertainty around dating the *CP*. It seems likely that most of Martial's work postdates the *CP*, even occasionally alluding to or quoting the *CP*.
30 Nisbet (2003, xv).

The *Carmina Priapea* are something new: a *libellus* of satiric epigrams. Epigram breaks up the monotone of a single text and, under the guise of light poetry, invites a polyvalence of meaning, as the poems can be read and re-read with and against each other, sequentially and non-sequentially, in varying cycles, just as the *Carmina Priapea* can and should be read. Satire, meanwhile, aims at social commentary and critique through biting description of social circumstances. The *Carmina Priapea* combine these techniques to invite and delight multiple readers: the *viri* who identify with Priapus and assert social and hierarchical norms; and the various members of the subordinate classes who see themselves acting successfully against Priapus, evading punishment and ultimately emasculating Priapus as their society emasculates them. The *Carmina Priapea* not only allow these multiple readings but link them with a strong central protagonist who, as Holzberg shows, develops over the course of the book from aggressively potent to pathetically impotent.[31] This evolving backdrop encourages multiple and subversive readings and re-readings by the very fact that it destabilizes the elite male gaze. Shadi Bartsch has done much to show the anxiety the senatorial class felt about the destabilization of their gaze under Nero and subsequent emperors, particularly the increasingly narrow distinction between the gazed-at subject and the gazed-at object.[32] As she puts it: 'because the gaze could be aggressive as well as admiring, destructive as well as productive, one needed to have control over its motivation, origin, and direction in order to maintain control over its effects – a control that the Roman upper classes practiced with varying degrees of success'.[33] And it is that control which gradually dissipates under the emperors. This anxiety is immediate under Nero and especially Domitian, who, under the guise of moral reforms, engaged in an active campaign of censorship in all senses of that word about the time when the *Carmina Priapea* were published. The elite male reader seeing Priapus's degradation would not, as Richlin asserts, feel that he was 'express[ing] dominance over him, superior over his wooden form'.[34] That is the straight reading. His position has become too precarious for such optimism. Instead, he would feel at the same time his identification with Priapus and the satirical commentary on the Priapic pose. We can see this quite clearly in the final two poems, 79 and 80:

Priape, quod sis fascino gravis tento,
Quod exprobravit hic tibi suo versu

---

[31] Holzberg (2005).
[32] See Bartsch (1998) and (2006).
[33] Bartsch (2006, 116).
[34] Richlin (1992, 125).

Poeta noster, erubescere hoc noli:
Non es poeta sarcinosior nostro.

Priapus, although you are burdened with an erect phallus, which our poet has blamed you for here in his verse, don't blush at it: you've got no more baggage than our poet!

CP 79

At non longa satis, non stat bene mentula crassa
Et quam si tractes, crescere posse putes?
Me miserum, cupidas fallit mensura puellas:
Non habet haec aliud mentula maius eo.
Utilior Tydeus qui, si quid credis Homero,
Ingenio pugnax, corpore parvus erat.
Sed potuit damno nobis novitasque pudorque
Esse, repellendus saepius iste mihi.

Dum vivis, sperare decet: tu, rustice custos,
Huc ades et nervis, tente Priape, fave.

Well, isn't it long enough, and quite the thick dick, and one which you'd think could grow if you handle it? Darn it all, the size dupes eager girls: this cock doesn't have anything bigger than that. Still, Tydeus was rather useful, who, if you believe Homer at all, was talented at fighting, though his body was small. But this novelty and embarrassment could wreck me and I've got to fight it off.

While you live, it is right to hope. You, rustic guardian, be present here and, taut Priapus, help my 'vigor'.

CP 80

In 79 the poet makes an ambiguous claim: 'I've made fun of your large phallus, but don't worry, it's not bigger than mine.' This is an explicit rendering of the identification of the elite male with Priapus, and it seems at first to support the Priapic pose, to remove anxiety over the gaze. But in 80 the poet is very clear that his phallus only looks like it should be large but actually is deceptive. We might say that it has been deflated by the gaze. This makes us reevaluate 79 and realize that the aggressive exterior Priapus shows – the Priapic pose – is just a pose, and that it can dissolve under a different gaze. This goes beyond expressing anxiety or modes of negotiating gazes that Bartsch identifies in Tacitus and Seneca. This suggests inevitability. And most telling is the author's solution: he published the *Carmina Priapea* anonymously.[35] The only way to protect himself was to become invisible.

Works Cited

Bartsch, Shadi. 1998. *Actors in the Audience*. Cambridge, MA: Harvard University Press.

———. 2006. *The Mirror of the Self: Sexuality, Self-Knowledge, and the Gaze in the Early Roman Empire*. Chicago: University of Chicago Press.

Bianchini, E. 2001. *Carmina Priapea*. Milan: Rizzoli.

Biville, F., E. Plantade and D. Vallat, eds. 2008. *'Le vers du plus nul des poètes …': nouvelles recherches sur les Priapées*. Lyon: Maison de l'Orient et de la Méditerranée.

Buchheit, Vinzenz. 1962. *Studien zum Corpus Priapeorum*. Munich: Beck.

Callebat, Louis. 2012. *Priapées*. Paris: Les Belles Lettres.

Clairmont, Richard. 1983. 'Carmina Priapea'. PhD diss., Loyola University. ProQuest (8317404).

Goldberg, Christiane. 1992. *Carmina Priapea: Einleitung, Übersetzung, Interpretation und Kommentar*. Heidelberg: Carl Winter Universitätsverlag.

Habinek, Thomas. 2005. 'Satire as Aristocratic Play'. In *The Cambridge Companion to Roman Satire*, edited by Kirk Freudenburg, 177–91. Cambridge: Cambridge University Press.

Holzberg, Niklas. 2005. 'Impotence? It Happened to the Best of Them! A Linear Reading of the *Corpus Priapeorum*'. *Hermes* 133: 368–81.

Höschele, Regina. 2008. 'Priape mis en abyme, ou comment clore le recueil'. In Biville et al. 2008, 53–66.

Kloss, Gerrit. 2003. 'Überlegungen zur Verfaserschaft und Datierung der *Carmina Priapea*'. *Hermes* 131: 464–85.

Mulvey, Laura. 1975. 'Visual Pleasure and Narrative Cinema'. *Screen* 16: 6–18.

Nisbet, Gideon. 2003. *Greek Epigram in the Roman Empire: Martial's Forgotten Rivals*. Oxford: Oxford University Press.

O'Connor, Eugene. 2019. '*Carminis Incompti Lusus*: The *Carmina Priapea*'. In *A Companion to Ancient Epigram*, edited by Christer Henriksén, 541–56. Hoboken: Wiley Blackwell.

Parker, Holt. 1997. 'The Teratogenic Grid'. In *Roman Sexualities*, edited by Judith P. Hallett and Marilyn B. Skinner, 47–65. Princeton: Princeton University Press.

Parker, W. H. 1988. *Priapea: Poems for a Phallic God*. London: Croom Helm.

Peirano, Irene. 2012. *The Rhetoric of the Roman Fake: Latin Pseudepigrapha in Context*. Cambridge: Cambridge University Press.

Plantade, E. 2008. '*Priapus gloriosus*: poétique d'un discours compensatoire'. In Biville et al. 2008, 99–120.

Prioux, E. 2008. '*At non longa bene est?* Priape face à la tradition du discours critique alexandrin'. In Biville et al. 2008, 157–82.

---

35 For more on pseudepigrapha, see Peirano (2012, esp. 66–80).

Richlin, Amy. 1992. *The Garden of Priapus: Sexuality and Aggression in Roman Humor*. New York: Columbia University Press.

Travillian, Tyler. 2017. '*Credere quis possit? Falcem subripuere*: An Alternative Reading of the *Carmina Priapea*'. *Sino-American Journal of Comparative Literature*, December: 5–43.

Vallat, Daniel. 2008. 'Épigramme et *variatio*: Priape et le cycle des dieux (Pr. 9, 20, 36, 39, 75)'. In '*Le vers du plus nul des poètes ...*': *nouvelles recherches sur les Priapées*, edited by F. Biville, E. Plantade and D. Vallat, 69–82. Lyon: Maison de l'Orient et de la Méditerranée.

———. 2012. 'Hors du jardin, hors de l'épigramme: pour une relecture métapoétique des *Priapées*'. *Bollettino di Studi Latini* 42: 15–28.

Young, Elizabeth. 2015a. 'The Touch of the Cinaedus: Unmanly Sensations in the *Carmina Priapea*'. *CA* 34: 183–208.

———. 2015b. '*Dicere Latine*: The Art of Speaking Crudely in the *Carmina Priapea*'. In *Ancient Obscenities: Their Nature and Use in the Ancient Greek and Roman Worlds*, edited by Dorota Dutsch and Ann Suter, 255–80. Ann Arbor: University of Michigan Press.

———. 2018. 'The Touch of Poetry in the *Carmina Priapea*'. In *Touch and the Ancient Senses*, edited by Alex Purves, 134–49. London: Routledge.

CHAPTER 12

What Are the Goals of Lucretius's De Rerum Natura?

James J. O'Hara

This chapter will explore some arguments in favor of an unpopular position: that in its original social and literary context Lucretius's *De Rerum Natura* may possibly have been seen as, and may even have been meant as, a virtuoso versification of a way of looking at the world in which the art and skill and reader's pleasure matter more than the content. Lucretius, to be sure, seems sincerely obsessed with the goal of convincing his reader to adopt Epicureanism, seems to be 'that extraordinary thing, a real didactic poem, the first since the fifth century', to quote Richard Jenkyns, who has also said that 'Lucretius is genuinely trying to write philosophy in verse, to expound, argue, and persuade, and no one, it seems, had seriously attempted that for nearly four hundred years.'[1] But there are some arguments and pieces of evidence that point in another direction, some newer or neglected arguments that I think can give fresh life to this old question. My hope is to give even those who resist thinking about this position some pause, and that thinking through the question will be useful, even if ultimately many or perhaps even most readers of this piece will not adopt it.

Among the points I will mention are: (1) Sedley's demonstration that Lucretius mainly followed only one text, Epicurus's *On Nature*, bringing his practice more in line with that of the Hellenistic practitioners of 'literary' didactic from whom he is usually so sharply distinguished;[2] (2) the problem of how readers of 'the first' 'real' didactic 'since the fifth century' would know how to handle it, and the suggestions about contemporary readers' horizon of expectations illustrated by Cicero's claim that the Hellenistic didactic poets Aratus and Nicander knew nothing about their subject matter when they wrote 'excellent, nicely ornamented verses' about them; (3) the further suggestions about contemporary expectations inherent in Philodemus's claim, contemporary with Lucretius, that poetry itself

---

1 Jenkyns (1998, 162) and (2007, 15).
2 Sedley (1998).

provides no benefit, but should 'imitate' or 'represent' the style of writing that actually seeks to teach; (4) Lucretius's ignoring, according to many but not all scholars, of most philosophical developments after Epicurus, with a focus here on his ridicule of the notion that the mind might be able to exist in the head; and (5) Horace's description in *Satire* 1.10 of how he came to write satire, which is basically that there was an opening in satire. As part of the larger context, I shall call attention to numerous Roman poets' evident fondness for writing challenging, surprising poems, which can make more plausible that writing and reading such a poem might have been Lucretius's goal and readers' expectation.

Since this is a volume dedicated to Jeff Henderson, I want to contextualize my questions by briefly reaching both back before and forward after Lucretius to mention questions about two other kinds of literature. One kind of literature is the Aristophanic comedy that plays such a central role in this volume, and to which Jeff Henderson has made so much of a contribution; the other is the Roman novel, which I associate with Jeff Henderson in a way few scholars do, because I am someone whose first encounter with the Roman novel came in a Michigan graduate proseminar with Jeff in the fall of 1981. It is also possible that the basic idea for this paper, although my memory on this point is not clear, comes from an off-hand comment, perhaps even a joke that he will not remember, made by Jeff in the 1981–2 academic year about Lucretius possibly being a Hellenistic (though Roman) poet who chose Epicureanism as the subject of his poem simply because he thought it would make for a good and unique poem.

Most readers of this volume will know better than I how questions have long been asked about whether the political message or the comedic or artistic goals of his plays were more important to Aristophanes. The question has evolved from old-fashioned intentionalist questions about what the poet's 'real' beliefs and sympathies were, to more subtle questions in recent years:

> earlier scholarship on politics in (or 'and') Aristophanes, which tended to focus on determining Aristophanes' 'actual' political views, has by now given way to approaches far more sensitive to how comic literary texts work and more attentive to the complexities of Athenian political structures and social dynamics.[3]

A reading that sees Aristophanes as more interested in comedy and laughter than in the 'teaching' that Aristophanes has characters say in the *Frogs* is the purpose of Athenian comedy and tragedy is not one that Jeff Henderson has promoted, but mine is a paper exploring rather than insisting on these

---

3 Foley and Rosen (2020, 7).

kinds of approaches to satiric and didactic texts. In brief: in favor of one or another version of the idea that the plays do not seriously advocate or seek to influence policies, views or political opinions are Gomme, Heath, Halliwell and Rosen, while on the other side are Ste Croix, MacDowell, Edmunds and Henderson.[4] Rosen, for example, argues 'that Aristophanes' attacks against Cleon can be regarded as an elaborate literary conceit with direct antecedents in the iambic ψόγος, and that the invective against Cleon in *Knights* in particular must be seen, to a great degree, as conventional'.[5] Henderson's Introduction to his Loeb, by contrast, says that 'Aristophanes' hostility to Cleon was but one element of his consistent tendency to espouse the social, moral and political sentiments of contemporary upperclass conservatives.'[6] Walsh's survey also describes a 'third way' taken by Goldhill and Platter and others that says the plays themselves stage this uncertainty about 'the specific socio-political orientation of Aristophanic comedy'.[7] The way that satirical poets play with the audience's or reader's uncertainty about its positions is also key to Rosen's book on the poetics of ancient satire, and is discussed also in Gellar-Goad's recent book on Lucretius and satire.[8]

For both Petronius and Apuleius, questions have been asked about the seriousness of their satire (for Petronius) and even religious conviction (for Apuleius). For Petronius's *Satyrica*, some readers will see guidance from the 'hidden author', to use the title of Conte's book, to know who is being sati-

---

4 Walsh (2009) offers a convenient survey.
5 Rosen (1988, 3).
6 Henderson (1998, 14). See too Martin (2021) for a description of 'complementary' chapters by Rosen and Henderson in Rosen and Foley (2020).
7 Platter (2007, 37).
8 Cf. Rosen (2007, 233): 'The satirical poet himself, as I have argued throughout this study, no doubt takes a wry pleasure in leaving some of his audience convinced of his didactic seriousness, some humored but still confused in their quest to pin down his "real" sentiments, and others simply scandalized by his ponēria … Juvenal's *Ninth Satire* is very much concerned not only with sorting through precisely these responses to satire and mockery, but also with articulating a fundamental insight that comedy and didacticism are, in the end, if not antithetical to one another, then certainly in constant tension.' Some of Rosen's ideas are developed and refined in the study of Gellar-Goad (2020) of Lucretius and satire; see, for example, Gellar-Goad (2020, 38): 'Do satirists mean what they say? Because of the personal voice of the satiric ego and the realism of satire's fictive world, the reader may understand the satirist's words as sincerely spoken and may take the satirist at face value as a moral didact. In other words, the audience may be tempted to take the satirist's seriousness seriously. But care is required, since the didactic pose may not be genuine and since the satirist is characterized by recurrent ponēria, Rosen's term for "forays into scandalous diction, compromised self-representation, and other similarly comedic gestures". This comic ponēria undercuts any enduring credence in the satirist's seriousness and moral superiority, as entertainment overtakes critique. In my view, the tension between righteousness and ponēria is a pivotal point for understanding the identity of the satiric persona'.

rized and with whom we should sympathize, but other modern readers have a more difficult time seeing any coherent moral positions being taken by the novel.[9] In his Introduction to the *Oxford Readings in the Roman Novel*, Stephen Harrison discusses possible responses to the surprisingly religious eleventh book of the other major Roman novel, Apuleius's *Metamorphoses*, and the problem of integrating it with the (at least on the surface) more playful first ten books. After noting the monumental impact of Winkler's *Auctor and Actor*, which argues that the work offers a kind of serious 'hermeneutic playfulness', Harrison suggests an alternative: the 'evidence can be made to argue strongly for a non-serious interpretation of [book 11] … [O]ne can jettison all serious notion of a genuine religious purpose, regarding the religious material as authorial manipulation and learning'.[10] This is a controversial and much debated position, and I am not sure it is one that I would adopt, but I think it certainly an approach worth keeping in mind while thinking about Apuleius and his remarkable novel.

In brief, my argument about Lucretius in this paper is this: just as some have found a way to see Apuleius's *Metamorphoses*, a novel written by a learned Neoplatonic scholar, as a virtuoso display of skill, style and learning rather than as a serious work of religion or philosophy, is it possible, and maybe even necessary, to think about whether Lucretius's *De Rerum Natura* may have been seen as a virtuoso versification of a way of looking at the world in which the art and skill matter more than the content.[11] Most of us assume that Lucretius, unlike most ancient practitioners of didactic, is a real, genuine, sincere, didactic poet, who is aiming to teach the thing

---

9 Conte (1996); scholars in the 1960s and 70s such as Sullivan (1967), Schmeling (1969), Walsh (1974) asked whether Petronius was an 'artist' or a 'moralist', that is, a serious satirist. For a brief survey see Harrison (1999, xxv), as well as Connors (1998, 6–12), and for more recent views see Schmeling and Setaioli (2011, xxx–xxxviii) on the genre of the *Satyrica*. Rimell (2002, 11) argues that 'as we swallow down Encolpius' adventures, we can never get "outside" the quandary of who our narrator really is, whether he is Petronius' foolish puppet, always silently mocked by a clever, detached author, or whether he is ever or always Petronius in disguise: ironic, satirical and double-edged'. Cf. Rosen and Gellar-Goad in previous note.
10 Harrison (1999, xxxiii), Winkler (1985); cf., for example, Harrison (2000-1, 246 and 248), which offers 'a view of *Metamorphoses* 11 which is fundamentally influenced by Winkler but which is even more sceptical and satirical' and suggests that 'Apuleius … is parodying [Aelius] Aristides' self-important and bizarre narrative of religious experience' in his *Sacred Tales*.
11 The first translator of Lucretius in English, Lucy Hutchinson, wrote in an introductory dedication that 'I abhorre all the Atheismes & impieties in it, and translated it only out of youthfull curiositie, to understand things I heard so much discourse of at second hand, but without the least inclination to propagate any of the wicked pernitious [sic] doctrines in it'. As the Oxford editors, Barbour and Norbrook (2012, *ad loc.*) note, 'Her insistence on the gulf between her current views and those of the youthful self who undertook the translation serves in effect to legitimize the circulation of her manuscript.'

that he says he is aiming to teach: Epicurean philosophy. There is a good brief discussion of the history of this idea, and how Lucretius's apparent earnest didacticism has bothered some critics, in Charles Martindale's *Latin Poetry and the Judgement of Taste: An Essay in Aesthetics*.[12] In being a real, genuine, sincere, didactic poet, Lucretius is thought to be different from all the 'didactic' poets of the last several centuries before he wrote, and from Roman didactic poets of the next several decades, whose poems may be teaching readers something, but are not teaching their nominal subject, since they do not offer real, complete instruction about astronomy or poisonous snakes or drugs or farming or picking up girls in Rome.[13] But, for Lucretius, is this assumption correct? How do we know that Lucretius is a 'real' didactic poet, and not a poet who has simply found versifying Epicurean doctrine a satisfying poetic challenge, writing for an audience that looked to poetry not for physics or philosophy, but for aesthetic beauty and pleasure (the last word of *DRN* 1.1 is *voluptas*) and demonstrations of literary skill?[14] Thinking about this possibility seems more important now in the light of some new or newish evidence, and some old evidence that

---

12 Martindale (2005, 182), for example, quotes Coleridge's famous claim that 'Whatever in Lucretius is poetry is not philosophical, whatever is philosophical is not poetry.'
13 Theorists of didactic distinguish between poetry that teaches what it professes to teach, poetry that teaches something other than its professed topic and poetry that merely pretends to teach; see especially Effe (1977), whose views have been often discussed, for example in Dalzell's (1996) survey of Latin didactic, and Annette Harder (1997) in a paper on Callimachus. Gellar-Goad (2020, 5) suggests that different readers may have used the *DRN* in different ways, covering all three of Effe's categories: 'By emphasizing the point of reception, the readers of *De Rerum Natura* …, we can allow for the poem to function as more than one kind of didactic simultaneously. For the philosophical novice eager to learn about Epicurus, there is a unity of Stoff and Thema, and the poem is sachbezogen. For readers who are acquainted with Epicureanism and read Lucretius as a Roman writing during the political and social crises of the late Republic, the poem's Epicurean Stoff is less important than the broader civic Thema behind it, so the poem is transparent. For Epicurean readers who know the philosophy and have withdrawn from public concerns, *De Rerum Natura* may be purely formal, a poetic tour de force on a topic new to the realm of Latin verse.'
14 Both goals, teaching philosophy and receiving credit for demonstration of literary skill in handling a difficult challenge, are prominent in the poet's comment on his work at 1.921–50 repeated with minor changes at 4.1–25. The view explored in my paper involves taking one of those claims, *primum quod magnis doceo de rebus et artis | religionum animum nodis exsolvere pergo* ('first, because I am teaching about great matters, and I proceed to free the mind from the tight bonds of superstition', 1.931–2), as less important, in a way that some may resist, and the other, *deinde quod obscura de re tam lucida pango | carmina, musaeo contingens cuncta lepore* ('second, because on such a murky subject I am fashioning such clear poetry, touching everything with the charm of the Muses', 1.933–4), as more in line with the poem's true goals. On the much discussed 1.921–50, see Goldschmidt (2020), Morrison (2020, 174–7), who suggests (177) that 'Some readers will have enjoyed the poem for the pleasures it produces as an aesthetic

can be looked at in a new way. The following pages, then, will present some reasons why Lucretius may have written – and perhaps more importantly, contemporaries may have thought it best to read him – with an eye mainly on aesthetic and poetic matters, and not philosophical content.

My paper will survey five arguments or pieces of evidence:

1. With our increased knowledge from new papyri of Epicurus and especially his treatise *On Nature*, it has now become possible to argue, as David Sedley does fairly convincingly in *Lucretius and the Transformation of Greek Wisdom*, that Lucretius used only this one text, the *On Nature*, as a source for almost all of the philosophical content of his whole poem. This changes things dramatically, I think, for someone who would want to argue for a purely or mainly literary or aesthetic approach to the poem. Sedley describes Lucretius, in the light of his own arguments about the poet's dependence on Epicurus, as a philosophical 'fundamentalist', or one devoted solely to the teachings of his third-century BCE master. If Lucretius followed only one source text, however, this also brings his practice more in line with that of the Hellenistic practitioners of 'literary' didactic from whom he is usually so sharply distinguished.[15] Lucretius's use of Epicurus may now be compared with Aratus's (likely) use of Eudoxus and Theophrastus, and Nicander's use of a Hippocratic treatise for his *Prognostica* and Apollodorus for his *Theriaca* and perhaps *Alexipharmaca*.[16] The idea that Lucretius was translating into Latin verse one treatise of Epicurus may have helped condition the expectations of Lucretius's readers about what kind of poem they were reading.

2. A more direct piece of evidence about reader's expectations comes from Cicero. I refer not to the most famous evidence from Cicero about Lucretius: Cicero and his brother Quintus are of course the only contemporaries of Lucretius who we know for a fact read his poem (which of course became very popular within a few years), because we have his letter to Quintus of February 54. Cicero praises the poem's flashes of *ingenium* and its *ars* and says nothing about its Epicurean content, which we know from his other writings Cicero would not have been a big fan of. But as evidence for readers' expectations of didactic I focus here not on that letter but on Cicero's discussion in *De Oratore* of the background and goals of Aratus and Nicander (1.69):

> object ...; others will have approached the poem primarily for its therapeutic or philosophical potential (and many readers will have combined these and other motivations).'

15 For recent discussion of Sedley's claim, see Morrison (2020), with further references.
16 Cf. Cameron (1995, 195); Kidd (1997, 14–18); Hunter (1995); Gow and Scholfield (2014, 18); Overduin (2015, 27–8); Bishop (2019, 50–1, with n. 26), who cites varying scholarly opinions on Aratus's sources.

Etenim si constat inter doctos, hominem ignarum astrologiae, Aratum ornatissimis atque optimis versibus, de caelo stellisque dixisse; si de rebus rusticis hominem ab agro remotissimum, Nicandrum Colophonium, poetica quadam facultate, non rustica, scripsisse praeclare, quid est, cur non orator de rebus eis eloquentissime dicat, quas ad certam causam tempusque cognorit?

If learned men agree that Aratus, who knew nothing about astrology, spoke about the stars and heavens in excellent, nicely ornamented verses, and that Nicander, who was as far removed from the farm as anyone, wrote outstandingly about agricultural matters by means of his poetic, not agricultural skill, then why shouldn't the orator be able to speak eloquently on those matters on which he has just studied up for a particular case and situation?[17]

The references in this passage to the ignorance of Aratus and Nicander concerning their subject matter, even if unfair to them, show what some contemporaries of Lucretius may have expected from a didactic poet. Cicero's claim comes from the biographical tradition of Aratus, from his reading of the first *Vita* of Aratus. That *Life of Aratus* goes so far as to claim that Antigonus ordered Aratus the physician and Nicander the astronomer to write poems on the other man's area of specialty. That story cannot literally be true, in the first place because Aratus and Nicander lived in different centuries. And of course, for Cicero (and his speaker Crassus) the story serves his own need to demonstrate that the orator must be ready to discuss any topic. But both the story and Cicero's adaptation of it tell us a lot about ancient and late Republican Roman expectations of didactic. It is often said that Lucretius reaches back for models to the classical practitioners of 'real' didactic, such as Hesiod and Parmenides and Empedocles, and that his poem is, to quote Richard Jenkyns again, 'that extraordinary thing, a real didactic poem, the first since the fifth century'.[18] But we should consider the practical problems faced by any author working in a familiar genre who wants his audience to respond to a poem differently from how they are used to responding to works in that genre, who wants them to take his 'content', as opposed to his form and style, more seriously than anyone

---

17 Cf. also *De Rep.* 1.22: *ab Eudoxo Cnidio ...; cuius omnem ornatum et descriptionem sumptam ab Eudoxo multis annis post non astrologiae scientia, sed poetica quadam facultate versibus Aratum extulisse* ('Eudoxus of Cnidus ..., whose entire arrangement and description [he said] Aratus had borrowed from Eudoxus and put into verse, not with any knowledge of astronomy, but with his own poetic talent'). On the story and its origins see Cameron (1995, 195), Bishop (2019, 50–1); Myers (2019) cites it in a discussion of didactic in Columella.
18 Jenkyns (1998, 162).

has for literally hundreds of years. This is a problem that one might have expected to be treated in the discussion of Lucretius in Martindale's *Latin Poetry and the Judgement of Taste: An Essay in Aesthetics*, whose chapter on Lucretius begins with a learned and valuable discussion of the history of the problem of whether poetry should aim to teach. But Martindale disappointingly does not mention Sedley's important argument in his *Lucretius and the Transformation of Greek Wisdom* about Lucretius's exclusive dependence on Epicurus's *On Nature*, and when he gets to Lucretius, Martindale says that it is 'obvious that he writes to persuade his reader to embrace his version of philosophical truth'. I always tell my students that when I see someone using the words 'obvious' or 'obviously' what it really means is 'I have no evidence for this.' Martindale follows up in a footnote with a use of the related word 'clearly'.[19] In the mid-50s BCE, if all of your readers expect your content to be mildly interesting, but subservient to literary questions of form and style, how do you get them to read you differently? I am not entirely kidding when I say that it is relevant here that Lucretius himself says in book 2 that there can be no unique thing in nature: *Huc accedit ut in summa res nulla sit una, | unica quae gignatur et unica solaque crescat* (2.1077–8). Earlier in book 2 he had discussed the practical problems that stand in the way of any hypothetical 'single unique thing': how could it come into being, how could it be fed and grow, how would the atoms of the unique thing wind up together (541–65)? These are similar to the questions that must be asked by proponents of the idea that you can write the first sincere didactic poem in centuries and have people understand what you are doing. Elsewhere Lucretius discusses another similar problem: in dismissing the myth that a single name-giver came up with the words for everything, he asks how the man could have made other people understand what he was jabbering on about (*DRN* 5.1041–55). In broader terms: can there be a truly unique thing in literature? Would not Romans (or Greeks) of Lucretius's day, in looking at real, sincere didactic, be likely to misunderstand it? The significant Empedoclean allusions in Lucretius's prologue would be a help, of course, and I am also – for purposes of this argument – understating the extent to which philosophical content was important in Aratus, Ennius, Cicero's *Aratea* and others; Hardie and Farrell and Myers have talked about this as background for Vergil and Ovid.[20] But Epicurean didactic poetry is all but unknown; Epicureans to some extent were opposed to poetry or to

---

19 Martindale (2005, 185, with n. 64). Martindale's chapter offers a number of excellent observations and readings; here as elsewhere Martindale is just excellent at challenging unsupported assumptions made by others.
20 Cf. Hardie (1986), Farrell (1991), Myers (1994) and much work influenced by them. But note that Myers often speaks of Ovid as positioning himself as a 'pseudo-scholar', and Johnson (1988), while rightly noting that Hardie's book 'seems to me one of the most interesting and valuable books on Vergil to have appeared in recent years', also says at

the use of it for serious matters. This idea, once perhaps overly stressed, has been modified somewhat by recent work, especially by people working on Philodemus, but it is important to note that this scholarship has contextualized and added further nuance to Epicurus's hostility to poetry, but it has not made that hostility vanish.[21] There are gentle philosophical lessons implicit in Philodemus's epigrams, as Sider notes, but there is no depiction of a didactic situation with teacher and student.[22] For Romans of Lucretius's day, the notion of an 'Epicurean philosophical epic' might well have sounded to Romans the way the phrase 'Amish rock video' would sound today.[23]

3. More on Epicureans: my third piece of evidence, also from the first century BCE, is a newish piece of evidence from Philodemus's *On Poems* book 5. It has been discussed in other contexts in recent years, but has not, I think, played much role in the debate about the function of didactic.[24] Like most Philodemus, it is challenging, and as often Philodemus can make the non-specialist feel humbled (*On Poems* V.25.30–26.11):

εἰ γὰρ καθὸ πόημα, φυσικὸν οὐδὲν οὔτε λέξεως οὔτε δι[α]γρήματος ὠφέλημα π[αρ]ασκευάζει – διὰ τοῦτ[ο] δὴ τῆς ἀρετῆς ἑστηκότες ὑπόκεινται σκ[οπ]οί, τῇ μὲν λέξει τὸ μ[εμι]μῆσθαι τὴν ὠφέλι[μα] προσδιδάσκουσαν, τῆς δὲ διανοίας τὸ μεταξὺ μετ[εσχη]κέναι τῆς τῶν σοφῶν καὶ τῆς τῶν χυδαίων. καὶ ταῦτ' ἔστιν, ἄν τε νομίσῃ τις ἄν τε μή, καὶ κριτέον ἐπὶ τ[α]ῦτ' ἐπανάγοντας.

… if a poem, qua poem (καθὸ πόημα), provides no natural benefit (ὠφέλημα) either in language or in content – therefore there so exist solid goals for goodness – for language, the imitation (μ[εμι]μῆσθαι) of language which teaches useful things in addition, and for thought, being intermediate between the thought of the wise and that of the uneducated. And these [*sc.* solid goals] do exist, whether one thinks so or not, and one must judge with reference to them.[25]

---

one point that he thinks Hardie is 'confusing Stoff with Gehalt' (cf. Gellar-Goad, quoted above, n. 13).

21 Cf. Asmis (1995), Goldschmidt (2020, 56), Nethercut (2020, 135–9), Morrison (2020, 157), all with further references.
22 Sider (1997).
23 Yes, Weird Al Yankovic made a 1996 song and video called 'Amish Paradise', but since Weird Al was not Amish and was not looking for converts, I think that helps rather than hurts my point – although I am certainly also not claiming that Lucretius is doing parody.
24 Armstrong (1993, 224).
25 Almost every word here is contested, and I mostly reproduce the text and translation of McOsker (2021, 142), except that in his text the quotation begins ε⟦υ⟧ \ἰ/ γὰρ {ϱι}καθὸ πόημα, which means that an upsilon has been corrected to an iota by a scribe, producing

Philodemus is not talking specifically about what we call didactic poetry, but more broadly all poetry that may seem to teach something. But I find this extremely interesting as near-contemporary evidence associating poetry not with instruction as a goal but with mimesis (μ[εμι]μῆσθαι), 'representation', 'portrayal' or even 'imitation' of instructional writing – the 'pretending to teach' that gives its title to a book I am writing on Roman didactic and satire.[26]

4. A fourth argument also follows from Sedley's book.[27] Sedley's argument that Lucretius is a 'fundamentalist' in his approach to Epicurean doctrine depends in part on the way in which Lucretius in following Epicurus closely engages mainly with the philosophical opponents of Epicurus, and either never or seldom addresses philosophical issues that date after the fourth century BCE. The philosophers he names and lampoons are all Presocratics, for example. This is a controversial topic, and there are many who argue that Lucretius makes subtle allusions to thinkers after Epicurus, including the Stoics, but in my view they are … pretty subtle.[28] Here I want simply to

---

the word translated as 'if', and that editors have deleted the οι. I am grateful to Professor Michael McOsker for answering some questions and showing me his work before it was published.

26 My book-in-progress, *Teaching, Pretending to Teach and the Authority of the Speaker in Roman Didactic and Satire*, after surveying Greek material in an introductory chapter, will discuss Lucretius, Vergil's *Georgics*, Horace's *Satires* and *Ars Poetica*, Ovid's *Ars Amatoria* and the *Satires* of Juvenal, with brief treatment of a number of other authors and texts. On the Philodemus passage, see Asmis (1991, 8–11), Armstrong (1993, 224), Janko (2000, 131), Blank (2019), Gellar-Goad (2020, 5) and McOsker (2021, 142); I also discuss this passage in a forthcoming chapter on Horace's *Ars Poetica* entitled 'Satire, Didactic, and New Contexts for Problems in Horace's *Ars Poetica*'. Blank summarizes: 'For poetry the aims should be to imitate the diction which also teaches useful things and to have a content which is between what wise and vulgar people would say (*Poem.* 5, xxv.30–xxvi.20 …). After all, the sage will rather express what is crucially useful for life in philosophical prose, while poetry will be a pleasant adjunct or pastime.' Nethercut (2020, 137) offers a novel reading. Yona (2018) is an extended argument for the influence of Philodemus on Horace's *Satires* – but also for a view of the *Satires* different from mine that takes them unambiguously seriously as philosophical satire and as moral criticism.

27 Sedley (1998).

28 Besides Sedley (1998), cf. Warren (2007, 22–7) for a brief summary of both sides, Furley (1966) arguing against engagement with the Stoics, and, for example, Asmis (1982), Gee (2013, 81–109) arguing in favor of such engagement. Fowler (2000, 140) is surely right to argue that regardless of whether any portion of the *DRN* is designed to refute the Stoics, the philosophical reception of the text will involve Roman readers in the context of Stoicism: 'for any plausible construction of a first-century BCE reader … Stoicism … will inevitably be a part of the mental habitus of such a reader, and will affect that reader's interpretation, and therefore ours if we choose to adopt such a perspective'. But we must be careful not to beg the question in a circular way: a reader steeped in Stoicism may think Lucretius is arguing with the Stoics, but only if he is in the habit of looking

cite the most startling example of Lucretius's sticking to arguments of an earlier age, where in arguing that the soul cannot survive outside the body, Lucretius says that to say that the soul or mind could survive outside the body would be as silly as saying the soul or mind could be located not in the chest but in the feet or shoulders or head. This first comes up in book 3's argument about the mortality of the soul. Lucretius first notes that trees cannot exist in the *aether*, nor clouds in the sea, nor fish in the fields, nor blood in sticks, nor sap in stones (3.784–6), because 'there is a definite and settled place in which each thing may grow and be contained' (*certum ac dispositumst ubi quicquid crescat et insit*, 3.787). It follows that the mind (as often, Lucretius blurs the difference between soul and mind) 'cannot arise without the body, and cannot exist by itself at a distance from the sinews and blood' (*sic animi natura nequit sine corpore oriri | sola neque a nervis et sanguine longius esse*, 3.788–9). He caps the argument with the familiar kind of syllogism in which he argues that if P is true than Q must be true, and since we know that Q is not true, it follows that P must be false (3.790–3):

> quod si posset enim, multo prius ipsa animi vis
> in capite aut umeris aut imis calcibus esse
> posset et innasci quavis in parte soleret,
> tandem in eodem homine atque in eodem vase manere.

> If that could happen (that the mind could live apart),
> the power of the soul/mind would sooner be able to be
> in the head or the shoulders, or would be accustomed to be born in
> the lowest part of the heels and in any random body part,
> since that would involve at least being in the same person and in the same vessel.

A version of these lines recurs in 5.131–8 when the poet is arguing against the idea that the earth or sun or stars could have a consciousness or be a god. In both passages, the idea that the mind could be in the head is cited as an idea that is so obviously false that it needs no argumentation. Mind in the head! What a kooky idea! Many scientists by this time knew that the brain was in the head, and there was at least debate among philosophers including Epicureans about where the mind was. For Lucretius in an a fortiori argument in the first century BCE to cite the idea of the mind being in the head as laughable is very strange.[29]

---

to poetry for philosophical arguments, rather than for *ingenium* and *ars*, the two things that Cicero, hostile to Epicureanism, praises in Lucretius in his letter to his brother.

[29] Campbell (1999), in a review of Sedley (1998), has an extensive discussion of Sedley's treatment of the argument about the soul in the head, but he focuses on the question of

5. From a couple of decades later, we should also consider Horace's description in *Satire* 1.10 of how he came to write satire. This is not a new piece of evidence, but I think it adds context to the others. In moving to Horace and the 30s BCE as I make an argument that Lucretius may have written his poem on Epicurean philosophy for artistic rather than philosophical reasons, I realize that can be seen as opening up a whole new can of worms. A counternarrative to my imaginings in this paper can be proposed in which Lucretius meant for his poem to be taken seriously as an argument in favor of Epicureanism, and was, and that in the next generation Vergil's *Eclogues* and especially Horace's *Satires* also explored or in the case of Horace actively lobbied for the Epicurean position.[30] In this chapter, I will avoid that issue for lack of space, or perhaps I will put it off for another day. Here I cite only Horace's idea of how he came to write satire. Like anything Horace writes about himself, we should not assume it is literally true, but I think it is fair to assume that the story in outline is at least one that a reader of the time would have found plausible (*Sat.* 1.10.31–5, 46–9):

> atque ego cum Graecos facerem, natus mare citra,
> versiculos, vetuit me tali voce Quirinus,
> post mediam noctem visus, cum somnia vera:
> 'in silvam non ligna feras insanius ac si
> magnas Graecorum malis implere catervas.'
> …
> hoc erat, experto frustra Varrone Atacino
> atque quibusdam aliis, melius quod scribere possem,
> inventore minor; neque ego illi detrahere ausim
> haerentem capiti cum multa laude coronam.

> And when I, though born on this side of the Adriatic, was making Greek
> versicles, Quirinus forbade me with these words,
> appearing to me after midnight, when dreams are true:
> 'It would not be crazier to bring lumber into the woods, than if
> you chose to supplement the great hordes of Greeks doing that.'
> …
> Poems in this genre, tried unsuccessfully by Varro Atacinus
> and a few others, were what I might write better,

whether Lucretius the man is ignorant of current debate about the location of the mind, and does nothing to counter the claim that the text of the *DRN* shows no knowledge of that debate. The same focus marks the brief treatment of this problem in O'Keefe (2020, 182–4).

30 Cf. especially Davis (2012) on the *Eclogues* and Yona (2018) on the *Satires*.

though less well than the inventor; nor would I dare to take from him the crown and all the accompanying praise that clings to his head.[31]

Horace says (no doubt facetiously) that as he was planning on writing 'Greek versicles' (*Graecos versiculos*), Quirinus or the deified Romulus came to him and said, in a scene resembling Callimachus's *Aetia* prologue and the contemporary Vergilian Sixth *Eclogue*, that Horace would be nuts to compete with the Greeks in that genre. Quirinus here is made to sound partly like Callimachus's Apollo, but also like a potential dissertation director talking to a modern graduate student in search of a topic. After a survey of choices made by other bad and then good poets, Horace says basically that there was an opening in satire: this was something that a few others had tried, without much success, and perhaps Horace could do better; note especially the rather Lucretian-sounding *corona* as a prize (49), which Lucretius attributes to Ennius, and then later himself.[32] Could this be what Lucretius was doing, or at least would be thought to have been doing by his first readers? Richard Jenkyns puts it well: 'What was the "gap in the market", so to speak, that Lucretius spotted?'[33]

From a certain perspective, every section of the Horatian corpus can be seen as a tour de force in terms of genres no Roman had mastered. If we return to epic now, one of the genres to which the *De Rerum Natura* belongs, and step back to take a larger view, we can observe that all of the extant long epics from 60 BCE to 10 CE are surprising and paradoxical: within a little over a half a century Rome sees an Epicurean philosophical epic by Lucretius, a Callimachean martial epic by Vergil (who had written earlier in the Callimachean opening to *Eclogue* 6 of how Apollo deterred him from writing epic) and a Callimachean *carmen perpetuum* in hexameter with strong elegiac features by Ovid (who had written earlier of how Cupid deterred him from writing epic). If we expand our time period by half a century we see Lucan writing a novel historical epic with little or no typical divine machinery. The other genre of the *De Rerum Natura*, didactic, shows a similar fondness for experimentation, with Vergil combining Hesiod, Aratus, Lucretius, numerous prose sources and Homer in the *Georgics*; Horace in the *Ars Poetica* writing a didactic satiric epistle; and Ovid in the *Ars Amatoria* bringing both elegiac subject matter and

---

31 On the passages see Gowers (2012, *ad loc.*), Scodel (1987), Zetzel (2002).
32 Cf. *Ennius ... qui primus amoeno | detulit ex Helicone perenni fronde coronam* ('Ennius, who first brought down from charming Helicon the crown of evergreen foliage', *DRN* 1.117–18), then *insignemque meo capiti petere inde coronam, | unde prius nulli velarint tempora Musae* ('to seek for my head a distinguished crown, from a place from which the Muses have never before veiled anyone's temples', 1.929–30 = 4.4–5), with Gowers (2012) on *Satire* 10.48–9.
33 Jenkyns (1998, 162).

the elegiac meter to didactic. Further, one aspect of Lucretius's poem that is not stressed enough is that the *De Rerum Natura* is far longer than any previous didactic poem, and, depending on how one views Empedocles, the *De Rerum Natura* is either the only or only the second didactic poem to comprise multiple books, and it smashes the previous record like Babe Ruth hitting home runs in the 1920s, or Bob Beamon long jumping in the Mexico City Olympics in 1968.[34]

In terms of content, Roman readers of didactic of the age of Cicero and the later Augustan age would have known Cicero's translation of Aratus that does promote Stoicism, but whose greatest impact was on Latin poetic style; Vergil's didactic poem on farming that Seneca tells us sought not to teach farmers but to delight readers;[35] Horace's *Ars Poetica*, which, even if not the complete parody that Bernard Frischer has intriguingly argued it to be, is certainly not a very dependable guide to becoming a poet like Horace; and Ovid's poem on the art of love that many have thought offers pretty poor advice.[36] Given that Lucretius's *De Rerum Natura* seems to have used one prose model as its main source the way that literary Hellenistic didactic poets did; that his contemporary Cicero said that Aratus and Nicander knew little about their subject matter but wrote with excellent poetic style; that another contemporary, the Epicurean Philodemus, says that poetry should 'imitate' the style of writing that actually seeks to teach without actually being useful; that Lucretius arguably ignores philosophical developments after Epicurus, and ridicules the idea of the mind being located in the head; and that Horace openly talks about being a poet looking for what one Lucretian scholar has called the 'gap in the market', how then do we think Lucretius's first readers reacted to his poem? At what point, if ever, would they realize that this was the first 'real didactic poem' in four centuries? Is that how Quintus and Marcus Cicero read it, and if so why does Marcus Cicero, who was hostile to Epicureanism, mention only the poem's *ingenium* and its *ars* and say nothing about its Epicurean content?

Some might respond to my arguments in this piece by saying that the *De Rerum Natura* simply 'feels' too sincere about Epicureanism for the poet to be interested mainly in literary matters. Here I return to Charles Martindale's claim that it is 'obvious' that the poet wants to convert us to Epicureanism. This feeling, I admit, could be right. I feel it. But an earlier generation felt it was equally 'obvious' that Catullus and the elegists,

---

34 On the size of the *DRN* see Sheerin (2015, 48 n. 6), with references.
35 Sen. *Ep.* 86.15: *ut ait Vergilius noster, qui non quid verissime, sed quid decentissime diceretur aspexit nec agricolas docere voluit, sed legentes delectare*, 'as our poet Vergil says, who looked for what he could most charmingly, not most truthfully, say, and wished not to teach farmers, but to delight readers'.
36 On the *Ars Poetica* see, for example, Frischer (1991), Ferriss-Hill (2019) and a forthcoming paper by me; on Ovid, Watson (2007), James (2008).

perhaps excluding Ovid, were obviously sincere about their great love for their elegiac girlfriends. The A. W. Allen article challenging this idea was published in 1950. Is it possible that the appearance of sincerity in Lucretius is merely the byproduct of a brilliantly successful style? Is Lucretius 'really' more devoted to Epicureanism than Tibullus is to Delia, or Propertius to Cynthia?

On balance, I think it's crucially important to keep in mind the possibility that Lucretius's *De Rerum Natura* might have been seen originally as a virtuoso versification of a way of looking at the world in which the art and skill mattered more than the content.

Works Cited

Allen, A. W. 1950. '"Sincerity" and the Roman Elegists'. *CP* 45: 145–60.
Armstrong, David. 1993. 'The Addressees of the *Ars Poetica*: Herculaneum, the Pisones and Epicurean Protreptic'. *Materiali e discussioni per l'analisi dei testi classici* 31: 185–203.
Asmis, Elizabeth. 1982. 'Lucretius' Venus and Stoic Zeus'. *Hermes* 110: 458–70.
———. 1991. 'Philodemus's Poetic Theory and *On the Good King According to Homer*'. *CA* 10: 1–46.
———. 1995. 'Epicurean Poetics'. In *Philodemus and Poetry*, edited by Dirk Obbink, 15–34. Oxford: Oxford University Press.
Barbour, Reid, and David Norbrook, eds. 2012. *The Works of Lucy Hutchinson*, vol. 1. Oxford: Oxford University Press.
Bishop, Caroline. 2019. *Cicero, Greek Learning, and the Making of a Roman Classic*. Oxford: Oxford University Press.
Blank, David. 2019. 'Philodemus'. *The Stanford Encyclopedia of Philosophy* (spring 2019 edn), edited by Edward N. Zalta. https://plato.stanford.edu/archives/spr2019/entries/philodemus/.
Cameron, Alan. 1995. *Callimachus and His Critics*. Princeton: Princeton University Press.
Campbell, Gordon. 1999. Review of *Lucretius and the Transformation of Greek Wisdom*, by D. N. Sedley (1998). *BMCR* 1999.10.29.
Connors, Catherine. 1998. *Petronius the Poet: Verse and Literary Tradition in the Satyricon*. Cambridge: Cambridge University Press.
Conte, Gian Biagio. 1996. *The Hidden Author: An Interpretation of Petronius's Satyricon*. Berkeley: University of California Press.
Dalzell, Alexander. 1996. *The Criticism of Didactic Poetry: Essays on Lucretius, Virgil, and Ovid*. Toronto: University of Toronto Press.
Davis, Gregson. 2012. *Parthenope: The Interplay of Ideas in Vergilian Bucolic*. Leiden: Brill.
Effe, Bernd. 1977. *Dichtung und Lehre: Untersuchungen zur Typologie des antiken Lehrgedichts*. Munich: Beck.
Farrell, Joseph. 1991. *Vergil's Georgics and the Traditions of Ancient Epic: The Art of Allusion in Literary History*. Oxford: Oxford University Press.

Ferriss-Hill, Jennifer. 2019. *Horace's Ars Poetica: Family, Friendship, and the Art of Living*. Princeton: Princeton University Press.

Foley, Helene P., and Ralph M. Rosen. 2020. 'Introduction'. In Rosen and Foley 2020, 1–8.

Fowler, D. P. 2000. 'Philosophy and Literature in Lucretian Intertextuality'. In *Roman Constructions: Readings in Postmodern Latin*, edited by D. P. Fowler, 138–55. Oxford: Oxford University Press.

Frischer, Bernard. 1991. *Shifting Paradigms: New Approaches to Horace's Ars Poetica*. Atlanta: Scholars Press.

Furley, D. J. 1966. 'Lucretius and the Stoics'. *BICS* 13: 13–33.

Gee, Emma. 2001. 'Cicero's Astronomy'. *CQ* 51: 520–36.

———. 2013. *Aratus and the Astronomical Tradition*. New York: Oxford University Press.

Gellar-Goad, T. H. M. 2020. *Laughing Atoms, Laughing Matter: Lucretius' De Rerum Natura and Satire*. Ann Arbor: University of Michigan Press.

Goldschmidt, Nora. 2020. 'Reading the "Implied Author" in Lucretius' *De Rerum Natura*'. In O'Rourke 2020, 43–58.

Gow, A. S. F., and A. F. Scholfield. 2014. *Nicander*. Cambridge: Cambridge University Press.

Gowers, Emily. 2012. *Horace: Satires Book 1*. Cambridge: Cambridge University Press.

Harder, Annette. 2007. 'To Teach or Not to Teach …? Some Aspects of the Genre of Didactic Poetry in Antiquity'. In *Calliope's Classroom: Studies in Didactic Poetry from Antiquity to the Renaissance*, edited by M. A. Harder, A. A. MacDonald and G. J. Reinink, 23–48. Leuven: Peeters.

Hardie, P. R. 1986. *Virgil's Aeneid: Cosmos and Imperium*. Oxford: Oxford University Press.

Harrison, Stephen. 1999. 'Some Twentieth-Century Views of the Roman Novel'. In *Oxford Readings in the Roman Novel*, edited by Stephen Harrison, xi–xxxix. Oxford: Oxford University Press.

———. 2000–1. 'Apuleius, Aelius Aristides and Religious Autobiography'. *Ancient Narrative* 1: 245–59.

Henderson, Jeffrey. 1998. *Aristophanes*, vol. 2. Cambridge, MA: Harvard University Press.

Hunter, Richard L. 1995. 'Written in the Stars: Poetry and Philosophy in the *Phaenomena* of Aratus'. *Arachnion* 2: 1–34.

James, Sharon L. 2008. 'Women Reading Men: The Female Audience of the *Ars Amatoria*'. *CCJ* 54: 136–59.

Janko, Richard. 2000. *Philodemus: On Poems Book 1*. Oxford: Oxford University Press.

Jenkyns, Richard. 1998. 'Response' (to 'The Didactic Poetry of Erasmus Darwin'). In *Form and Content in Didactic Poetry*, edited by Catherine Atherton, 161–9. Bari: Levante.

———. 2007. 'Introduction'. In *Lucretius: The Nature of Things*, translated by A. E. Stallings. London: Penguin.

Johnson, W. R. 1988. Review of *Virgil's Aeneid: Cosmos and Imperium*, by P. R. Hardie (1986). *CJ* 83: 269–71.

Kidd, D. A. 1997. *Aratus: Phaenomena*. Cambridge: Cambridge University Press.

McOsker, Michael. 2021. *The Good Poem According to Philodemus*. Oxford: Oxford University Press.

Martin, Richard. 2021. Review of *Aristophanes and Politics: New Studies*, edited by Ralph M. Rosen and Helene P. Foley (2020). *BMCR* 2021.04.36.

Martindale, C. 2005. *Latin Poetry and the Judgement of Taste: An Essay in Aesthetics*. Oxford: Oxford University Press.

Morrison, Andrew. 2020. 'Arguing over Text(s): Master-Texts vs Intertexts in the Criticism of Lucretius'. In O'Rourke 2020, 157–76.

Myers, K. S. 1994. *Ovid's Causes: Cosmogony and Aetiology in the Metamorphoses*. Ann Arbor: University of Michigan Press.

———. 2019. '"Pulpy Fiction": Virgilian Reception and Genre in Columella *De Re Rustica* 10'. In *Reflections and New Perspectives on Virgil's Georgics*, edited by Bobby Xinyue and Nicholas Freer, 129–38. London: Bloomsbury Academic.

Nethercut, Jason. 2020. 'Lucretian Echoes: Sound as Metaphor for Literary Allusion in *De Rerum Natura* 4.549-94'. In O'Rourke 2020, 124–39.

O'Hara, James J. Forthcoming. 'Satire, Didactic, and New Contexts for Problems in Horace's *Ars Poetica*'.

O'Keefe, Tim. 2020. 'Lucretius and the Philosophical Use of Literary Persuasion'. In *Approaches to Lucretius: Traditions and Innovations in Reading the De Rerum Natura*, edited by Donncha O'Rourke, 177–94. Cambridge: Cambridge University Press.

O'Rourke, Donncha, ed. 2020. *Approaches to Lucretius: Traditions and Innovations in Reading the De Rerum Natura*. Cambridge: Cambridge University Press.

Overduin, F. 2015. *Nicander of Colophon's Theriaca: A Literary Commentary*. Leiden: Brill.

Platter, Charles. 2007. *Aristophanes and the Carnival of Genres*. Baltimore: Johns Hopkins University Press.

Rimell, Victoria. 2002. *Petronius and the Anatomy of Fiction*. Cambridge: Cambridge University Press.

Rosen, Ralph. 1988. *Old Comedy and the Iambographic Tradition*. Atlanta: Scholars Press.

———. 2007. *Making Mockery: The Poetics of Ancient Satire*. Oxford: Oxford University Press.

———. 2020. 'Accessing and Understanding Aristophanic Politics'. In Rosen and Foley 2020, 9–23.

Rosen, Ralph M., and Helene P. Foley, eds. 2020. *Aristophanes and Politics: New Studies*. Leiden: Brill.

Schmeling, Gareth. 1969. 'Petronius: Satirist, Moralist, Epicurean, Artist'. *CB* 45: 49–50, 64.

———, with the collaboration of Aldo Setaioli. 2011. *A Commentary on the Satyrica of Petronius*. Oxford: Oxford University Press.

Scodel, Ruth. 1987. 'Horace, Lucilius, and Callimachean Polemic'. *HSCP* 91: 199–215.

Sedley, D. N. 1998. *Lucretius and the Transformation of Greek Wisdom*. Cambridge: Cambridge University Press.

Sheerin, W. H. 2015. *The Language of Atoms: Performativity and Politics in Lucretius' De Rerum Natura*. Oxford: Oxford University Press.

Sider, David. 1997. *The Epigrams of Philodemos: Introduction, Text, and Commentary*. Oxford: Oxford University Press.

———. 2005. 'Posidippus on Weather Signs and the Tradition of Didactic Poetry'. In *The New Posidipppus: A Hellenistic Poetry Book*, edited by Kathryn J. Gutzwiller, 164–82. Oxford: Oxford University Press.

Sullivan. J. P. 1967. 'Petronius: Artist or Moralist?' *Arion* 6: 71–88.

Walsh, P. G. 1974. 'Was Petronius a Moralist?' *G&R* 21: 181–91.

Walsh, Philip. 2009. 'A Study in Reception: The British Debates over Aristophanes' Politics and Influence'. *Classical Receptions Journal* 1: 55–72.

Warren, James. 2007. 'Lucretius and Greek Philosophy'. In *The Cambridge Companion to Lucretius*, edited by S. Gillespie and P. Hardie, 19–32. Cambridge: Cambridge University Press.

Watson, L. 2007. 'The Bogus Teacher and His Relevance for Ovid's *Ars Amatoria*'. *RhM* 150: 337–74.

Winkler, J. 1985. *Auctor and Actor: A Narratological Reading of Apuleius's The Golden Ass*. Berkeley: University of California Press.

Yona, Sergio. 2018. *Epicurean Ethics in Horace: The Psychology of Satire*. Oxford: Oxford University Press.

Zetzel, James E. G. 1998. '*De Re Publica* and *De Rerum Natura*'. In *Style and Tradition: Studies in Honor of Wendell Clausen*, edited by Peter Knox and Clive Foss, 230–47. Leipzig: De Gruyter.

———. 2002. 'Dreaming About Quirinus: Horace's *Satires* and the Development of Augustan Poetry'. In *Traditions and Contexts in the Poetry of Horace*, edited by T. Woodman and D. Feeney, 38–52. Cambridge: Cambridge University Press.

CHAPTER 13

Not So Funny After All:
On Deconstructing (and Reconstructing)
the Text of Petronius
John Bodel

Stemmata quid faciunt? How much, really, can the transmission and recension of a text affect our understanding of it?[1] Quite a bit, as it turns out. The *Satyrica* of Petronius provides a case in point. All that survives of what was evidently once a long narrative work has been aptly characterized by the leading modern editor of the text as 'not at all a narrative but rather a collection of disjointed pieces, mutilated excerpts' that 'seem to be in many places the end-product of methodical attempts to shorten or remove sections' from the original.[2] The resulting text has thus in places seemed 'funny', in the sense of appearing 'odd' or 'not right', and has encouraged readings of the work that range from taking the abrupt snippets of narrative as part of a literary technique designed to reflect disintegration as a worldview to suggesting that the search for meaning in the text is illusory to diagnosing disruption and smoothing away inconsistencies in order to align the fragmentary sections more squarely with what are considered the work's narrative norms.[3] No part of the surviving text has seemed 'funnier' in this respect than the episode that immediately precedes the *Cena Trimalchionis* in our texts (16–26.6), in which the protagonists, Encolpius, Giton and (here) Ascyltus encounter a local priestess of Priapus, Quartilla,

---

1 Juvenal 8.1 refers to the Roman aristocratic practice of representing family 'trees' of ancestors in the atrium; see Bettini (1991, 167–76) and Flower (1996, 211–12). The modern use of the arboreal metaphor to characterize the relationships among families of manuscripts has a long history going back, ultimately, to Politian; see Ginzburg (2004: 545–56).
2 Schmeling (2020, 23).
3 Zeitlin (1971) is a classic statement of the first position. Slater (1990, 249–50) believes that the text invites aporia. Smoothing the narrative has been the most common approach; for an extreme case, Gaselee (1909); for a recent one, Jensson (2004). The circularity inherent in the procedure renders suspect even a sensitive application of the principle (as, for example, by Sullivan below).

and her entourage, outside Naples.⁴ How we respond to the Quartilla episode inevitably depends upon how we understand the character of the narrative at this point, and here, unfortunately, many of our most basic questions remain unresolved.

In 1971 Helmut van Thiel published a short monograph in which he proposed that the text of Petronius, as we have it, preserves some of the badly damaged fragments out of order; that the source of some of the dislocations can be identified; and that the narrative can therefore be restored in places to its original form.⁵ Part of van Thiel's argument involved an elegant demonstration that the manuscript family of longer excerpts (L), long thought to derive directly from the archetype, instead represented a composite edition put together from a missing, but incomplete, manuscript or manuscripts (Λ), a collection of *florilegia* (φ), and one or another of a long recognized family of manuscripts of shorter excerpts (O). The smoking gun in van Thiel's dramatic exposure of the missing hyparchetype Λ emerged in the form of a cluster of short passages in the middle of the episode known as the *Cena Trimalchionis*, which is preserved nearly in its entirety only in a single manuscript, the famous *codex Traguriensis* (H) that became separated early (before 800 CE) from the other surviving manuscripts and reappeared only in the seventeenth century as an independent witness to an early stage of the tradition.⁶ After the first ten chapters of this episode, the Long and Short excerpts and the *florilegia* among them preserve a mere nine short excerpts, three from a single chapter. Of the three passages in chapter 55 recorded in the Long excerpts (L), the *florilegia* preserve one, the Short excerpts (O) the other two, the only two passages it preserves from the entire *Cena*. This pattern of overlapping citations strongly suggests that the family of Long excerpts was not itself a source of the Short excerpts and the *florilegia*, as had previously been supposed, but was instead compiled from them and from some other manuscript that provided long stretches of continuous narrative not preserved in the Short excerpts or *florilegia*, that is, Λ.⁷

If the creator of L was not primarily an excerptor but a compiler, who pulled together as many fragments of Petronius's already badly damaged

---

4 Schmeling (2011, 45): 'The Quartilla episode is the most lacunose in a lacunose text and also presents structural problems: we do not know (and suspect the worst) if the order of fragments as we have them in this episode is P's order; we do not know if the whole episode belongs between the episode of the stolen cloak and the Cena.' See below, n. 9.
5 van Thiel (1971); cf. van Thiel (1983).
6 For a brief overview and proposed stemma, see Schmeling (2003, 469–74). How long ago learned opinion about Petronius's Latinity became fixed on the Short and Long fragments may be seen in the controversy regarding the authenticity of the Trau manuscript at the time of its discovery: see Pace (2018).
7 van Thiel (1971, 17–20) and (1983, 6).

narrative as possible, then we need to reconsider the principles and methods that informed the composition of this edition. Whereas the working practices of excerptors and lexicographers (for example, a tendency to work from the beginning of a source and to note mainly first instances of phenomena of interest) are generally recognized and can at times be used to help reconstruct the works they excerpted, the practices of compilers are more variable and unpredictable.[8] In the case of L, van Thiel argued, the compiler's sources included a manuscript made by a scribe with grammatical and lexical interests that exhibited a preference for rare or unusual words or expressions but had little concern for context, as well as another manuscript that preserved long stretches of continuous narrative no longer available to us (Λ), and one or more manuscripts of the O family that eschewed sexual content and favored verse. Where Λ overlapped with any of the shorter excerpts (in manuscripts of the O family, the *florilegia*, or the lexical excerpts), the compiler of L knew with certainty where they belonged in the text. Where it did not, and the excerpts were handed down without context, the compiler may have inserted them in places that seemed appropriate but which are not in fact correct. That this is in fact the case, van Thiel argued, is demonstrated precisely by the Quartilla episode (16–26.6).[9]

The episode begins after a lacuna with two and a half chapters of continuous narrative (16.1–18.6), followed by three chapters of short isolated fragments, fifteen in all, of between one and twelve lines in length (18.7–21.7), before the continuous narrative resumes (22–6, with one marked lacuna after 23.1). In the first of the short excerpts a woman (evidently Quartilla) claps her hands and erupts into laughter and is followed by her maid (Psyche) and a young girl with them (Pannychis), to the astonishment of the protagonists, who marvel at the sudden change of mood (18.7–19.1). Thereafter follow nine short excerpts involving the same actors, now engaged in a different activity (some sort of erotic ritual of penitential submission and bondage, 19.2–20.7), before a tenth excerpt describes Giton at last willingly giving in to laughter and kisses from the girl (20.8). As van Thiel sees it, the first and tenth excerpts, which appear

---

8 For the practices of excerptors, see, for example, Keyser (1996) on Nonius Marcellus's quotations of Sallust. For compilers, Oikonomopoulou (2017) notes the aim among the writers of miscellanies during the second and third centuries for variety and their usually disingenuous claims of nonchalance with regard to arrangement.

9 van Thiel (1971, 76–8 [Anhang 3]), (1983, 5–6). For the setting of the Quartilla episode – probably near the Neapolitan end of the *crypta Neapolitana* (fr. 16), a subterranean gallery that linked Naples and Puteoli, where a small shrine to Priapus has been found – see Jensson (2004, 127) and Vannini (2010, 5–6 and n. 16). The arguments of Sgobbo (1930, 354–61), followed by Sullivan (1968, 35, 46), for transposing the Quartilla episode to before the encounter with Agamemnon at the school of rhetoric (1–6) raise more problems than they resolve; see Jensson (2004, 127–35).

one after the other in manuscripts of the Short excerpts (O), should be read as continuous text, without the excerpts inserted between them by the well-meaning but misguided compiler of L, who injected extraneous material into a coherent narrative.[10]

The seamlessness of the supposed juncture in the O excerpts is upon first inspection striking, and, seen in isolation, one could readily imagine the two fragments originally appearing as continuous text.

18.7–19.1: Complosis deinde manibus in tantum repente risum effusa est, ut timeremus. Idem ex altera parte et ancilla fecit, quae prior venerat, idem virguncula, quae una intraverat. [19.1] Omnia mimico risu exsonuerant, cum interim nos quae tam repentina esset mutatio animorum facta ignoraremus, ac modo nosmet ipsos, modo mulieres intueremur.

20.8: Ac ne Giton quidem ultimo risum tenuit, utique postquam virguncula cervicem eius invasit et non repugnanti puero innumerabilia oscula dedit.

Then she clapped her hands and suddenly burst into such a peal of laughter that we were frightened. The maid who had entered first behaved in the same way on the other side of us, and so did the little girl who came with Quartilla. The whole place rang with the laughter of low mime, and while we were in the dark as to the reason for this sudden change of mood, we kept looking now at each other, now at the women. | In the end even Giton did not hold back his laughter, especially after the little girl threw her arms around his neck and gave the compliant boy countless kisses.[11]

Considered within a wider context, the join may seem less compelling. One difficulty is precisely the issue of continuity and repetition. Already at the end of the long passage of continuous narrative that begins the episode (16.1–18.4) Quartilla had made an abrupt transition from tears to laughter (*ex lacrimis in risum mota*) and had lavished affectionate caresses on Encolpius (*mulier basiavit me spissius et … descendentes ab aure capillos meos lenta manu duxit*, 18.4), which renders less plausible the suddenness here of Quartilla's laughter (*repente*) and the women's change of mood (*repentina mutatio*), both having been established earlier. What is more, laughter appears frequently throughout the episode, including in the two

---

10 van Thiel (1971, 33–4) and (1983, 6).
11 Translations of Petronius, here and elsewhere, from Schmeling's Loeb (2020), in places slightly adapted.

isolated fragments that immediately precede 20.8 in our texts. In the first (20.6), which incorporates a lacuna noted in all our manuscripts, a maid, betrayed by Encolpius's laughter (*ancilla risu meo prodita*), claps her hands (as Quartilla had earlier, in 18.7) and begins affirming that she had placed something (*apposui quidem <*>*).[12] In the second (20.7), a mere five words with lacunae on either side, someone laughs in an attractive way (*non indecenti risu latera commovit*). If the subject of this sentence were anyone other than the maid – Quartilla, for example, as the current arrangement of fragments suggests – then the two fragments together would anticipate and thus adequately motivate the statement that not even Giton in the end restrained his laughter (20.8). Of course, the compiler of L, looking to place fragments of similar content together in order to piece together the original narrative, might have positioned both fragments before 20.8 with precisely that intent, but erroneously. Perhaps so, but that cannot explain why the very next fragment attested in the O family, after three pages of mostly continuous text preserved only in the Long excerpts (L), resumes the same theme of Giton laughing:

24.5: Stabat inter haec Giton et risu dissolvebat ilia sua.

While all this was going on, Giton was standing there, splitting his sides in laughter.

In this case, we have more than a couple of isolated fragments to establish the context, since the O family here overlaps with the L family and runs continuously up to just before the beginning of the *Cena* at 26.7. Indeed, only a single, eight-word excerpt – *abiecti in lectis sine metu reliquam exegimus noctem* – preserved in isolation only in the L family (26.6), intervenes. That a compiler of L mistakenly inserted extraneous material into an originally continuous narrative seems, on this evidence, less plausible than that an excerptor of the O family selectively edited out passages considered scurrilous or distasteful, with the intention of creating the appearance of a seamless narrative – a Bowdlerizing technique that aimed to conceal what it expurgated. Either procedure, or even a combination of both, could explain the peculiar composition of our narrative, and on the present evidence it is impossible to decide which or what combination of them is more likely to be correct.

---

12 Schmeling (2020) translates *prodita* as 'encouraged' in order to suit the context, but the word more plausibly points to a deception revealed, as for example might pertain to Psyche's surreptitious besmirching of Ascyltus's inert body with blackface and phalluses at 22.1.

Selective excerpting or methodical compiling are not the only textual conundrums that the transmitted fragments of the Quartilla episode present. The nefarious work of an anonymous Carolingian interpolator has also been suspected. The idea that a single learned scribe of the early ninth century was responsible for supplementing the text with a number of clarifying glosses originated with Eduard Fraenkel but was first articulated and acted upon by Konrad Müller, under Fraenkel's influence, in his *editio maior* of Petronius published in 1961, in which dozens of such suspected glosses are athetized.[13] In subsequent editions (especially those of 1965, 1978 and 1983), Müller backed away from many of Fraenkel's bolder suggestions, and the issue of interpolations in the text of Petronius, never at the forefront of critical interest, receded further into the background. Once established, however, as it had been definitively by Fraenkel and others, the existence of interpolation in the text of Petronius has never been doubted. Before the pendulum of critical opinion swung fully back to the more conservative equilibrium where it rests today, J. P. Sullivan rounded up a generous collection of some 290 suspected instances in the text of Petronius and proposed a six-fold categorization of them according to presumed source, ranging from simple scribal dittographies to explanatory relative clauses designed to stitch together pieces of the narrative.[14] The latter category is of particular interest. Of twenty-two possible interpolations within the Quartilla episode, the highest density per chapter of any extant section of the *Satyrica*, Sullivan classifies no fewer than four, out of a total of only a dozen in the entire work, as belonging to the category that points to an effort to tie together the narrative, making the Quartilla episode also the most heavily sutured part of the text.[15] Taken together, these signs both of selective cutting and pasting of fragments of narrative and of attempts to stitch together the disparate pieces have encouraged critics to venture further here than elsewhere in the narrative in rearranging the fragments in order to reconstruct the plot.

13 Müller (1961, xxxvii, xxxix–xlvii, lii). Müller dedicated the work to Fraenkel, *unico magistro*.
14 Sullivan (1976) offers his categories as tentative and allows alternative and overlapping ascriptions of putative origins. The two most important general conclusions to be drawn from his survey are that interpolations probably entered the text at different times from different sources and there is little evidence that any derives from a manuscript that preserves more of the narrative than what we have (103–4). Many of the ascriptive glosses Sullivan attributes to Jacques Cujas and his circle in the sixteenth century. More recently, John of Salisbury in the twelfth century has emerged as a plausible candidate; see di Simone (1998) and Vannini (2010, 58 and 152).
15 Sullivan (1976, 106–22). The 'connective' interpolations identified by Sullivan, all involving relative clauses and all but the second considered highly probable, are found at 16.3, 20.2, 22.5 and 25.2. The others of this type (ascriptive relative clauses, a subset of Sullivan's category D) occur at 31.1, 40.5, 57.1, 70.12, 74.5, 96.1, 111.13 and 131.10.

Gaselee, Sullivan and Schmeling all remark two unusual features of the episode: a disconcerting oscillation in mood, which alternates between laughter and distress, and a curious doubling of events: there are two unsuccessful attempts to arouse Encolpius's penis (20.2, 23.5) and two outbreaks of laughter by Giton (20.8, 24.5); twice Giton willingly succumbs to a girl's seduction (20.8, 26.3); twice a *cinaedus* appears (21.2, 23.2); and twice the protagonists drift off to sleep (21.7, 22.1).[16] Each scholar offers a different explanation. For Schmeling, 'the series of paired events could be overemphasized to the reader because of the lacunose state of the text, or P. could have had some structure in mind, which because of the state of the text we can recapture only in a series of pairs'.[17] Sullivan (following Gaselee) believed that many of the duplications were due to the interpolation into the text of an excerptor's abbreviated summaries and that the transmitted text could be explained or justified with minimal adjustment, specifically by the simple repositioning of one group of unplaced fragments (20.5–8) to slightly later in the episode (after 21.3).[18] For Gaselee, whose arguments in his unpublished Cambridge dissertation of 1909 are reported by Sullivan, the disruptions to the narrative of the Quartilla episode imported into our text went far deeper and were multiple and various, ranging from the simple interpolation of extraneous scribal notes to the misplacement of isolated fragments to the intrusion into the text of brief summary statements meant to replace episodes more fully reported and contextualized in other excerpts. His reconstruction assigns very little authority to our transmitted text and proposes a radical rearrangement of the fragments that have been handed down, with the aim of reducing duplication and (in his view) clarifying the narrative sequence of the episode. The main changes consolidate two of the notable repetitions (the two *cinaedi* and two outbursts of Giton's laughter) and place the mock wedding of Giton and Pannychis much earlier in the episode.[19]

Others have proposed different solutions. Vincenzo Ciaffi and Edward Courtney would remove the inconsistencies and explain the duplications

---

16 Gaselee (1909, 1–7); Sullivan (1968, 51); Schmeling (2011, 58 *ad* 19.6).
17 Schmeling (2011, 58).
18 Sullivan (1968, 52–3) recognizes that any reconstruction of this damaged episode must remain speculative and claims for his only 'that it gets rid of the strange dramatic movement and the more unconvincing repetitions, without altering the order of the fragments more than seems strictly necessary'. He also suggests (1968, 52 n. 1) that fragment 28, nine hexameters on the story of Midas's secret, 'might fit somewhere in this episode' and allows (1968, 53) that 'the disorders of the whole episode [may] go far deeper than our reconstruction assumes'.
19 Gaselee's 'Excursus (I) on the Order of the Fragments, Chapters 19–26', pp. 1–7 of his unpublished dissertation (1909), is summarized by Sullivan (1968, 51 n. 1), who details the order Gaselee proposed: 19.5, 20.2 (*sollicitat*), 20.2 (*ancilla*), 21.3, 20.8, 24.5–26.10, 21.4, 21.7, 20.3, 20.5, 21.1, 20.7, 19.6, 23.2–23.5, 20.4, 20.1, 21.2, 22.1–23.1, 26.6.

by positing a large gap in the narrative after 21.3, during which both time and place change, to the next day at Quartilla's house, where the revelry is renewed and many of the earlier scenes are recalled.[20] To both, the portentous nature of 21.3, in which two persons (apparently Encolpius and Ascyltus) swear lifelong secrecy about a horrible secret, seem to mark the end of an episode. In its current position, the fragment immediately follows, and thus seems to refer to, a fragment in which a catamite (*cinaedus*) assaults Encolpius and Ascyltus (*nos*) (21.2), an event that could certainly qualify, in Encolpius's eyes, as worthy of being kept secret. This fragment too, it may be noted, pairs with an earlier scene, when Quartilla first confronts the two with their inadvertent violation of the rites of Priapus, and Encolpius swears that no one of them will divulge the secrets (18.3). Here the passage is contextually grounded in the long stretch of continuous narrative preserved in both the L and the O families of manuscripts at the start of the Quartilla episode, so its position is secure.

Gottskálk Jensson, who is inclined to accept as genuine many of the explanatory glosses athetized in this episode by Müller, likewise posits a change of venue (from the boys' lodging back to the shrine of Priapus) and a lacuna earlier in the episode, after 20.4, which describes Psyche (*ancilla*) binding the protagonists' hands and feet. Thereafter, he believes, the bound captives are brought back to the shrine of Priapus, where a second round of revelry ensues on the same day.[21] Costas Panayotakis sees the episode arranged as a theatrical production in three acts, set in a room (*cella*) within an inn (*deversorium*) (16.1–21.4); in a neighboring dining room (*proxima cella, triclinium*) (21.5–26.3); and in a bedroom (*cubiculum*) (26.3–26.6).[22]

By positing at least one change of venue and a large lacuna somewhere in the episode, all four effectively opt for the first of Schmeling's proposed explanations – that the pairing of events is exaggerated by the lacunose state of the text. A defense of this position might point to other recurring motifs in the narrative as a natural feature of Petronius's picaresque travelogue and a concession to the exigencies of the plot. Petronius was not a first-rate author, this line of thinking goes (and Sullivan explicitly says), and

---

20 Ciaffi (1955, 31–40); Courtney (2001, 68). Sullivan too (1968, 52) believes that a change in venue and 'a perhaps considerable lacuna' are needed to explain a transition between the scenes in the *deversorium* and the later scenes in a dining room (*triclinium*); he would place both after 21.4–7, in which Quartilla reminds the company that an all-night vigil is owed to Priapus.
21 Jensson (2004, 129–30): 'a considerable amount of text may be missing in this most fragmentary part of the episode (19.6–21.3)'. But, as he notes (2004, 130 n. 294), Petronius often effects such transitions of scene and changes of venue crisply, in a single sentence, so we need not on that count imagine a large amount of text to have fallen out here: cf. Jensson (2004, 134 n. 303).
22 Panayotakis (1995, 31–51); cf. Brozek (1972, 287).

had recourse to certain narratological devices that he deployed repeatedly and at times monotonously in order to advance the plot. Perhaps so. But the second of Schmeling's possible explanations – that Petronius had some more systematic structure in mind, which because of the state of the text we can now discern only through a series of pairs – deserves more serious consideration than it has received.

Schmeling does not say where the idea of a systematic structure to the work comes from, but it no doubt springs in part from the classic demonstration by Louis Callebat of the complementary techniques of linking and framing that Petronius and later Apuleius employed to give shape to the amorphous and open narrative form they were creating.[23] The first, through the device of a recurring character or a parallel situation, joined independent units of narrative loosely together like links on a chain; the second, created by stories set within stories or bookending of narrative units into episodes, formed coherent self-contained units capable of being arranged independently. The two techniques were the warp and woof of the narrative fabric of the *Satyrica*. Later, in calling attention to the structural parallels that link the Quartilla episode with a sequence of scenes involving an old woman, Oenothea (136.5–138.1), Schmeling shows how the techniques of framing (internal parallels mark off both episodes as units) and linking (parallelism of context – unwitting offenses against Priapus, the reactions of the priestesses, emoluments) work to juxtapose two episodes otherwise distant and distinct from each other within the narrative.[24]

He may also have been thinking of the brilliant insight of Tom Hubbard, who noted the systematic way that certain scenes within the *Cena* seem to recur in a series of concentric frames. Hubbard believed that the process of framing governed the architecture of the entire work and extended beyond the *Cena* to include the Quartilla episode as well as the scenes following the banquet episode.[25] More plausibly, the 'second dinner' initiated within the *Cena* after the abortive escape attempt (74), which Hubbard pairs with the scenes involving Quartilla, reflects back on the ring structure within the banquet episode itself, as a kind of recursive coda, and thus figures the metaphor of Trimalchio's house as a labyrinthine underworld from which the heroes are unable to escape.[26] The device of concentric framing, in other words, is specific and peculiar to the *Cena* episode, where it reinforces the representation of the setting as a box-like trap. Outside of the episode, the framing device has no obvious relevance and, as outlined

---

23 Callebat (1974).
24 Schmeling (2011, 531–2).
25 Hubbard (1986, 194–203), on the *Cena*, and Hubbard (1986, 203–10), on the controlling structure of entire work. The latter view has found no followers.
26 Bodel (1999, 44–5).

by Hubbard, no convincing explanation.[27] This does not mean that paired details have no significance – they might, for example, point to the conflation of two similarly constructed but otherwise independent episodes, as with the parallel elements of characterization identified by Schmeling between the Quartilla and the Oenothea episodes. Or they might serve some other literary purpose, like concentric framing within the *Cena* episode, that reinforces or replicates the intent of the narrative.

I want to consider this last possibility here. If we approach the question of the relation of the narrative structure to the author's literary aims by putting the latter first – that is, if we begin by considering the *mise en scène* and asking what contemporary social type is targeted, and only then consider how any observable narrative devices (in this instance, parallel or paired narrative details) may have served the goals of the broader satiric portrait – we may find that a possible solution to many of the puzzles of the episode presents itself. For it is clear that each of the major surviving episodes of the work revolve around a central figure and that Petronius painted these figures with careful attention to the contemporary social and cultural setting, so that they emerge less as Theophrastan character types than as fully fleshed individuals from the world of Neronian society. Humor emanates from the poignancy with which topical details from current events and contemporary life are mapped onto timeless types. With Trimalchio, the peculiarly constrained social circumstances of a Roman ex-slave in the economic boom world of the late Julio-Claudian era fit seamlessly with the caricature type of the boorish host, for which the essential characteristics had been sketched by Theophrastus (in *Char.* 4, 16, 21, 27) and given Roman coloring by Horace (in his *Cena Nasidieni*, *Sat.* 2.8). With Eumolpus, the timeless type of the amateur versifier fond of his own voice fit well onto the *captator* of legacy hunters (cf. Theophr. *Char.* 23; Hor. *Sat.* 2.5) in a Crotonian land of the dead (116.9), the role Eumolpus plays (it seems) to its inevitable conclusion in an elaborate *Scheintod* in the final remaining fragments of our text. With more minor characters – Agamemnon, Lichas, Tryphaena, Oenothea – the portraits are less elaborate but no less specific in representing generic character types (the rhetorician, the ship captain, the hedonist, the drunken old woman) with contemporary features.[28]

For Quartilla the particular features of the contemporary figure (the independent woman in a powerful public position, 18.6) grafted easily onto the timeless type (the sex-crazed voluptuary); her role as priestess of

---

27 Despite Rimell (2002, 169, 201–2).
28 One pairing that bears further consideration is that of the two magically empowered women (witches) with sexual designs on Encolpius, Quartilla (16.2) and Circe (127.6), and their adjutant maids, Psyche and Chrysis, each of whom furthers her mistress's aims while at the same time satisfying her own.

Priapus further combined her vital character trait – lust – with her public office by linking the latter to the cult of a notoriously ithyphallic and comical deity (cf. Hor. *Sat.* 1.8).²⁹ The association with Priapus advances a leitmotif that many have seen as the driving narratological device of the work – a representation of Encolpius's persistent impotence and Odyssean wanderings as caused by the wrath of Priapus.³⁰ Illuminating as they are for setting the scenes with Quartilla into their broader narratological context, these recognized features fail to account for the immediate circumstances that underlie the portentous epiphany of Quartilla at the start of the episode (16.2–17.1) and the specific event alleged to have motivated her intervention. Encolpius, Ascyltus and Giton had disrupted a ritual in front of a crypt (16.3) and had thus inadvertently (16.4, *errorem*; 17.6, *imprudentes*) become privy to secret nocturnal rites known to only a few (17.9); now a dream-induced vision has driven Quartilla to seek through them a cure for her malarial fever (17.7, 18.3, 19.2).

Malarial fever, like lust, is intrinsic to Quartilla's being. Together the two conditions allow a novel twist on the conventional figuring of love as a disease by appealing to a strand of popular medical wisdom which held that fever in women could be cured by sexual intercourse.³¹ This sort of quackery suited the portrait well, since it provided a specious motive not only for Quartilla's lust but also for the erratic mood swings that characterize her behavior. Celsus informs us about the nature of fevers (*febres*), of which he distinguishes three types: the kind that occur randomly and variously and can recur daily (*cotidiana*); the type that occur every other day (*tertiana*), of which there are two varieties, a milder and a more pernicious sort, which experts called ἡμιτριταῖον, 'quasi-tertian'; and a type that occurs every third day, which tends to have simpler characteristics (*quartana*).³²

---

29 Sullivan (1968, 122–3) sees the type in more conventional terms, as simply that of 'the hypocritical woman who masks sexuality beneath the guise of religion'. For Richlin (1992, 194) Quartilla is 'a monster of orgiastic religiosity', but in the end 'her voyeuristic pimping of her maid Pannyche to Giton makes her a standard *lena* (or *socrus*)'. Plaza (2000, 77 n. 236) recognizes Quartilla's role as priestess of Priapus as essential but misses its significance for her characterization. For Priapic humor in Roman literature, see Richlin (1992, esp. 64–80).
30 For example, Herter (1932, 315–17); Courtney (2001, 152–7); cf. Schmeling (2011, xxii–xxv).
31 Martial 11.71 imagines a neglected wife preferring death to sex with her elderly husband as a cure for her hysteria. Even more apposite is the opinion of an otherwise unknown physician, Icatidas, recorded by Pliny the Elder (*NH* 28.83), that sex could cure quartan fever in a woman beginning to menstruate. Cf. further Galen 8 p. 420 Kuhn with Kay (1985, 222–3); Ach. Tat. 5.26.2 with Schmeling (2011, 51); and below n. 33 on Quartilla's name.
32 Celsus, *Med.* 3.3.1–3. For ἡμιτριταῖον cf. Hipp. *Epid.* 1.2; Galen 17(1) p. 233 Kuhn; LSJ Suppl. 69 *s.v.*

Quartilla's name recalls the last type, *quartana*, but she claims to suffer from the form that recurs every other day (*tertiana*, 17.7, 18.3, 19.2), evidently the acute version of it, the quasi-tertian, which, according to Celsus, occupies thirty-six of every forty-eight hours and is never fully in remission but only abates somewhat.[33] Thus, toward the end of the episode, just before the wedding of Pannychis and Giton, Quartilla fondles Giton and anticipates enjoying his member as an appetizer the next day, since on that day she has already taken on an ass (Ascyltus?) (24.7). The alternation of days in the recurrence of Quartilla's fever and her proposed daily treatment of it provide a narratological context for repeated sexual encounters of the promiscuous sort depicted in the most fragmentary section of the episode (19.6–21.4). Her role as priestess of Priapus provides the interpretive lens through which we can make sense not only of the orgiastic horseplay but also of the mercurial shifts in mood that characterize her behavior and the peculiar iteration of incidents that stand out in our reconstruction of the episode.

According to Diodorus, Priapus was naturally linked with Dionysus in myth, since men under the influence of wine experience erections – a condition that afflicts Encolpius only rarely and never in our episode. Called by some Ithyphallus, by others Tychon, he received honor not only in the rites of Dionysus but in those of most of the other gods as well, always with laughter and jesting (μετὰ γέλωτος καὶ παιδιᾶς).[34] His rites, as practiced by Quartilla, were nocturnal and secret and liable to ridicule (17.9). The violation of them committed by the protagonists was visual – they had witnessed activities (evidently sexual activities) they were not meant to see (17.8) – but their response to what they saw showed them to be young men of a certain sophistication (*iuvenes tam urbanos*, 16.4). The theme of sexual voyeurism, clearly implied in the *error* imputed to Encolpius and Ascyltus (16.4), if not actually described in parts of the narrative now lost, sets up another pairing, with the voyeuristic foreplay instigated by Quartilla with

---

33 For Quartilla's name, 'Quartan Fever Lady', see Prag and Repath (2009b, 13). Pathology of *quartana*: Celsus, *Med*. 3.2. For malaria in the coastal regions of Campania, see Sallares (2002, 85, 250 n. 43).

34 Diod. 4.6.1–4: ... ἔν τε ταῖς τελεταῖς οὐ μόνον ταῖς Διονυσιακαῖς, ἀλλὰ καὶ ταῖς ἄλλαις σχεδὸν ἁπάσαις οὗτος ὁ θεὸς τυγχάνει τινὸς τιμῆς, μετὰ γέλωτος καὶ παιδιᾶς παρεισαγόμενος ἐν ταῖς θυσίαις (4.6.4). The name 'Tychon', when applied to Priapus (Strabo 13.1.12), identified him as a δαίμων associated with Aphrodite, who gave small gifts to mortals (*Anth. Pal.* 9.334). The name was also used for Hermes (*I.Magn.* 203), possibly in his a role as ψυχαγωγός; cf. LSJ *s.v.* In confusing Priapus with the ithyphallic fertility deity of the Egyptians, Min, and associating him with the myth of Osiris (4.6.3), Diodorus links Priapus with the resurrection ideology common to several of the mysteries. Herter (1932, 287–8) doubts the veracity of Diodorus's report, but see Burkert (1987, 104–5); cf. Juv. 6.314–17, on rites of the Bona Dea performed by *attonitae ... Priapi maenades*; below n. 35.

Encolpius while watching the imminent consummation of the coerced marriage of Giton and the seven-year-old virgin Pannychis at the end of the episode (26.4–5).[35] Insofar as we can hypothesize the trajectory of the plot, the two scenes of voyeurism seem to have framed the Quartilla episode, the first providing a shadow version of a parodic rite of passage (initiation to sex) actualized at the end, in the same way that, within the *Cena Trimalchionis*, the faintly funereal entrance of the central figure (28.4–5) foreshadows the enactment of his own mock funeral at the end.[36]

With the introduction of Priapus Ithyphallus, all the elements are present for a full-scale parodic representation of Quartilla's treatment of her medical condition as coinciding with her functions as high priestess of a cult comically associated with sex. The suspected excesses of the devotees of Dionysus, father of the ithyphallic Priapus and perceived threat to moral order in southern Italy at least since the time of the Bacchanalian affair of 186 BCE, provide a plausible context for many of the more peculiar details of the orgiastic sequences of the episode, and the primary and essential feature common to the group of cults recognized in antiquity as 'mysteries' – voluntary initiation – may help to explain the apparent iteration of detail. The more we learn about the so-called 'mystery cults', and the more closely we attend to the narratological features of the ancient novels, both Greek and Roman, the further we move away from the divergent but equally influential views of Cumont and Merkelbach and the closer we come, under the pervasive influence of social anthropology, to recognizing (after van Gennep) the tripartite structures common to both, as rites of passage, from separation through liminality to incorporation and integration.[37] Indeed, one literary critic has gone so far as to propose a new model for reading the ancient novels that recognizes as central and essential the life-crisis rite of passage that the discovery of sexuality and first sexual experience represent.[38]

---

35 Sullivan (1968, 238–53) investigates the theme of scopophilia (as he styles it) in all possible manifestations and concludes that it provides insight into Petronius's psychosexual predilections. The focus on 'secrets' in the Quartilla episode, Sullivan (1968, 246) believes, may be 'susceptible of deeper interpretation'. Richlin (2009, 93) similarly adopts a meta-reading of the motif: 'arguably, the whole of the *Satyrica* constitutes a sort of spying on things usually unseen'. Whatever their wider implications, both details serve the satiric depiction of a mystery cult of Priapus. The notorious violation of the rites of the Bona Dea in 62 BCE by P. Clodius Pulcher provided an obvious comic foundation: cf. Cic. *Att.* 1.13.3, 1.14.1–5, 1.15.1–6; Plut. *Caes.* 10.6.

36 Both episodes, in any case, culminate in a ritual enactment of a major rite of passage, the pseudo-marriage (sexual initiation) of Giton and Pannychis (26.1–4) and the mock funeral of Trimalchio (78.1–8).

37 For the Greek novel, see Lalanne (2006). For the Roman novel, see the next note.

38 Bierl (2013), advocating a 'bio-ritual' approach and analyzing Apuleius's *Metamorphoses* through this lens. See also Alvar (2008, 158–9).

If reading the ancient novels as rites of passage has replaced reading them as mystery texts, initiation, as a concept, remains central to both approaches. For Merkelbach, the novels were coded narratives that provided literary entertainment superficially but were fully comprehensible only to initiates. For the rite-of-passage school, 'initiation', in the form of sexual discovery, provides the thematic center around which all novel narratives revolve.[39] Strictly and originally *vox propria* for the experience of undergoing the mysteries of Eleusis or Samothrace, 'initiation', in the syntagm 'initiation rites' (*les rites initiatiques*), was first applied metaphorically to the coming-of-age ceremonies of Native Americans in the early eighteenth century and was later picked up and extended to any puberty rite by ethnographers and folklorists such as Frazer and van Gennep in the nineteenth and early twentieth centuries.[40] By further extending the metaphor, popular usage has nowadays diluted the concept to meaning, at times, little more than a first experience of something.

'Mysteries', on the other hand, has never enjoyed any generally agreed definition, either in antiquity, when the religious form was variously described, but not explained, by the terms μυστήρια, τελεταί and ὄργια in Greek, *mysteria*, *initia* and *sacra* in Latin, or today.[41] The trend in recent decades has been to focus on commonalities and experiential similarities – the phenomenological model laid out by Walter Burkert thirty-five years ago has been widely influential – and to recognize that 'mystery cults', by centering on a direct personal experience of the divine, had always formed a vibrant alternative mode of religiosity in Greco-Roman life.[42] As a result, for all their myriad differences, 'mysteries' today are generally understood more as a collection of practices than as a specific secret or set of secrets,

---

39 Merkelbach (1962, esp. the preface); Bierl (2013, 84–5); Alvar (2008, 158).
40 Graf (2003) provides an illuminating history of the concept. Jesuit Father Joseph-François Lafiteau in 1724 first characterized the coming-of-age ceremonies he had witnessed among the Iroquois and the Huron by applying to them the terminology used by Cicero and Varro (*initia*, translating the Greek *mysteria*) and Suetonius (*initiatio*) to describe ritual introduction to the mysteries of Eleusis and Samothrace.
41 For the problem of definition, see, for example, Sfameni Gasparro (2006, 189–91); Bowden (2010, 14–15), who skirts the question; Bremmer (2014, xi–xiii); Belayche and Massa (2021b, 12–16).
42 Wellman (2005). For the phenomenological approach, see Burkert (1987, 4); Burkert's (1987, 11) often quoted definition of mysteries as 'initiation rituals of a voluntary, personal, and secret character that aimed at a change of mind through experience of the sacred' would parodoxically exclude the mysteries of Eleusis and Samothrace, which evidently did not involve any change of mind; see Bremmer (2014, xi–xii). Bowden (2010, 15) adopts anthropologist Harvey Whitehouse's concept of different ways of religiosity to distinguish the imagistic mode of the mystery cults from the doctrinal modes of Judeo-Christian as well as traditional Greco-Roman civic theology. Belayche and Massa (2021b) provide a helpful overview of recent developments in this field.

and the tendency nowadays is to identify a coherent (if open) set of general characteristics rather than to try to formulate a comprehensive definition of the form. That is probably how the mysteries were viewed and identified by outsiders in antiquity as well, in much the same way as secular Westerners today can identify as acts of devotion a variety of behaviors and practices engaged in by religious Christians, Jews and Muslims without knowing (or needing to know) the significance of any of them or the particular orthodoxies of any individual sect.

So we, like Petronius's original readers, may recognize in the worship of Priapus as practiced by Quartilla all the signs of initiation into a mystery cult without needing to understand the meaning of any of particular act. Bremmer in his recent study of the phenomenon identifies nine general characteristics. These can serve as a sort of field guide for identifying members of the species: first and foremost, secrecy and an emotionally heightened initiatory ritual seem to have been essential; these are followed closely by voluntary membership and nocturnal rites. Less universal but notable in many cults are preliminary purification, an obligation to pay for participation (metaphorically but in many cases also literally) and promised rewards (in this life or the afterlife). The older mysteries were located in specific sites at various distances outside but near cities and, with the exception of the (later) cult of Mithras, which was exclusively male, they were ecumenical and all-encompassing, being open to male and female, slave and free, young and old, citizen and non-citizen.[43]

In the Quartilla episode, we find no indications of preliminary purification or promised rewards (in this life or the afterlife), but Encolpius pays for his participation in loss of dignity and self-respect (21.3), and many of the other features that characterize the form can be readily identified.[44] Secrecy lies at the heart of the rites that have been violated (17.8-9, 20.3), and the violation itself takes the form of an illicit witnessing of something meant not to be seen (17.4, 17.8); this emphasis on optics accords not only with the imagistic mode of religiosity characteristic of the way mysteries imprinted themselves in individual minds but with the importance of seeing and visualization for the *way* they encoded their 'mysteries'.[45]

---

43 Bremmer (2014, xii–xiii): 'The fact that the Greeks and Romans called all these rituals *Mystêria* suggests that they saw above all similarities.' Belayche and Massa (2021b, 24-5) distribute these features into four ontologically distinct classifications ('items') that group six of the nine characteristics into the first category ('ritualistic') and assign one each to the other three: 'interpretative' (rewards promised, eschatology); 'topographical' (older mysteries outside cities); and 'sociological' (open to all). The rationale of this classification is unclear.

44 Cf. Bremmer (2014, 4, 68, 82, 89) on pay and (2014, 138-9) on symbolic costs.

45 See Bowden (2010, 15-18); Belayche and Massa (2021b, 5-12).

The rites violated were nocturnal (17.9, 21.7), and Encolpius's participation in the potentially traumatic ritual that will absolve him of his sin is voluntary, in full knowledge of the potential harm to himself and his companions (*vel periculo nostro*, 18.3). This last point is important, since many of the emotionally heightened experiences of those undergoing initiatory rituals were physically taxing, disconcerting or frightening, and in order for us to recognize the passages describing these perceptions in the Quartilla episode as functionally different from the many other places in our surviving text where Encolpius the narrator articulates similar feelings, we need to remember that he has subjected himself and his companions to these minor traumas willingly and knowingly. The location of Quartilla's rites – before a crypt (16.3) in a shrine to Priapus (17.8) – answers well to the topographical and morphological features characteristic of the places where mysteries were celebrated, and the diversity of participants in the sexual escapades depicted (adults and children, male and female, free and slave, straight and queer) reflects the worst suspicions of Roman critics about the practices initiates engaged in.[46]

The stage is fully set, in other words, for a 'Quartilla mime' centered around bawdy parody of the ritualistic behaviors of initiates into the mysteries.[47] Within this setting, many of the more peculiar incidents of the episode may be seen to conform to popular expectations (if not the reality) of what initiation into mysteries entailed. Here, the very secrecy of the mysteries allowed Petronius to focus on superficial features of the sort that attracted popular comment without needing to specify any particular eschatology or soteriology. Thus, the 'sudden change of attitude' (*tam repentina ... mutatio animorum*) manifested in Quartilla and her entourage by their abrupt explosion into laughter out of tears, explicitly remarked by Encolpius (19.4) as puzzling, may or may not be seen as reflecting the sort of revelatory 'change of mind' that Burkert regarded as fundamental to the initiatory experience; but the abrupt shifts of mood that characterize the behavior of Quartilla and her maids at the start of the episode (17.6, 18.4), which consistently produce wonder and fear in Encolpius (18.2, 18.7, 19.1), reflect well the

---

46 Initiations into mysteries often involved allusion to (if not actual enactment in) crypts and caves; see Bremmer (2014, 11–12, 103, 130–1, 176, 182). For Roman suspicion that the mysteries involved sexual excesses, see Burkert (1987, 104–5); Bowden (2010, 213); Bremmer (2014, 11–13).
47 See Panayotakis (1995, 37–9) on the scenographic presentation of the episode; cf. Schmeling (2011, 49) on 17.3, *manibus constrictis*. Later Eumolpus explicitly characterizes his plot to deceive the legacy hunters of Croton as a mime (117.4), and mime is evoked directly in the Quartilla episode at 19.1, *omnia mimico risu exsonuerant*, a phrase often taken to encapsulate the tone of the entire *Satyrica* (see above, p. 181); see Schmeling (2011, 55 *ad loc.*); Plaza (2000, 81–2).

emotional swings described by ancient initiates.[48] As with the initiation of Lucius into the rites of Isis in the final book of Apuleius's *Metamorphoses*, the process is set into motion by a dream vision sent to the priest who will induct the novice into the mysteries. Quartilla's incubation-induced vision (of Priapus?) ordering her, in the formulaic phrase (*iussa sum*, 17.7), to seek out the culprits thus hints at an initiatory context from the outset.[49] With Encolpius and his companions maintaining silence (*tacentibus adhuc nobis*, 17.1) up to the point of his promise on their behalf to preserve the secrets of Priapus and further to comply with the cure prescribed by Quartilla's incubatory vision, the initiatory setting is further established.[50]

At this point the staging of the initiation proper begins with the outburst of mimic laughter by Quartilla and her entourage noted earlier (18.7–19.1), followed by Quartilla's announcement that she has shut off the lodgings from all other 'mortals' (*mortales*, a religiously portentous term; cf. 104.5) in order to receive her cure without interruption (19.2). With this spatial segregation she converts the inn into a τελεστήριον, a place for initiation into mysteries. The announcement causes bewilderment and consternation in Ascyltus and Encolpius (19.3) and, briefly, a determination to resist (19.4–5), which is quickly lost somewhere in the lacuna that marks the beginning of the most choppy section of the narrative preserved in the Longer excerpts (19.6–21.3). The first fragment (19.6) describes a sensation of astonishment and loss of nerve and a vision of imminent death – evidently reactions of the three initiands. This is the first clear allusion to one of the hallmark metaphors used by ancient writers to describe the experience of initiation: a voluntary death, or near death, leading to a spiritual rebirth.[51] Thereafter the isolated snippets of text present vignettes of hazing of a sort familiar from contemporary American collegiate initiations –

---

48 Burkert (1987, 11, 89–92). Dio of Prusa mentions 'darkness and light appearing in sudden changes' (σκότους τε καὶ φωτὸς ἐναλλὰξ αὐτῷ φαινομένων, *Or.* 12.33); Plutarch (fr. 178 Sandbach) describes the experience of 'tiresome walking in circles, some frightening paths in the darkness that lead nowhere, then ... panic and shivering and sweat and amazement. And then some wonderful light' (πλάναι τὰ πρῶτα καὶ περιδρομαὶ κοπώδεις καὶ διὰ σκότους τινὲς ὕποπτοι πορεῖαι καὶ ἀτέλεστοι. . .φρίκη καὶ τρόμος καὶ ἰδρὼς καὶ θάμβος. ἐκ δὲ τούτου φῶς τι θαυμάσιον ἀπήντησεν, translation by Burkert).

49 Cf. Apul. *Met.* 11.6.3, a double-dream vision, as with Tryphaena's and Lichas's double dream involving epiphanies of Priapus and a statue of Neptune 104.1–2; 11.13.1. Strabo 14.1.44 describes a *Ploutonion* near Nysa with a wondrous cave (ἄντρον θαυμαστὸν) known as the *Charonion*, where those sick and seeking to be cured consulted priests who incubated in or near the cave and prescribed cures based on their dreams. Cf. Renberg (2017, 295–7, 613 n. 1) on Quartilla's incubation.

50 As noted already by Weinreich (1909, 182–3), who cites the miraculous door-opening and epiphany of Psyche, the incubation dream and the *pervigilium Priapi*.

51 See, for example, Apul. *Met.* 11.23.6–8; Plut. fr. 178; Burkert (1987, 75, 91–2, 99–101); Bremmer (2014, 120–2).

ritualized 'torture' and humiliation, required consumption of narcotics or inebriants and compulsory sexual performance – all of which are found also in ancient testimony about mystery cults.[52]

Encolpius begs Quartilla not to torture them (20.1); her maid Psyche prepares a space for the initiation (20.2) and binds the initiands' hands and feet (20.4); someone tries unsuccessfully to stimulate Encolpius's penis (20.2); Ascyltus covers his head in his cloak (apparently out of fear or shame) (20.3) and demands his share of an aphrodisiac (*satyrion*) that Encolpius has entirely consumed (20.5–6). Under its influence, Quartilla's flanks, rippling with laughter, now seem to Encolpius attractive (20.7), and Giton succumbs willingly to the flirtatious kisses of the child Pannychis. In the next fragment the mood shifts abruptly: the initiands are being assailed – Psyche pokes Encolpius in the cheeks with a hairpin; Pannychis assaults (sodomizes?) Ascyltus (*Ascylton opprimebat*) with a cosmetics brush soaked in aphrodisiac – and want to cry out for help, but their isolation precludes assistance (21.1).[53] Finally, a catamite clad in a chestnut-brown cloak sexually assaults Encolpius and Ascyltus until Quartilla, wielding a whalebone crop, grants them remission (21.2). The two victim initiands swear to each other never to reveal 'such a horrible secret' (*tam horribile secretum*, 21.3) – evidently the experiences just undergone, rather than the original violation of the rite of Priapus, for which Encolpius had already pledged their silence (18.3) – and the first stage of the initiation comes to a close.

Among the features most characteristic of initiation into the mysteries during the imperial period was iteration, whether optional (as in the case of repeat visits to the Eleusinian and Samothracian mysteries, where initiates observed the rites as ἐπόπται rather than undergoing them a second time) or more commonly, it seems, if not mandatory, at least encouraged by systems that ranked adherents according to their advancement through various stages of initiation. This was certainly the case with the hierarchical all-male cult of Mithras and with the mysteries of Isis as encountered by

---

52 For 'hazing'-type practices in mystery initiations, cf., for example, the flagellation scene in the Villa of the Mysteries frieze with Burkert (1987, 95–6, 104) and Bremmer (2014, 107); Dem. 18.259, on Dionysiac initiations in which the initiands, seated, are smeared with a mixture of clay and chaff; Ach. Tat. 5.23.6 and Plaut. *Aul.* 408–9 for ritual beatings (the latter a Bacchanal banquet); Livy 39.15.9 (cf. 39.10.7, 39.13.10), implying, apropos of the notorious Bacchanalian affair of 186 BCE, that initiands to the Bacchic mysteries were sodomized; Bremmer (2014, 135–6), on flogging, bondage and the threat of violence in Mithraic initiation; Burkert (1987, 104–8) on the role of sex, often intensified by prolonged abstinence in preparation for initiation; Burkert (1987, 108–9) on drugs, perhaps underestimating the significance of intoxicants: see Bremmer (2014, 40–1) on the heavy consumption of wine at the rites of the Kabeiroi at Samothrace.
53 The verb *comprimo*, with its cognates (here *opprimo*), was the standard Latin euphemism for the penetrating role in sex; see Adams (1982, 182–3).

Lucius in Apuleius's *Metamorphoses*.[54] Initiands to the Eleusinian mysteries traditionally underwent two stages of initiation over two successive nights.[55] As the most widely known and enduring mysteries of the ancient world, the ritual practices at Eleusis would have formed a recognizable model for a two-stage initiation to the rites of Priapus and a fitting paradigm for Quartilla's daily treatment of her quasi-tertian malarial fever. The blending of the two models also provides a plausible motive for the repetition, with variation, of several of the incidents recounted in the first stage of initiation and thus a ready explanation for many of the puzzling duplications in the narrative.

The break between the two stages of initiation that falls in the lacuna after Encolpius and Ascyltus swear to maintain their 'horrible secret' (21.3) need not mean a loss of much text or a long passage of time.[56] Indeed, the fatigue and general dissipation of the revelers (21.5, 21.7, 22.4) suggest that only brief respite is given to the celebration. The move to a new dining service laid out in the adjacent room (21.5) serves as the formal marker for the beginning of the second stage, which Quartilla identifies as the all-night vigil of Priapus (*Priapi ... pervigilium*, 21.7).[57] When Encolpius describes himself and his companions as having been 'initiated' (*initiati*) into the new meal by a remarkable appetizer (21.6), the poignancy of the metaphor would not have been lost on the Roman reader, and the groundwork is laid for a repetition of the initiatory process.[58]

---

54 For Lucius's three-stage initiation, see Apul. *Met.* 11.21-2, 27, 29 with Burkert (1987, 17); cf. Burkert (1987, 8, 18) on the *taurobolium*, which had to be repeated every twenty years, like a vaccine. Mesomedes, *Hymn* 5.10 (to Isis), with Bremmer (2014, 12) and below, n. 63, on the stages of initiation into the mysteries of Isis. Theophr. *Char.* 16.12 shows the superstitious man undergoing initiation every month. What had been caricature in the late fourth century BCE had become reality by the first century CE. Cf. also Plut. *Mor.* 81d-e and Theon of Smyrna, *Expositio Rerum Mathematicarum* pp. 14.8-16.2 Hiller, with Belayche and Massa (2021a, 41 n. 1).

55 Bremmer (2014, 9-10) follows Mommsen in hypothesizing that the two stages of initiation must have been different and that the ceremonies we know of should therefore be distributed over the two nights. This need not imply re-enactment of a linear narrative, as with the Eleusinian mysteries or the fictional mysteries of Glycon fabricated by Alexander of Abonuteichos (Luc. *Alex.* 38-9), but might mean no more than a heightened or intensified reiteration or variation of the previous night's experiences.

56 *Pace* Ciaffi and Courtney, who posit a large lacuna here and a change of both venue and date; see above at n. 20.

57 For the importance of communal dining and feasting in the mysteries, see Burkert (1987, 109-12). The *pervigilium*, though celebrated in a variety of contexts, was particularly associated with Bona Dea (originally), Venus, Ceres and Dea Dia – all female deities involved with mysteries or sex; see Schmeling (2011, 64) for references.

58 The metaphorical use of *initiatus* in antiquity was not common (see *TLL s.v.* 'initio') and led Otto Jahn to propose emending the text here to *invitati*.

So, in place of bondage (20.4) and physical violation (21.1), harassment of the initiands now takes the form of body shaming and mockery: a maid (Psyche?) smears an unconscious Ascyltus with blackface and paints his torso with penises (22.1). A catamite returns and forces himself on Encolpius with increased vigor and urgency (23.2–5) but, as before (20.2), Encolpius's organ fails to respond (23.5). Quartilla again intervenes to orchestrate the catamite's performance, dictating the measure of sexual harassment to be inflicted on each initiand (24.4; cf. 21.2). The motif of Encolpius misunderstanding the drinking ritual here hinges on a double entendre of the sort that represents the sort of debunking demystification of the sacred object that preoccupied Christian critics of the mysteries and, we must suppose, ordinary skeptics: when Encolpius learns that an *embasicoetan* is to be administered, no doubt remembering the cup of *satyrion* he had consumed earlier (20.6–7), he imagines a phallus-shaped drinking vessel modeled in such a way as to implicate the drinker in a visual simulation of fellatio (21.1), when in fact it is the unwelcome attention of a catamite that is prescribed (24.2).[59] Giton's inopportune outburst of laughter at his companions' discomfort recalls the earlier scene in which he had been last to join in the laughter of communal merriment (20.8) and leads directly to Quartilla incorporating him into her initiatory ritual, on Psyche's suggestion, because, as she remarks, the occasion (of Encolpius's and Ascyltus's initiation) is opportune (*quia bellissima occasio est*, 25.1), for the deflowering of the girl Pannychis.[60]

The unholy marriage of the adolescent Giton and the girl Pannychis (about seven years old) (26.1–4) marks the culmination of the initiatory ritual and the conclusion of the Quartilla episode. Within the framework of the entire Quartilla story, as I have interpreted it, the voyeuristic observation by Quartilla and Encolpius of the newlyweds copulating (26.4–5) recalls the illicit observation by Encolpius and his companions of Quartilla's Priapic rites (involving some sort of sexual activity) in a part of the text now lost, but which may be presumed to have marked the introduction of Quartilla into the narrative.[61] Within the narrower context of the scenes at the inn, the sexual union of the virgin Pannychis and Giton recalls in more intensified form the affectionate kisses lavished

---

59 For *embasicoetan*, see Schmeling (2011, 71 *ad loc.*).
60 See Plaza (2000, 78–80) for the tone of Giton's laughter and his unusually dominant role in this episode. Just as Psyche's name reminds us of initiation, Pannychis's name evokes the *pervigilium Priapi*: cf. *Anth. Pal.* 5.200.3–4 with Schmeling (2011, 75 *ad* 25.1).
61 See above, at n. 35. As with Trimalchio and Eumolpus, the first impressions the narrator has of Quartilla are formed from visual observation. The poignancy of the bookending may have been enhanced by the inversion of Quartilla's role from object to agent of voyeurism. Giton is about sixteen years old (97.2).

by her on him earlier (20.8). In both cases, Giton is characterized as a not unwilling participant (*non repugnanti puero*, 20.8; *non repugnavit puer*, 26.3), further linking the two scenes. As with the *embasicoetan* scene, in Petronius's telling, two details presented independently or incidentally in the first stage of the initiation are combined and intensified in the second: Encolpius drinking the aphrodisiac (20.6–7) and the attack of the catamite (21.2), two separate events in the first initiatory stage, are brought together in the second stage in Encolpius's misapprehension of the ritual prescription of an *embasicoetan* (24.1–3). Similarly, Giton's initial outburst of laughter, prompted by the girl's kisses (20.8), is expanded and elaborated by Quartilla's and Psyche's interventions (24.5–25.1) into the full final scene, which is initiated by another outburst of Giton's laughter (24.5) and leads to the mock wedding that crowns the episode (26.1–5).

Above all, the mock wedding of Pannychis and Giton completes the arc of narrative that incorporates the initiation parody proper, which is formalized by Encolpius's assent to follow Quartilla's prescriptions (18.2–3) and begins in earnest with the disconcerting and frightening mimic laughter that precedes Quartilla's announcement that she has cut off the inn to outsiders (18.7–19.1). We have no direct written testimony of ritual marriage forming part of any initiation ritual into a mystery cult, but a variety of indications suggests that symbolic marriage and even ritual weddings were recognized features of the ceremonies. The famous painted frieze in a dining room of the Villa of the Mysteries at Pompeii provides vivid if enigmatic evidence in a chronologically and geographically relevant context for ritual marriage forming some part of the Dionysiac mysteries.[62] The Cretan poet Mesomedes, a freedman of the emperor Hadrian, in explicating the stages of initiation to the mysteries of Isis according to those of the Eleusinian mysteries, lists first an 'underground wedding song' (χθόνιος ὑμέναιος), the meaning of which is uncertain and disputed but which evidently formed an integral part of the ceremony, since it involved the ἀνάκτορον, a small chapel at Eleusis where the mysteries were celebrated.[63] The all-male cult of Mithras would seem to have allowed little opportunity to exploit marriage symbolism, but the second of the seven grades to which initiates could aspire was that of 'Bridegroom' (*Nymphius*), a status that apparently placed the initiand in a subservient position, and we cannot exclude the possibility that some sort of marital union was

---

62 Burkert (1987, 105); Bowden (2010, 130–3).
63 Mesomedes, *Hymn* 5.10 (to Isis); cf. Bremmer (2014, 12–13), contesting an interpretation of Burkert. For the Eleusinian ἀνάκτορον, Bremmer (2014, 9).

imagined.⁶⁴ Finally, the performative aspect of the mock wedding of Pannychis and Giton finds intriguing parallel in the mysteries devised on the model of the Eleusinian mysteries by the religious entrepreneur Alexander of Abonuteichos around the middle of the second century.⁶⁵ Celebrations were to take place annually over three days, the last of which culminated in a live re-enactment of a mystical union between himself and Selene, in accordance with a story he had propagated some years previously in establishing his reputation as a divine seer. On the occasion witnessed by Lucian, Alexander as hierophant lay out in full view, pretending to sleep, while stage machinery lowered from the roof 'as if from heaven' a beautiful woman, Rutilia, the wife of an imperial freedman, who was genuinely in love with Alexander, and the two then engaged in amorous kisses and embraces in full public view, as Lucian twice remarks, and would have gone further, he implies, had there been fewer torches present.⁶⁶ This performance took place a hundred years after the time when figures like Quartilla and Trimalchio populated the cultural world of the Roman Bay of Naples, where some eastern cults had well-established roots already in the first century BCE and others blossomed from the Augustan period on, but there is no reason to doubt that similar public performances were known already in the Neronian age.⁶⁷

Recognizing the mock wedding of Pannychis and Giton as the culmination of a carefully crafted parody of a two-stage initiation ritual into the mysteries of Priapus does not represent a radically novel interpretation of the episode – hints of an initiation parody are noted in passing by many critics – nor does it solve every narrative puzzle that the transmitted fragments present. The characterization of the maid who paints the unconscious Ascyltus with blackface and penises as the one 'who had been so rudely rejected' (22.1) is oddly indirect if referring to Psyche, who has already been named (at 20.2 and 21.1) and may allude to a different

---

64 Hieron. *Epist.* 107.2. The seven grades of membership seem to have been most actively observed at Rome and in Italy; for their significance and groupings, see Bremmer (2014, 133–8) and Bremmer (2014, 134–5) for the *Nymphius*.
65 Luc. *Alex.* 38–40, with Chaniotis (2002, 77–9).
66 Luc. *Alex.* 39. For the story established earlier: 35. Alexander is accused by Lucian also of hypocritically sodomizing boys under religious pretexts while advocating abstinence (41) and of openly seducing married women to impregnate them (42).
67 In the Augustan era, the annual games of Flora (April 28 to May 2) included five days of licentious theatrical performances involving naked women (Ov. *Fast.* 4.946, 5.331–56; Mart. 1 Pref.); the 'Laureolus' mime, in which an actor playing a historical bandit was mock-crucified with great gore, was well known by the time of Gaius (Joseph. *AJ* 19.94; Suet. *Gaius* 56.2); and public punishments involving sexual humiliation and torture became common during the Flavian era: see Coleman (1990, 60–6) and Wiseman (1999).

servant involved in an episode of the narrative now lost. The intrusion of the two Syrians intent on robbery (22.3) would seem to contradict the declaration by Quartilla that she had closed off the inn to outside mortals (19.2), were it not the case that the entire party had fallen into an inebriated stupor (22.2–5) and whatever precautions Quartilla might have taken may be presumed to have lapsed. Quartilla's apparent failure to take notice of Giton until halfway through the second stage of initiation (24.5), when his laughter had already attracted Encolpius's attention earlier (20.8), is not as peculiar as some critics have imagined, since the activities of slaves, especially other people's slaves, often fell beneath the notice of slave-owners.

The advantages of the interpretation advanced here, on the other hand, are several. Taking seriously Quartilla's designated role as a priestess of Priapus, and thus a μύστης, a guide, to the mysteries of Priapus, allows Petronius to motivate her lust by combining cleverly a bit of contemporary medical wisdom about the pathology of malaria, particularly of the 'quasi-tertian' sort (flare-ups every other day, with fever persistent for most of the two-day period) with popular beliefs about the practices associated with initiation into the mysteries (nocturnal rites and advancement in stages). Acknowledging the range of behaviors attested in or suspected of initiation into the mysteries – humiliation, bondage, compulsory public sex, physical and sexual abuse, body modification, symbolic death – enables us to make sense of many of the more sensational tidbits of narrative preserved in our fragments. And appreciating the structural similarities between the two-stage debauch orchestrated by Quartilla, with a transition from one *cubiculum* to another marking a momentary pause in the festivities (21.5–6), and the two-stage initiation ritual of the Eleusinian mysteries, the best known of all ancient mystery cults, provides contextual justification for the otherwise puzzling duplication of detail – in the secrecy sworn about shared experiences (18.3, 21.3), in Giton's laughter (20.8, 24.5) and compliant seduction (20.8, 26.3), in the assaults of the catamite (or catamites) (21.2, 23.2) and in the unsuccessful attempts to arouse Encolpius's penis (20.2, 23.5).

This last understanding, finally, takes us back to the very real problems with the text of this portion of Petronius's narrative, as it has come down to us in its most disturbed sections (19.6–21.3), and the various solutions critics have proposed to resolve its presumed difficulties. Most of the latter involve excising some phrases and clauses as interpolations, transposing one or more fragments, or hypothesizing major changes of location and time in missing parts of the text – all with the aim of reducing the apparent duplications and streamlining the narrative. If the interpretation advanced here is sound, none of these measures is necessary in order to explain the intentional, not incidental, duplications of detail in the satiric presentation of a two-stage ritual initiation into the mysteries of Priapus. On this reading, very little editorial intervention and only a moderate amount of speculative filling-in of gaps in the narrative are needed in order to make sense of the fragments in the order transmitted, and to render the episode, as a whole, not so funny after all.[68]

Works Cited

Adams, James N. 1982. *The Latin Sexual Vocabulary*. Baltimore: Johns Hopkins University Press.
Alvar, Jaime. 2008. *Romanising Oriental Gods: Myth, Salvation, and Ethics in the Cults of Cybele, Isis and Mithras*, translated by Richard Gordon. Leiden: Brill.
Aragosti, Andrea, Paola Cosci and Annamaria Cotrozzi. 1988. *Petronio: l'episodio di Quartilla (Satyricon 16–26.6)*. Bologna: Pitagora.
Belayche, Nicole, and Francesco Massa, eds. 2021a. *Mystery Cults in Visual Representation in Graeco-Roman Antiquity*. Leiden: Brill.
———. 2021b. 'Mystery Cults and Visual Language in Graeco-Roman Antiquity: An Introduction'. In Belayche and Massa 2021a, 1–37.
Bettini, Maurizio. 1991. *Anthropology and Roman Culture: Kinship, Time, Images of the Soul*, translated by John Van Sickle. Baltimore: Johns Hopkins University Press.
Bierl, Anton. 2013. 'From Mystery to Initiation: A Mytho-Ritual Poetics of Love and Sex in the Ancient Novel – Even in Apuleius' *Golden Ass*?'. In *Intende Lector: Echoes of Myth, Religion, and Ritual in the Ancient Novel*, edited by Marilia P. Futre Pinheiro, Anton Bierl and Roger Beck, 82–99. Berlin and Boston: De Gruyter.
Bodel, John. 1999. 'The *Cena Trimlachionis*'. In *Latin Fiction: The Latin Novel in Context*, edited by Heinz Hofmann, 38–51. London: Routledge.
Bowden, Hugh. 2010. *Mystery Cults of the Ancient World*. Princeton: Princeton University Press.
Bremmer, Jan. 2014. *Initiation into the Mysteries of the Ancient World*. Berlin: De Gruyter.
Brozek, M. 1972. 'Szenereibeschreibungen bei Petronius'. *Eos* 56: 285–91.
Burkert, Walter 1987. *Ancient Mystery Cults*. Cambridge, MA: Harvard University Press.
Callebat, Louis. 1974. 'Structures narratives et modes de representation dans le *Satyricon* de Pétrone'. *Revue des Études Latines* 52: 281–303.
Chaniotis, Angelos. 2002. 'Old Wine in a New Skin: Tradition and Innovation in the Cult Foundation of Alexander of Abonouteichos'. In *Tradition and Innovation*

---

68 In the fall of 1978 and spring of 1979 Jeff Henderson and I spent many hours over pool tables in the Michigan Union discussing Delta blues and problems in the text history of Petronius, a then popular topic around Angell Hall. This essay is offered in fond memory of those conversations and less than adequate tribute to the Aristophanic spirit that inspired them. Gareth Schmeling read a draft and offered encouragement and sage advice with his customary generosity.

in the Ancient World, edited by Edward Dąbrowa, 67–85. Cracow: Jagiellonian University Press.

Ciaffi, Vincenzo. 1955. *Struttura del Satyricon*. Turin: Università di Torino.

Coleman, Kathleen M. 1990. 'Fatal Charades: Roman Executions Staged as Mythological Enactments'. *JRS* 80: 44–73.

Courtney, Edward. 2001. *A Companion to Petronius*. Oxford: Oxford University Press.

di Simone, Marina 1998. 'Le didascalie nel testo del *Satyricon* e la costituzione degli *excerpta longa*: percorsi di lettura'. *SCO* 46: 933–53.

Flower, Harriet I. 1996. *Ancestor Masks and Aristocratic Power in Roman Culture*. Oxford: Clarendon Press.

Gaselee, Stephen. 1909. *Some Unpublished Materials for an Edition of Petronius*. Unpublished diss. Cambridge University Library [*non vidi*].

Ginzburg, Carlo. 2004. 'Family Resemblances and Family Trees: Two Cognitive Metaphors'. *Critical Inquiry* 30: 537–56.

Graf, Fritz. 2003. 'Initiation: A Concept with a Troubled History'. In *Initiation in Ancient Greek Rituals and Narratives*, edited by David B. Dodd and Christopher Faraone, 3–24. London: Routledge.

Herter, Hans. 1932. *De Priapo*. Giessen: Töpelmann.

Hubbard, Thomas. 1986. 'The Narrative Architecture of Petronius's *Satyricon*'. *L'Antiquité Classique* 55: 190–212.

Jensson, Gottskálk. 2004. *The Recollections of Encolpius: The Satyrica of Petronius as Milesian Fiction*. Groningen: Barkhuis.

Kay, Nigel M. 1985. *Martial Book XI*. Oxford: Oxford University Press.

Keyser, Paul 1996. 'Nonius Marcellus' Quotations of Sallust'. *Wiener Studien* 109: 181–226.

Lalanne, Sophie. 2006. *Une éducation grecque: rites de passages et construction des genres dans le roman grec ancien*. Paris: Découverte.

Merkelbach, Reinhold. 1962. *Roman und Mysterium*. Munich and Berlin: Beck.

Müller, Konrad. 1961. *Petronii Arbitri Satyricon*. Munich: Ernst Heimeran.

———. 1995. *Petronius Satyricon Reliquiae*, 4th edn. Stuttgart and Leipzig: Teubner.

Oikonomopoulou, Katerina 2017. 'Miscellanies'. In *The Oxford Handbook to the Second Sophistic*, edited by Daniel S. Richter and William A. Johnson, 447–59. Oxford: Oxford University Press.

Pace, N. 2018. 'New Evidence for Dating the Discovery at Traù of the Petronian *Cena Trimalchionis*'. In *Cultural Crossroads in the Ancient Novel*, edited by Marília P. Futre Pinheiro, David Konstan and Bruce D. MacQueen, 209–20. Berlin: De Gruyter.

Panayotakis, Costas. 1995. *Theatrum Mundi: Theatrical Elements in the Satyrica of Petronius*. Leiden: Brill.

Plaza, Maria. 2000. *Laughter and Derision in Petronius' Satyrica*. Stockholm: Almquist & Wiksell.

Prag, Jonathan, and Ian Repath, eds. 2009a. *Petronius: A Handbook*. Oxford: Blackwell.

———. 2009b. 'Introduction'. In Prag and Repath 2009a, 1–15.

Renberg, Gil. 2017. *Where Dreams May Come: Incubation Sanctuaries in the Ancient World*. Leiden: Brill.
Richlin, Amy. 1992. *The Garden of Priapus: Sexuality and Aggression in Roman Humor*. Rev. edn. Oxford: Oxford University Press.
———. 2009. 'Sex in the *Satyrica*'. In Prag and Repath 2009a, 82–100.
Rimell, Victoria 2002. *Petronius and the Anatomy of Fiction*. Cambridge: Cambridge University Press.
Sallares, Robert. 2002. *Malaria and Rome: A History of Malaria in Ancient Italy*. Oxford: Oxford University Press.
Schmeling, Gareth. 2003. 'The *Satyrica* of Petronius'. In *The Novel in the Ancient World*. Rev. edn., edited by Gareth Schmeling, 457–90. Leiden: Brill.
———, with the collaboration of Aldo Setaioli. 2011. *A Commentary on the Satyrica of Petronius*. Oxford: Oxford University Press.
———. 2020. *Petronius: Satyricon, Seneca: Apocolocyntosis*. Cambridge, MA: Harvard University Press.
Sfameni Gasparro, Giulia. 2006. 'Misteri e culti orientali: un problema storico-religioso'. In *Religions orientales – culti misterici: neue Perspektiven – nouvelles perspectives – prospettive nuove*, edited by Corinne Bonnet, Jörg Rüpke and Paolo Scarpi, 181–210. Stuttgart: Franz Steiner.
Sgobbo, Italo. 1930. 'Frammenti dello libro XIV delle "Saturae" di Petronio', *Rendiconti dell'Accademia dei Lincei* 6.6: 354–61.
Slater, Niall. 1990. *Reading Petronius*. Baltimore: Johns Hopkins University Press.
Sullivan, John P. 1968. *The Satyricon of Petronius*. London: Faber and Faber.
———. 1976. 'Interpolations in Petronius'. *Proceedings of the Cambridge Philological Society* 22: 90–122.
Thiel, Helmut van. 1971. *Petron: Überlieferung und Rekonstruktion*. Leiden: Brill.
———. 1983. 'On the Order of the Petronius Excerpts'. *Petronian Society Newsletter* 15: 5–6.
Vannini, Giulio. 2010. *Petronii Arbitri Satyricon 100–115: edizione critica e commento*. Berlin: De Gruyter.
Weinreich, Otto. 1909. *Antike Heilungswunder*. Giessen: Topelmann.
Wellman, Tennyson J. 2005. 'Ancient *Mysteria* and Modern Mystery Cults'. *Religion and Theology* 12: 308–48.
Wiseman, Timothy Peter. 1999. 'The Games of Flora'. In *The Art of Ancient Spectacle*, edited by Bettina Bergmann and Christine Kondoleon, 194–203. New Haven: Yale University Press.
Zeitlin, Froma. 1971. 'Petronius as Paradox: Anarchy and Artistic Integrity'. *TAPA* 102: 631–84.

Index

Note: n denotes a note.

Accius, Lucius, 67
Aeschylus, 40, 64–5, 67, 68
agency, 10, 20, 24, 28, 30, 34, 76n, 83n, 110–11, 197n
Alcibiades, 31n, 54, 62
Alexander of Abonuteichus, 196n, 199
allusions, literary, 59, 60n, 131, 132–5, 137, 140–1, 155, 167, 169; *see also* intertextuality
Apocrypha, 119–23
apotheosis *see* divinization
Apuleius, 162, 163, 194, 195–6
Aratus, 160, 165–6, 173
Aristophanes
  Acharnians, 4, 11–12, 113n
  Amphiaraus, 45
  Assemblywomen, 9
  Birds, 8, 9, 10, 19, 20, 21–32, 33–4, 38–9, 40–1, 42–4, 46, 49–62, 70
  Frogs, 161
  in Plato, *Symposium*, 49, 57–62
  Knights, 162
  Lysistrata, 4, 8–10, 13, 30, 32–3, 39n, 65
  Peace, 6–7, 10, 38–9, 40–2, 43–4, 46, 56
  Wasps, 5–6, 10, 11
  Wealth, 39n, 45–6
  Women at the Thesmophoria, 9, 30, 43n, 104–5, 111n
Aristotle, 67, 69, 96, 97–8
asebeia, 40–1, 43, 45, 46

Athena, 29–30
awe, religious, 98, 124, 125, 128
body
  after death, 72, 106–7, 119, 120, 122–3, 128
  and gender *see* gendered bodies
  and soul, 120, 122–3, 170
  as index of ethical qualities, 83, 86–7, 104–5, 116, 119, 120, 124, 128

Celsus, 188–9
Cicero, 67–8, 135–6, 140, 160, 165–6, 173
cinaedus see homosexuality, male
Comedy, New, 3, 12, 14–16, 65–6, 73n, 136, 140–1
Comedy, Old, 3, 8, 27n, 30, 39–40, 44–5, 46n, 54, 65–6, 73n, 110–11, 112, 113
cosmology, 91–2, 93–4, 98, 100
costume, theatrical, 3, 4, 6, 14, 16, 110, 111, 113, 116
Cratinus, 44–5, 105, 108, 109, 111–16

Democritus, 98–9
didactic genre, 160, 161–70, 172–3; *see also* poetry, didactic utility
Dionysus
  in Cratinus, *Dionysalexandros*, 112–14
  rites of, 190, 195n, 198

divinization
  apotheosis, 30, 31–2, 54, 57–8, 119–21, 122–3, 124, 126, 128–9
  human desire for, 54, 55, 57–8, 59, 124–5, 128–9

elegy, Roman, 8, 172–3, 174
Eleusinian mysteries, 39, 40, 57, 191, 195–6, 198, 199, 200
Empdocles, 167, 173
Ennius, 67, 172
Epicureanism, 160, 161, 164, 167–8, 171, 173–4
Epicurus, *On Nature*, 160, 165, 167
epigram, 144–5, 155–6, 168
eros
  as Eros, 49, 58, 132–3, 136–8, 139
  political, 49, 58–61
  romantic, 49, 57–8, 59, 60, 61–2, 66, 69, 132, 136, 138–9
Euelpides (*Birds*)
  disappearance, 50, 54–5
  treatment of Procne, 8, 26, 28, 34
Euripides
  as Aristophanic character, 30, 111n
  Helen, 9, 64, 65, 66, 108–11, 113, 115
  Hippolytus, 64, 119, 123–9
  Ion, 64, 65, 66, 71
  Iphigenia Among the Taurians, 64, 66, 67, 68
  Phoenician Women, 127–8
  Suppliants, 68, 69, 98

gaze
  female, 147–8, 152, 153–4
  male scopophilic, 3–11, 12–13, 26, 27–8, 29, 30, 146, 147–8
  male narcissistic, 148–9, 150–1
  voyeuristic, 148, 189–90, 197
gendered bodies
  chastity and virginity, 119, 120, 124–8, 146–7
  men's bodies and masculinity, 145, 148–9, 150–1, 152
  women's beauty and danger, 103–4, 105–16

  women's bodies as sexualized objects, 3, 5–6, 10, 26–9, 30, 146, 147–8, 150
  see also costume; gaze
gendered sexualities
  masculinity and impotence, 144, 153, 154, 156, 184, 188 195, 197, 200
  masculinity and sexual dominance, 145, 148–51, 152
  women and transgressive desire, 110–11, 146–9, 153–4, 187–9
  see also gaze; homosexuality, male
gendered speech
  men's speech and sociopolitical control, 20–3, 25–6, 145
  women and controlled speech, 20, 23–6, 30–1
  women and transgressive speech, 20, 23, 29, 30–1, 32–3
  women without speech, 3, 4, 5–10, 20, 22, 25n, 30, 34
genre
  and ancient literary criticism, 67–8, 135–6, 160–1, 165–6
  and audience/reader expectations, 34, 38, 43, 65n, 160–1, 165–7, 173
  canons and textual transmission, 64, 66
  comedy vs tragedy, 20, 21, 23, 59n, 65–6, 110–11
  play and innovation, 131–2, 135, 136–41, 154–6, 171–3

Helen, 65, 96, 103–4, 105–16
Henderson, Jeffrey, 1–4, 6, 7–9, 11, 16, 31n, 39–40, 46n, 53–4, 62, 73n, 87, 90, 109n, 110–11, 161–2
Heracles, 65–6, 73, 86–7
Hermes, 105–7, 114–16
Herodas, 12–14
Herodotus, 96, 113n
Hesiod
  Muses in, 56, 95–6, 131, 133–5, 141
  Pandora in, 105, 115, 116

Hippolytus, 64, 119, 123–8, 147
Homer, heroic values, 76, 77, 78–9, 82, 86–7
homosexuality, male
  and social hierarchy, 61, 145n, 149, 150–1
  pathic (*cinaedus*), 60–1, 145n, 149, 150–1, 152–4, 195, 197, 198
  pederastic relationship, 49, 59, 61
Horace, 145n, 152, 161, 171–2, 173
Hypereides, 13–14
humor
  mockery of real persons, 9, 29, 39–40, 55, 60–1, 104–5, 162
  of reversed expectations, 112–13, 154
  sexual, 4–15, 28, 42, 145
  see also satire; parody

initiation, ritual, 190–201
intertextuality, 19–20, 96, 127n; *see also* allusions, literary
Isis, 194, 195–6, 198

laws and justice, 50–3, 61, 90, 92, 94–5, 100
Lucian, 105–7, 108, 116, 199
Lyly, John, 103–4
Lysias, 40
Lysistrata, 4–5, 9–10, 33, 39n, 65

Mary, the Virgin, 119–23, 124–6, 128–9
Megarian farce, 11
metapoetry, 21, 22, 25, 33–4, 95–6, 111n, 144, 155
mime, 12–14, 193, 194, 199n
Mithras, 192, 195, 198–9
Muses, 56, 95, 131, 133–5, 141
mystery cults, 39, 40, 45, 57, 190–201
myth (*mythos*)
  and Christian syncresis, 122–3
  and (narrative) fiction, 131, 134, 135–8, 141
  philosophical, 49, 57–62, 95
  political, 55, 58, 59, 60

  rationalization of, 96, 97, 98
  reception and innovation, 34–5, 103–4, 105–16

narrative
  and pleasure, 91, 96, 97–8, 100, 132, 134, 137, 138
  rhetorical categories of, 135–6, 141
  structural devices, 138, 184–5, 186–7, 188, 190, 191–2, 196, 200
  utility of, 137
  truth value of, 131, 134–5, 136, 138–9, 141
Nemesis, 114, 119, 125
Neronian culture, 155–6, 187, 199
Nicander, 160, 165–6, 173
Nicias, Peace of, 31n, 39, 46
novel, ancient, 131–41, 144, 162–3, 186–7, 190–1; *see also* Apuleius; Petronius

Ovid, 107–8, 113, 116, 172–3

Pacuvius, 67, 135
Pan, 136–7, 139
Pandora, 105, 115, 116
Paris, 67, 108, 112–13, 114
parody
  of genre, 111n, 114, 139, 163n
  of ritual, 38–9, 41–45, 163n, 193, 198–9
Peisetaerus, 8, 22–3, 28, 29–30, 31–2, 33, 38–9, 41, 42–4, 46, 51–6, 58, 60, 61–2
Pericles, 111, 114
Petronius, 162–3, 178–201
Philodemus, 160–1, 168–9, 173
Pindar, 55, 96–7
Plato
  Republic, 54, 95
  Symposium, 49, 57–62, 66
Plautus, 12, 14–16, 65–6
poetry
  and artistic/aesthetic value, 160, 163, 164, 165, 171–2, 173
  and lies, 95–6, 97

INDEX 207

and mimesis, 160–1, 168–9, 173
didactic utility of, 91n, 163–4, 166, 167–8, 169, 171, 173
sociopolitical power of, 55–7, 61–2, 91, 95, 134, 161
politics
  and eros, 49, 58–61
  and role of poetry, 55–7, 61–2, 95, 134, 161
  as context of aristophanic comedy, 31–3, 39–40, 44, 45–6, 49, 54, 57
  democratic and tyrannical, 51, 52, 53–4
  of Aristophanes, 33, 46, 53n, 54, 161–2
  see also laws and justice; myth, political use of; religion, political use of
Pollio, C. Asinius, 68
Priapus, 144–57, 185, 186, 188, 189–201
Procne, 8–10, 13, 19–21, 23–30, 32–4
Prodicus, 98, 99
props, theatrical, 6n, 26–7, 28, 45, 109, 115

reception, 33–5, 57, 104, 109n, 111–16
recognition scenes, 65, 67, 68–9, 71, 73, 140
religion
  Christian syncresis, 123
  norms and comedy, 29–30, 38–9, 40–1 43–4, 46; *see also* parody, of ritual
  political uses of, 51, 55, 60, 91, 95
  rationalization of, 90, 91, 92, 95, 98–9, 100, 101
  ritual, 5, 38–9, 41–5, 46, 190–201
  see also divinization; mystery cults
rites of passage, 190–2, 200; *see also* initiation
Romilly, Jacqueline de, 66–8, 71, 73

satire, 31n, 38, 56–7, 73n, 154–6, 161, 162–3, 169n, 171–2, 187
Seneca (the Younger), 66, 68, 173
Sextus Empiricus, 90, 92–3, 135–6, 140
sexuality *see* gendered sexualities
Sicilian Expedition, 31–3, 39, 44, 45, 46, 49, 54, 57
sophists, 91, 96, 98, 99, 101
Sophocles
  Ajax, 65, 68, 73
  Oedipus at Colonus, 65, 69, 71–3
  Oedipus the King, 67
  Philoctetes, 65, 73, 76–88
  Tereus, 19–21, 22–3, 25, 29, 30–1, 33–5, 59n
  Tyro, 65, 69–71
speech *see* gendered speech
Stoicism, 169, 173
storytelling *see* narrative

taboo, religious, 38n, 124–5, 128
Terence, 136, 140
Tereus, 8–9, 19–23, 24–5, 26, 28, 29, 30, 34, 59
textual transmission, and interpretation, 64, 66, 91, 98, 120–2, 178–86, 200–1
theology, 90–3, 120–1, 122–3, 126n
Theophrastus, 187, 196n
theosis *see* divinization
Thucydides, 137, 139
tragedy, Greek, 64–71, 73; *see also* genre, comedy vs tragedy
tragedy, Roman, 66, 67–8, 135
Transitus Mariae (apocrypha), 119, 120–3
Trimalchio (*Satyricon*), 186, 187, 190
Trojan War
  and Helen, 104, 107, 108, 110, 113, 114, 116
  and heroism, 76, 77, 78–9, 87
  and Peloponnesian War, 111, 113
Trygaeus (*Peace*), 6–7, 38–9, 41–4, 46

EU representative:
Easy Access System Europe
Mustamäe tee 50, 10621 Tallinn, Estonia
Gpsr.requests@easproject.com

www.ingramcontent.com/pod-product-compliance
Lightning Source LLC
Chambersburg PA
CBHW051123160426
43195CB00014B/2326